THE TWO GANDHIS

"Eknath Easwaran's great achievement is telling an international audience about an Islamic practitioner of pacifism at a moment when few in the West understand its effectiveness and fewer still associate it with anything Islamic."

—THE WASHINGTON POST

"With the renewed interest in India . . . comes this remarkable account of Ghaffar (Badshah) Khan, the Muslim holy man known as the 'Frontier Gandhi.'"

—SAN FRANCISCO CHRONICLE

"The essence of Khan's story . . . is that the true nature of Islam is nonviolent."

—CHRISTIAN SCIENCE MONITOR

"This book is a must for every Muslim. The life of Khan can change and will challenge many readers in the Middle East."

—MUBARAK E. AWAD, *Palestinian Center for the Study of Nonviolence, Jerusalem*

"This extraordinarily interesting book of Eknath Easwaran will be very helpful in making the phenomenon of Islam more understandable."

—HELMUT SCHMIDT,
FORMER CHANCELLOR OF GERMANY

"Few are aware of the nonviolent tradition in Islam. Fewer still know the story of its greatest modern exemplar, Abdul Ghaffar Khan, better known as Badshah Khan. Easwaran's excellent biography deserves the widest possible reading."

—FELLOWSHIP

"A vivid portrait of a too-little known associate of Gandhi, Abdul Ghaffar Khan, a charismatic pacifist Muslim who led the Pathans of India and Pakistan in a nonviolent resistance to British rule."

—BOOKLIST

I have one great desire.

I want to rescue these gentle, brave, patriotic people from the tyranny of the foreigners who have disgraced and dishonored them.

I want to create for them a world of freedom, where they can live in peace, where they can laugh and be happy.

I want to kiss the ground where their ruined homes once stood, before they were destroyed by savage strangers.

I want to take a broom and sweep the alleys and the lanes, and I want to clean their houses with my own hands.

I want to wash away the stains of blood from their garments.

I want to show the world how beautiful they are, these people from the hills, and then I want to proclaim: "Show me, if you can, any gentler, more courteous, more cultured people than these."

–BADSHAH KHAN

THE TWO GANDHIS

NON-VIOLENT SOLDIERS:

The Frontier Gandhi—Khan Abdul Ghaffar Khan

and Mahatma Gandhi

Eknath Easwaran

JAICO PUBLISHING HOUSE

Ahmedabad Bangalore Chennai
Delhi Hyderabad Kolkata Mumbai

Published by Jaico Publishing House
A-2 Jash Chambers, 7-A Sir Phirozshah Mehta Road
Fort, Mumbai - 400 001
jaicopub@jaicobooks.com
www.jaicobooks.com

Published in arrangement with
Nilgiri Press
P.O. Box 256
Tomales, California 94971, USA
www.easwaran.org

To be sold only in India, Bangladesh, Bhutan,
Pakistan, Nepal, Sri Lanka and the Maldives.

THE TWO GANDHIS
ISBN 978-81-8495-041-0

Originally published as *Nonviolent Soldier of Islam*

First Jaico Impression: 2009
Third Jaico Impression (New Cover): 2011

Printed by
Trinity Academy For Corporate Training Limited, Mumbai

Table of Contents

Quotations at the head of each chapter are from Badshah Khan.

Certain passages which appear in italic type have been dramatized. Sources for these incidents are cited in the Sources & Historical Notes, p. 235.

Nonviolence for the Twenty-first Century

The present-day world can only survive the mass production of nuclear weapons through nonviolence. The world needs Gandhi's message of love and peace more today than it ever did before, if it does not want to wipe out civilization and humanity itself from the earth's surface.

—BADSHAH KHAN, *message to the author, 1983*

AS THIS BOOK enters its second edition, at the turn of the millennium, the world confronts an ever-widening nuclear arms race and the terrible loss of life in the Balkans and Africa. No region of the globe is exempt from the scourge of violence. While nations gauge whether to squander their resources on nuclear weapons or the new "poor man's" arsenals of biological war, fear of different races, religions, nationalities, and ethnic identities continues to fan the flames of hatred and violence around the world.

Badshah Khan offers the twenty-first century a way out. A devout Muslim and devoted ally of Mahatma Gandhi, this true freedom fighter struggled for the rights of his people for almost eighty years without ever wielding a weapon.

"Today's world is traveling in some strange direction," he told an interviewer in Afghanistan in 1985. "You see that the world is going toward destruction and violence. And the specialty of violence is to create hatred among people and to create fear. I am a believer in nonviolence and I say that no peace or tranquility will descend upon the people of the world until nonviolence is practiced, because nonviolence is love and it stirs courage in people."

In the fervent hope that it may spread the message of this great

Muslim leader to every country and language and religion on earth, I offer this little book to the world.

—EKNATH EASWARAN

Preface

During the early years of the Second World War, I was a graduate student at the University of Nagpur. Lying as it does near the geographical center of India, Nagpur is a major junction for trains coming from every direction: from Madras in the south, Bombay in the west, Calcutta in the east, and Delhi in the north.

But the real center of India at the time was Sevagram ashram, near a town called Wardha about ninety miles to the south of Nagpur, where Mahatma Gandhi lived with his closest followers. The leaders of India's independence movement visited often to seek guidance, and the Working Committee of the Indian National Congress party met there frequently.

The result was that the whole constellation of India's leaders passed through my city of Nagpur on their way to Wardha. On weekends I used to go down to the railway station to see the men and women who were leading our country to freedom.

I saw them all: Jawaharlal Nehru, who became our first prime minister; Sardar Patel, later our first home minister and Gandhi's trusted lieutenant; Maulana Azad, the great Muslim leader. I remember the austere Acharya Kripalani eating a bagful of potato chips. I saw Mrs. Sarojini Naidu, a talented poet and dedicated patriot; C. V. Rajagopalachari, a brilliant lawyer and statesman; Rajendra Prasad, who became India's first president – and, on one special occasion, Khan Abdul Ghaffar Khan.

Badshah Khan had become a real favorite of mine. Stepping down from the third-class carriage, this majestic Pathan from India's North-West Frontier Province looked something of a giant to me. His many years in prison had taken their toll, but his six-foot- three-inch frame still looked powerful and he carried it with a stately grace. Yet he was so reserved, so unassuming, even child-like. There was a simplicity about him that made me want to sit down with him and have a quiet chat.

I did not have the nerve to approach him on that occasion. I was young and reticent myself. But that brief encounter confirmed everything I believed of him. Of all the brilliant leaders around Gandhi, Badshah Khan was the one who most appealed to me because he not only understood Gandhi's teachings but followed them completely. Formerly a wealthy landowner, he had handed his holdings over to his sons and dedicated his life to the service of God and his own impoverished people. Clothed in simple home-spun cotton, carrying only a small bag with him, he looked more like a *fakir,* a religious renunciate, than the renowned leader of one hundred thousand nonviolent Pathans.

Shortly after I saw him, Badshah Khan showed his true mettle. It was a period of great anxiety for Indians because the Japanese had advanced to within a thousand miles of our eastern border, seemingly poised to attack. The Congress Working Committee met at Wardha and, in their first open opposition to Gandhi, declared that India must be prepared to defend itself militarily. But Badshah Khan would not go along. He resigned immediately, explaining that his nonviolence was not a policy, to be used when expedient, but an article of faith. For him, as for Gandhi, nonviolence had become a way of life. Later, when the Working Committee changed its position, Badshah Khan and Gandhi rejoined it – on their own terms.

I confess that at the time it bothered me a great deal that among all those leaders who were eager to follow Gandhi into the independence struggle, only a few like Badshah Khan were willing to follow his lead in other matters. Perhaps that is why he came to occupy such a large part of my affection. He had joined Gandhi in 1919 without conditions, and since that time nothing ever changed his resolve to stick by him and put his teachings into practice. I admired the other Indian leaders, but most of them did not fully understand the spiritual basis of Gandhi's work – and honestly admitted it. Badshah Khan not only understood, he lived to the letter what Gandhi taught.

For some time, I had been trying to understand the source of Gandhi's power. How had such a small man become such a powerhouse? Badshah Khan offered a clue, for he was obviously following Gandhi's spiritual disciplines as well as his politics.

It took me a long, long time to understand that the answer lay in Gandhi's renunciation of every self-centered impulse in his personality: as he put it, in "reducing himself to zero." For years the idea made little sense to me. But Badshah Khan's words were simpler: what drew him to Gandhi, he used to say, was Gandhi's ability to submit his will to God. This gave me a clue. Badshah Khan's heroic, decades-long efforts to forget himself in the service of God through the service of his people were a vivid illustration of how the deepest human resources can be released in anyone with the discipline and courage to dig for them.

*

When India gained independence, Badshah Khan's Pathan homelands became part of Pakistan. There, as in British India, he spent much of his time in prison as he continued to press for the same basic rights for his people. When I moved to the United States I lost track of him, except on those rare occasions when the world took note. In 1962, Amnesty International drew attention to his plight by naming him Prisoner of the Year. Twenty years later, learning that he had been jailed yet again in Peshawar at the age of ninety-three, I tried to do what was within my own reach to place him in the world's eyes, getting him nominated for the Nobel Prize and writing this book. Reviewers were fascinated by the story, and Badshah Khan got full-page treatment in a sensitive piece in the *New Yorker* when I was interviewed for "Talk of the Town." But it all seemed written on water.

Yet the world was changing. In 1979 the Soviet Union had invaded Afghanistan, bringing that unfortunate pawn in the

"Great Game" back into global affairs after a century of obscurity. The Pathans found themselves celebrated in the news as guerrilla "freedom fighters." Thus, when Abdul Ghaffar Khan died on January 20, 1988, at the age of ninety-eight, he finally gained the attention of the world's wire services and the *New York Times*.

On the day of his funeral, Soviet-held Afghanistan opened its border to Pakistan for the first time since the occupation to allow thousands of Pathan mourners to walk seventy miles over the Khyber Pass carrying Badshah Khan's coffin to his home in Islamabad, where he had asked to be buried. Inside Afghanistan the mourners were joined by thousands more, while the Pathan guerrillas declared a day's cease-fire so that all could honor this "king of khans." Like Gandhi, Khan Abdul Ghaffar Khan brought people together even in his death.

But only for a day. Soon after this the Soviet army pulled out; but today, ten years later, the massacres of civil war continue. The Taliban – themselves mostly Pathans – have not brought peace. They and rival guerrilla factions still bomb each other by turns, taking countless innocent lives among women and children.

These are people noted for their courage, who would rather die than be driven to submission. No outside power is going to force them to lay down their guns. Peace can only be made by the Afghans themselves – which requires even higher courage than killing. Gandhi was once asked if he really thought nonviolence was the best way to resolve conflicts. "No," he replied. "Nonviolence is not the best way. It is the only way." Violence provokes more violence. Only what Gandhi called "the nonviolence of the brave" can break this cycle and move the hearts of the violent to peace.

Even now this can be done. Badshah Khan is not dead. His example is a living force which can come to life to inspire and lead people wherever they turn to nonviolence with faith and courage.

This is not a message merely for Afghanistan. Wherever civil war or ethnic violence rages, but especially in the Middle East, Badshah Khan offers a path to peace. A devout Muslim, he showed in his life a face of Islam which non-Islamic countries seldom see, proving that within the scope of Islam exists a noble alternative to violence. His nonviolent army, the "Servants of God," was entirely

Muslim, and based upon the ancient Islamic principles of universal brotherhood, submission to God, and the service of God through the service of His creatures.

"It is my inmost conviction," Badshah Khan said, "that Islam is *amal, yakeen, muhabat*" – selfless service, faith, and love. *Yakeen,* faith, is an unwavering belief in the spiritual laws that underlie all life, and in the nobility of human nature – in particular, in the ability of every human being to respond to spiritual laws. It implies a profound belief in the power of *muhabat,* love, to transform human affairs, as Badshah Khan, like Gandhi, demonstrated with his life. This is not the sentimental notion of love portrayed in films. It is a spiritual force which, when drawn upon systematically, can root out exploitation and transform anger into love in action.

Badshah Khan based his life and work on this profound principle, raising an army of courageous men and women who translated it into action. Were his example better known, the world might come to recognize that the highest religious values of Islam are deeply compatible with a nonviolence that has the power to resolve conflicts even against heavy odds.

In Israel and Palestine, India and Pakistan, Iraq and Iran and the Balkans, select groups of nonviolent freedom fighters can march into opposing territories just as Mahatma Gandhi did in India's epic Salt March in 1930. As with any other kind of fighting, this requires training – strenuous inner training of the mind, the heart, the will. It cannot be done without faith and courage. Fortunately, in every great religion there are powerful spiritual disciplines that can provide the basis of such training. Badshah Khan's legacy to the world was to show how this can be done within Islam.

Nearly seventy years have passed since the Salt March, but the world remains blind to the power of nonviolence, which could end war once and for all. This book is dedicated to the men and women who can take humanity further by practicing war without violence.

– EKNATH EASWARAN

The Two Gandhis (Kanu Gandhi)

AUGUST 14, 1947

Prologue

SMILING IN SPITE of the stifling heat, Louis Francis Albert Victor Nicholas Mountbatten, great-grandson of Queen Victoria and viceroy of the Indian Empire, sat on a raised dais overlooking the crowded Karachi assembly hall. He did not wish to rush matters. For the past six months he had had too little time to do anything else. As India's last viceroy, he had been granted the full plenipotentiary powers of a head of state by the Attlee government in London, and had arrived in New Delhi with fourteen months to disengage the British Raj from India. He had already managed it in less than six.

Now, with independence only hours away, Mountbatten would proclaim to the packed hall of the Pakistani assembly His Majesty King George VI's good wishes for the fledgling republic. He seemed determined to give the moment its proper polish. Yet despite his apparently unhurried calm, Mountbatten was still walking a tightwire. He was presiding over the tormented birth of not one country but two: Pakistan had been carved away from the rest of India in the two separate corners of the subcontinent where Muslims predominated over Hindus.

It had been three and a half centuries, almost to the year, since the British came to India; it had been two centuries since they established military control. From the beginning the Indian people had chafed with increasing bitterness under the British yoke, and the parts of the country that had been longest under colonial rule had histories of rebellion and reprisal. Then, in the last thirty years, Mahatma Gandhi had captured the Indian imagination with an unprecedented challenge: to make the British "quit India" and to see them depart as friends. It was the only nonviolent overthrow of an imperial power in recorded history, and its success had focused the attention of the world on this day.

Tall, turbaned Punjabis in the colorful assembly milled with the khans and chieftains of the wild tribes of the south. Baluchis, Sindis, and Pathans checkered the room. In the hall were almost all the prominent Muslim leaders – Liaquat Ali Khan, Khwaja Nazimuddin, Iskander Mirza, and, at the viceroy's side, Mohammed Ali Jinnah, soon to become governor-general of the world's first Islamic republic.

Yet one prominent Muslim was absent. Abdul Ghaffar Khan had baffled the British and electrified Indians by raising an army of one hundred thousand nonviolent soldiers out of one of the world's most violent peoples, the Pathans. The villagers of his North-West Frontier Province revered him as a saint and called him Badshah Khan, the "king of khans." Throughout India he was known as the Frontier Gandhi because he, of all Gandhi's followers, best mirrored the fullness of Gandhi's way.

To Mountbatten, it must have seemed ironic that the man who had done more than any other Pakistani Muslim to fuel the freedom struggle should be absent at its consummation. Under the circumstances, however, the viceroy would not have been surprised. Khan, a devout Muslim, had opposed partitioning India to create a separate Muslim state.

Mountbatten nodded to the stately Jinnah and stood up. The chattering crowd stilled to listen to the king-emperor's message of good will.

Only hours later Mountbatten was aboard his Royal Air Force York on its way to New Delhi. There, at midnight, the ceremony of independence would be repeated. Across the night air the low, thin wail of a conch shell proclaimed the birth of the Indian Republic. The cry that had roused India's millions to revolution and freedom built to a roar over the city: *Mahatma Gandhi ki jai!* Victory to Mahatma Gandhi!

Yet Gandhi was five hundred miles away. Declining to attend the ceremony – India's partition had been too high a price to pay for freedom – he had spent the eve of independence in prayer and fasting.

And while Gandhi fasted in Calcutta, the "Frontier Gandhi" was finishing his evening prayers near his home village in Pakistan. His palms lifted to the pale sky, Badshah Khan turned toward Mecca and chanted verses from the sacred Koran, as uncounted millions had chanted them before him. Their deep, slow music stirred the air: *Bismillah ir-Rahman ir-Rahim* . . . "In the name of God, most compassionate, most merciful. . ."

Khan raised himself from the small prayer carpet. Looking out across the sprawling Peshawar valley to the scarred hills and ridges of the Khyber, he scarcely heard the tumult of celebration building in his village. Freedom for him would be measured by how quickly the lot of the desperately backward Pathans in hundreds of villages spotting the valleys and low hills would improve. Ignorant and provincial, most Pathans still lived in poverty and fear. *Badal,* the obligation of revenge, ran deep in their blood and almost daily stained the social netting with violence between brothers, rivals, families, and clans – and in defending their homelands against the British invaders. Pathan life, and history, were awash in blood.

*

> To have to carry destruction, if not destitution, into the homes of some hundreds of families is the great drawback of border warfare, but with savage tribes, to whom there is no right but might, the only course open as regards humanity as well as policy, is to make all suffer.

> If objection be taken to the nature of punishment inflicted as repugnant to civilization, the answer is that savages cannot be met and checked by civilized warfare, and that to spare their houses and crops would be to leave them unpunished and therefore, unrestrained. In short, civilized warfare is inapplicable.

Sir Neville Chamberlain was commander of the Punjab Frontier Force when he sent this dispatch to London during a punitive campaign against the Pathans in 1859. The words distill the attitude that most British held ever since. Less than civilized, subhuman, the Pathan was a "savage," a "brute," "cruel as a leopard," a "treacherous murderer." Khan's people commanded the attention – and the wrath – of the British Empire solely because they happened to inhabit the mountains around the strategic Khyber Pass. The Khyber was the gateway to India, the greatest source of wealth in the Empire. The British were determined to hold it at any cost – and the Pathans, for whom independence was everything and warfare a way of life, were equally determined to win their freedom.

The Pathans had carried the stamp of fear and hatred ever since the bone-chilling January morning in 1842 when the sole English survivor of the forty-five-hundred-man "Army of the Indus" rode into Fort Jalalabad. The eighty-odd years of guerrilla warfare that followed hardened these feelings into an article of faith. The British sent scores of expeditions into the Pathans' hills, shelled their strongholds, burned (and later bombed) their villages, beat, flogged, and jailed Pathans by the thousands. In between, in times that passed for peaceful, they tried to bribe them into submission. But nothing worked for long. The Pathan homeland remained the only part of the British Empire never to be fully subjugated. Throughout the Raj's tenure, it would be safe to say, no Englishman slept a night in a Frontier town or village – or even within an army cantonment – without the lurking menace of a bullet crashing from a distant lookout or the sudden, silent descent of a razor-sharp dagger.

The British counted on only one certitude on the Frontier: that the peace would break, and that British columns would once again have to file into the desolate hills. Among British soldiers stationed across the earth's five continents, the North-West Frontier Province was called simply "the Grim."

But it would not be the Pathans' sharpshooting or cunning or violent heroics that would finally drive the British from the Frontier. No amount of sniping or suicidal assaults could match the weaponry and will the Empire had at its command. Only a historical mutation, a reversal of the rules themselves, could finally thwart the imperial will and send the British home.

It was left to Gandhi to supply the innovation – nonviolent warfare – and to Badshah Khan to provide the surprise. History played a great trick upon the empire builders of the Raj when it brought forth from the heart of "the Grim" a man who combined Pathan fire with the tempering spirit of a dove. It was utterly improbable. No one could have anticipated that such a phenomenon – a Muslim St. Francis – would emerge from the seething Pathan badlands. That it did, and that it burst into a broad and mighty force, stands as one of history's most extraordinary – and most neglected – moments.

Khan's backward tribesmen turned the tables on the British. These same maligned Pathans stirred the whole Indian subcontinent when they put down their daggers and handmade rifles and faced, without retaliating, the worst the armies of a baffled, panicking empire could deal out.

It was severe in the extreme. In 1930, at the height of the Indian nonviolence movement, a British report less polished than Sir Neville Chamberlain's but more candid would conclude: "The brutes must be ruled brutally and by brutes." In British eyes, Khan's nonviolence was nothing more than a camouflage. A nonviolent Pathan was an impostor; they had seen too many of the Empire's finest cut down on too many nameless crags to think otherwise. Gandhi's nonviolence was one thing: a bitter nuisance, perhaps, but consistent at least with the image of the peaceable Hindu. A nonviolent Pathan was unthinkable, a fraud that masked something cunning and darkly treacherous.

During the Indian freedom struggle, therefore, Khan and his nonviolent army found themselves the target of savage repression. On occasion the entire province was even sealed off from the eyes of the world, leaving government forces a free hand to crush the movement in whatever way they could. The impression that the British were fair and easygoing opponents in India is based largely upon the ignorance in which the treatment of Khan and his people has been shrouded. Throughout the thirties and early forties, Pathans had to endure mass shootings, torture, the destruction of their fields and homes, jail, flogging, and humiliations. Khan himself spent fifteen years in British prisons, often in solitary confinement: in effect, in jail one day for every day that he was free. But the Pathans remained nonviolent and stood unmoved – suffering and dying in large numbers to win their freedom.

Even Indians, themselves engaged in the same nonviolent struggle, were astonished. Jawaharlal Nehru, India's first prime minister, found it incredible that "the man who loved his gun better than his child or brother, who valued life cheaply and cared nothing for death, who avenged the slightest insult with the thrust of a dagger, had suddenly become the bravest and most enduring of India's soldiers." In one of history's more improbable turnabouts, it was left to Khan's ragged tribesmen to explode the myth that nonviolence works only for those who are already peaceful.

Gandhi had long claimed that nonviolence was more truly the province of the daring and the undaunted: and surely no people on the face of the earth was more daring or dauntless than the Pathans. Even the average tribesman prefers death to dishonor. But not even Gandhi would have predicted that the evidence to back up his claims would come from these swaggering sharpshooters. He knew the odds against such a miracle: "That such men," he said, "who would have killed a human being with no more thought than they would kill a sheep or a hen should at the bidding of one man have laid down their arms and accepted nonviolence as the superior weapon sounds almost like a fairy tale."

Gandhi, a truth-loving man, was never nearer the truth. Like many such tales, the story of Abdul Ghaffar Khan has hidden within it the seeds of a deeper truth, of which our explosive, tottering world stands much in need. It is time the tale was told.

Part One

The Khyber Pass, 1895. Previous pages: British army in Kabul , 1879
(Both photos National Army Museum, London)

CHAPTER ONE : JUNE, 1897

The Jubilee

O Pathans! Your house has fallen into ruin. Arise and rebuild it – and remember to what race you belong.

JUST AFTER eleven o'clock on the morning of June 22, 1897, Queen Victoria touched her fingers to the brass transmitting key in the telegraph room at Buckingham Palace and started to click out a message to the 372 million subjects of the British Empire. It was the morning of her Diamond Jubilee – sixty years on the British throne. "From my heart I thank my people," the Queen-Empress tapped with a trace of nervousness. "May God bless them."

Within minutes the Queen's message was humming toward the telegraph offices of British possessions throughout the Empire: westward to Ireland, Canada, and Newfoundland, Trinidad and Tobago, the Virgin Islands, Barbados, the Bahamas, the Leeward and Windward Islands, Ascension, Bermuda, British Guiana, Honduras, and the Falklands; eastward to Gibraltar and Malta in the Mediterranean; then on to Nigeria, Egypt, Gambia, the Gold Coast, Rhodesia, Cape Province, Somaliland, Uganda, and Zanzibar, to Aden on the Red Sea, to Mauritius and the Seychelles in the Indian Ocean, and then to India, Ceylon, Burma, Malaysia, Hong Kong, and Singapore; from there to Australia, North Borneo, Papua, Fiji, Pitcairn, and two dozen other island groups in the South Pacific. All these were under some form of British rule – as nation-states, colonies, protectorates, suzerainties, island fortresses, and isolated coaling stations – flying the Union Jack and governed by white military officers or civil servants speaking crisp Queen's English.

Her message finished, Victoria, dressed in black, stepped into an open landau drawn by eight cream-colored horses. Joined by a procession of fifty thousand troops from every corner of the Empire, she made her way through the London streets to St. Paul's Cathedral for a thanksgiving service.

Victoria – and all England – had much to be thankful for. The world had never before seen anything to match the power, the scope, the pure dazzle of the British Empire. Flung across every continent and ocean of the world, its possessions covered one fourth of the earth's land mass. The well-being of one quarter of the entire population of the earth was its sworn responsibility. It was a stupendous, if sprawling, success. One good reason: Britain's navies ruled the seas. At any given moment her ships were carrying four hundred thousand passengers and crew to and from every imaginable port, rock fortress, steaming island settlement, or up-country trading post in Europe, Asia, Africa, America, and the South Seas. For every thousand tons of shipping that passed through the Suez Canal during the year of the Jubilee, seven hundred came on British ships.

England itself was securely in conservative hands. Lord Salisbury's cabinet, elected two years earlier, included two marquesses, two dukes, an earl, a viscount, three barons, and three baronets: a government whose aristocratic credentials made it the perfect mirror for the burst of "new imperialism" which spread over England that smiling summer. The Jubilee morning marked the zenith of the Empire. For those who attended, the Jubilee itself was proof enough that England was favored among the nations of the world. "The sun never looked down until yesterday upon the embodiment of so much energy and power," one paper crowed. Another commentator estimated that the Jubilee would be "the costliest event in the world's history." The premiers of eleven colonies rode in parade with Victoria, as did twenty-three princesses, a grand duke, forty Indian maharajas, and a crown prince. The fifty thousand troops who marched were thought to form the "largest military force ever assembled in London." Onlookers caught the sweep of the Empire just from reading the names of the regiments: Canadian Hussars, New South Wales Lancers, Trinidad Light Horse, the Zaptichs of Cyprus, the Jamaica Artillery, the Bengal Lancers, the Bikaner camel troops, the Royal Nigerian Constabulary.

The clear, shimmering skies – "Queen's weather" – remained bright until sunset. Troops filed past, drums beat, a thousand Union Jacks snapped in the breeze. And at the end of the procession, while millions cheered, Victoria passed, alternately weeping and waving. "No one ever, I believe, has met with such an ovation as was given me," the Queen wrote in her journal after returning to the palace. And she was probably right.

Caught up in the heady brilliance of the day, it would have been difficult for any Englishman not to believe that Great Britain was destined – indeed, called – to rule. In a thousand dark corners of the earth, the rule of law would prevail while ignorant savages were enlightened and their burdens eased – all through the power and good offices of the British Empire. A former civil servant in India told the House of Commons that there was "a cherished conviction shared by every Englishman in India, from the highest to the lowest, by the planter's assistant in his lonely bungalow and by the editor in the full light of his presidency town, from the Chief Commissioner in charge of an important province to the Viceroy upon his throne – the conviction in every man that he belongs to a race which God has destined to govern and to subdue."

And who could argue with the notion? On this halcyon June day, it would have been difficult for even the sourest anglophobe to disagree. There had been nothing like this since the days of Rome. Pax Britannica reigned. The Empire was secure.

*

In one of the remoter corners of the Empire that June morning – next to a green field in the northwest tip of British India – one of Victoria's younger subjects, the seven-year-old Abdul Ghaffar Khan, was working mightily to stop a log floating in the shallows of the river Swat. The sun was bright, the air over the valley morning-cool. Behind the boy, the fields of his father's farm stretched wide and green toward the ridges of the Khyber Pass.

Ghaffar Khan had probably never heard of Victoria. Here on the North-West Frontier the British political agent was king, and a remote woman monarch on a throne thousands of miles away could not have meant a great deal even to an educated Pathan. At the moment, what mattered to the boy was a log curling away from the bank into the current.

"Ghaffar!" The word fell faintly over the river, like a chime struck far away. The boy swirled his stick closer to the log.

"Ghaffar!" It hovered again, then vanished. The boy kept swirling.

It was not unusual for Ghaffar Khan to have to be called more than once. He was an intense boy who easily lost himself in the green world of his father's farm – in the fields of cane and cotton, the orchards of plum, peach, orange, and persimmon – and the slow, dark waters of the river Swat.

Ghaffar was the youngest child in the family of Behram Khan. He had two sisters and an elder brother, Abdul Jabar, who was attending the Edwardes Memorial Mission High School in Peshawar, the provincial capital. Ghaffar did not get to see him much. But now it was June and school was out, so he and his brother had been spending long, languid hours along the river, occasionally rafting over to the tiny island in the middle. When he was alone, as now, he would often walk into the village where his friends lived. He especially liked the sons of the laborers and craftsmen – uncommon for a khan's son – and two of his best friends were bhangis, *sweepers.*

This fragrant morning seemed made for churning the river water with a stick, so he had left the farmhouse early and settled down near the shallows, where the ducks and wild swans fed. Then he saw the log, too tantalizing a treasure to pass up.

"Ghaffar!" This time the call cracked the air like a rifle shot and the boy snapped around. It was his father calling. He jumped onto the thread of path that skirted the river and sprinted toward the farmhouse through a cane row.

Behram Khan was standing near the oak gate, a basket of unleavened bread balanced on his head. "Ghaffar!" he boomed when he saw the boy. "Let's go. I need your help." Some travelers had spent the night in their guest house and needed to be fed.

Behram Khan came from a line of Pathan farmers who had settled in the rich Peshawar Valley many decades before. They had given up the independence of the theoretically free but generally poor tribes of the hills to prosper in a "settled" area – under the yoke of British rule. For strategic reasons the British had divided the Frontier into three geographic groups: the Agencies in the north, the so-called settled districts between the Indus River and the hills, and the "free" areas along the western border where the Pathans were left to govern themselves under *Pushtunwali*, "the Law of the Pathans."

That Jubilee summer perhaps two million Pathans lived on the Frontier, divided into dozens of tribes and subgroups. Among larger tribes were the Afridis, who were paid by the British to "guard" the Khyber Pass (from their own marauding), and the Mohmands and Yusufzais, who lived in the mountainous provinces north of Peshawar. South of the Khyber, next to the Afridis, lived the Orakzais. Further south were the Waziris and Mahsuds, perhaps the fiercest and most volatile of the Pathan tribes.

The Raj "subsidized" these tribes, paying them to keep the peace. The British generally left them alone, unless they caused trouble – which was often. During the four decades of their rule on the Frontier, the British had sent fifty expeditions into the "free" territories to punish rebellious tribes. The policy never really worked, but it was better than all-out war.

Behram Khan's tribe, the Mohammedzais, was smaller than most Pathan tribes and was generally prosperous and peaceful. Behram Khan himself was wealthy. He owned all the fields that stretched beyond the big farmhouse and along the river Swat. Furthermore, he was the khan – the chief – of Utmanzai, a village about twenty miles north of Peshawar.

Utmanzai was a prosperous village, with wide lanes and two-storied houses made of thick timbers and clay. It lay almost at the geographical center of the North-West Frontier Province, midway between the Chinese border on the north and the barren southern deserts of Baluchistan bordering Iran. North of the village were the mountainous regions of Swat, Dir, Buner, and Bajaur, thickly forested and laced with tumbling rivers. Around Peshawar the hills gave way to the wide river bottoms of the Peshawar and Kurram valleys. East of Utmanzai was the broad Indus River and beyond it, India. If the young Ghaffar Khan and his father had stopped and looked west as they walked toward their guest house that June morning, they would have seen the tanned, bare hills of the Khyber Pass, the gateway between central Asia and British India.

Travelers from any of these areas might have been found staying in Behram Khan's guest house. Most likely, however, they would be from the North, since Utmanzai lay along one of the main roads between Peshawar and the northern highlands. Wherever they were from, whatever their intent, the Pathan social code of *melmastia*, hospitality, dictated that they be treated as honored guests, entitled to food and lodging. Every Pathan village has at least one guest house or *derah* for this purpose. Wealthier Pathans like Behram Khan built their own, for a large, comfortable derah – with good food, amply given – is the key to status in a Pathan village, and khans commonly competed to attract the men of the village to share their hospitality. It was in the derahs that villagers gathered to chat, smoke tobacco from a common water pipe, and sip hot green *qahwa* tea from a hissing samovar. These evening get-togethers could go on far into the night. Exhilarated by the strong tea and companionship, the men would tell stories, sing songs together, or simply tease and bluster. Sometimes Behram Khan would lie back on his pillow and tell about his grandfather, Abaidullah Khan, who had gone to the gallows for Pathan honor.

Honor! Probably no word stirs a Pathan more deeply. No matter what his station in life, honor has long been the true calling of a Pathan. And God help the British, the men would agree, if all the Pathan clans – Afridi, Mohmand, Yusufzai, Mahsud, Waziri, Mohammedzai, Orakzai – ever set aside their differences and rose as one nation to drive the foreign unbelievers from their homelands. In the firelight, a trace of blood lust would steal across the dark, gleaming faces as they elaborated the unspeakable fate that awaited the British. Life without freedom made little sense to a Pathan – for without freedom, how could there be honor?

It was not unusual on such occasions for some robed figure to bring out a *surnai* and fill the evening with haunting, flutelike music. Another might begin to chant – slowly, with a measured rhythm – a poem of the immortal Khushal Khan:

> The young men have dyed red their hands
> As the falcon dyes his talons in the blood of his prey!
> They have reddened their pale swords with blood:
> They have made the tulip-bed blossom
>   in the middle of the summer.

Behram Khan's guest house was long and low. Ghaffar always approached the building with suppressed excitement, for he never knew what tall, turbaned strangers might have spent the night. He might find a blue-eyed Afridi down from the Khyber, or a Yusufzai in white pyjamas from one of the terraced farms of the Malakand, or a Swati on his way to the big city – hair scented, eyes darkened with collyrium, a rose tucked behind his ear and a rifle slung over his shoulder. Or it might be a Hazara from the far north, beardless and with slanted eyes. They were all Pathans: they bantered in the same Pushto that Ghaffar's own Mohammedzai clan spoke, and they all loved to sit in a circle and share a water pipe and the news.

Behram Khan had many servants, but he carried food to his guests himself and served it with his own hands. The code of hospitality did not demand this, and no other khan of the district was known to practice it. But the devout khan told his sons, "An unknown traveler is a guest sent to us by God. I will serve him myself."

That day of June 1897 the derahs of Utmanzai would have been humming with news of much greater interest than a remote queen's diamond jubilee. Mohmands or Swatis from the north, visiting Behram Khan on their way to Peshawar, would have talked excitedly of Mullah Mastun, a firebrand priest who had recently returned from a pilgrimage to Afghanistan and was now touring the mountain areas north of Utmanzai to preach that the time had come to turn out the British. The Prophet himself had told him the hour had come. Mullah Mastun promised that "he would throw stones into the Swat River and they would become artillery shells to fling back at the infidel."

Behram Khan would not have been surprised. Pathan mullahs often urged their followers to take up arms. But the last uprising in Chitral, two years earlier, had brought out a British force of fifteen thousand troops and convinced the British that they needed more forts and roads up there. It didn't seem likely that the northerners would have forgotten all of that so soon. To Behram Khan, it must have seemed just one more call to revolt in the long history of rebellion since the British took control of the Frontier some fifty years before.

Chitral, ca. 1890 (National Army Museum)

The Shahur Pass, Waziristan (Holmes)

CHAPTER TWO : JULY, 1897

Children of the Prophet

The history of my people is full of victories and tales of heroism, but there are drawbacks too. Internal feuds and personal jealousies have always snatched away the gains achieved through vast sacrifices. They were dispossessed only because of their own inherent defects, never by any outside power – for who could oppose them on the battlefield?

IN THE BEGINNING, at least, the British had no intention of creating an empire. One thing simply led to another. They had not even gone to India for conquest. "Trade, not property" was the official policy of the East India Trading Company when it was formed in 1599, inaugurating Britain's long association with India. Nevertheless, the Company's officers eagerly took advantage of the opportunities for expansion that presented themselves, and by the early part of the nineteenth century the Company's board of directors had become holders of the greatest imperial possession in the world – the "jewel in the crown of the Empire" – India.

It all began because of a five pounds sterling change in the cost of pepper. That was how much the Dutch privateers who controlled the Indian spice trade suddenly raised their price. Feeling the increase unwarranted, a group of London merchants formed the East India Trading Company in September 1599. Three months later Queen Elizabeth signed a charter that granted the new company "exclusive trading rights with all countries beyond the Cape of Good Hope for an initial period of fifteen years." In August 1600, the Company landed its first ship on the west coast of India, near Bombay. The Redcoats had come – on business.

Quickly gaining rights to trading depots near Bombay, Madras in the south, and Calcutta in the east, the Company soon had ships bringing to England great quantities of spices, gum, sugar, raw silk, and muslin cotton, and then sailing back with English manufactured goods. Local rulers, finding their presence profitable, welcomed the traders.

Inevitably rivalries formed. The Company soon found itself forced into local politics to protect its commercial interests. It hired its own army of white mercenaries and Indian sepoys, and before long, ambitious Company governors – in spite of official Company policy – had seized control over land. Thus was set in motion an irreversible process of conquest which led, ultimately, to the Indian Empire.

In 1757 a young Company colonel, Robert Clive, defeated the army of a local ruler in Bengal, opening northern India to the dominance of British influence. Almost imperceptibly the Company's officers were turning from merchants to imperialists. Believing that "no greater blessing may be confirmed on the native inhabitants of India than the extension of British authority," ambitious governors extended their control to include Mysore and Travancore in the south, Hyderabad and Maratha in Central India, and finally most of the Deccan, Bengal, and the great Gangetic plain. By the early 1800s the Company controlled three quarters of the Indian land mass and possessed some seventy-five thousand British and Indian employees, an army larger than any military force in continental Europe, and annual profits that often exceeded the revenues of Great Britain itself. Only the Royal Navy had more ships.

Along with spectacular success came corruption and mismanagement – and, eventually, restriction. Politicians in London grew uneasy with the somewhat indefensible fact that one hundred million people were being ruled by the board of directors of a private company. India had become the most stupendous commercial enterprise in history. Gradually the British government curbed the company's monopolies and trading rights and made the governor-general a virtual government appointee. The East India Company became officially what it had long been in practice: an instrument of British foreign policy.

Conquest was a heady wine, and by the early nineteenth century it had become a habit which the empire builders in London and on the Indian subcontinent found no reason to shed. They used outright invasion only after they had persuaded themselves – or at least the public – that British control was in the best interests of everyone concerned. Annexation followed a pattern described by a critic of British expansionism: "First an English Resident (often forced upon the country), then advice urgently pressed, then complaint of misgovernment constantly published, then interference, then compulsion, then open annexation."

No one was fooled. Trading missions to virgin Indian territory inevitably led to takeovers. "The evil is already done," a local chieftain told Alexander Burnes, the first Englishman to visit Sind along the Indus River. "You have seen our country." He was right. Ten years later, in 1843, the Company governor-general, Lord Ellenborough, ordered General Charles Napier "to pick a quarrel with the amirs [of Sind] and occupy their brigand-infested land."

Occasionally the Company overreached itself in spectacular fashion. One instance of crucial significance to the Pathans was the attempt of Lord Ellenborough's predecessor, governor-general Lord Auckland, to remove the amir of Afghanistan – the Pathan homeland – and establish a permanent British presence in Kabul. Armed with guidelines to "interfere decidedly in the affairs of Afghanistan," Auckland created the "Army of the Indus," a staggering assemblage of fifteen thousand troops and an equal number of horses, mules, camels, and elephants. On October 1, 1838, Auckland declared in a manifesto that the Afghan ruler had "avowed schemes of aggrandizement and ambition injurious to the security and peace of the frontier of India" – and invaded the country. The First Afghan War thus opened with a particularly sweet victory for the British, the first military success of the young Victoria.

But success was short-lived. The Afghans, many of whom were Pathans, had not been defeated but had simply withdrawn to the safety of mountain strongholds. In the winter of 1841 they stormed the British Residency, killing the Resident and forcing the troops to evacuate.

On January 6, 1842, the British force of forty-five hundred troops and twelve thousand camp followers set out from Kabul for the frozen passes that led back to India. Afghan and Pathan tribesmen swept down on the column, routing the entire army. On a freezing day in mid-January Dr. William Brydon, a medical officer with the army and its sole survivor, rode into Fort Jalalabad, only half alive. "Thus is verified," wrote a civilian captive who was later rescued, "what we were told before leaving Cabul: that Mahommed Akbar would annihilate the whole army except one man, who should reach Jalalabad to tell the tale."

The next summer an Army of Retribution forced its way back into Kabul long enough to set it on fire, then marched "as swiftly as terrain and dignity permitted" over the passes of the Safed Koh and back into British India. The governor-general announced, in as imperious a manner as he could muster under the circumstances, that he "would leave it to the Afghans themselves to create a government amidst the anarchy which is the consequence of their crimes."

Though the defeat did clip the pride of the Empire momentarily, it did not clip its wings. Before the decade was out, the Company's armies had won two wars with the Sikhs, annexed Sind, the Punjab, and Rajputana, and inherited from the Sikhs the nettlesome but strategic strip of land between the Indus and the Afghan border that came to be called the North-West Frontier.

By the mid-1850s the East India Trading Company had become what amounted to a sovereign power. Only the emperor of China and the czar of Russia ruled over more people than the Company's governor-general.

In 1857 the Indian army rebelled against its British officers, and in the rising that followed the British very nearly lost India altogether. The "Great Indian Mutiny," as the British called it, caused enough bad feeling for the Company in London that it was dissolved by royal decree in 1858 and its responsibilities handed over to the queen-empress herself. "John Company," as it was called, passed into history, and the British Raj was born – or at least made official.

For the British there would be more victories, a few setbacks, and nothing but trouble on the North-West Frontier. But the four decades between the Mutiny and the Diamond Jubilee saw a steady expansion of Great Britain's possessions in India and the consolidation of old ones. In 1897 of the 372 million subjects of the Empire, 308 million lived in India. With seemingly limitless raw materials and millions of consumers for British manufactured goods, India was unlike any other part of the Empire. It had been in British hands for so long that it was part of the national consciousness. Many Indians had come to value the status and material benefits the Empire gave them as subjects.

India's future must have looked supremely bright during the Jubilee summer, especially from the windows of the viceroy's palace in Simla. The lessons of the "Mutiny" had been well learned, and the Indian army had since proven its loyalty more than once. The country was at peace. Even the Frontier had been quiet for a few years.

*

July 28, 1897, was hot on the Frontier and the sun was almost straight overhead as Behram Khan and Ghaffar walked down the main street of Utmanzai, past the shops of traders and craftsmen that lay on either side. A month had passed since the Jubilee. The street was quiet; most of the villagers had gone to their fields. They passed the shoemaker, then two brothers working a large loom made from poplar branches, then the potter, then the coppersmith. Each of them nodded as the khan walked by.

"Pe kher rale?" *they pealed from behind wide smiles. "How are you?"*

"Stre mashe," *Khan called back with a smile.* "Stre mashe: *I hope you are not tired."*

Behram Khan would have stayed to talk had he not wanted to get home. These craftsmen were his equals: all Muslims, despite differences in wealth and status, are equal according to Islamic law. He might easily have spent the evening sitting around a water pipe, smoking tobacco with the shoemaker or the coppersmith. But now he kept on walking.

He was coming from the village guest house, where travelers from

Swat and Bajaur had brought portentous news. All month the khan had been hearing that trouble was brewing in the north. Now it seemed imminent. Mullah Mastun had succeeded in raising a large army of followers, and no one knew what might happen next. From what these travelers were saying, violence could break out at any moment. Behram Khan wanted to talk the matter over with his family.

The khan and his son approached the old defense wall of Utmanzai. Children scurried past them across the wide lane, seeking narrow strips of shade to rest in below the wall. With their watchtowers, Pathan villages often looked like walled medieval cities. From the square windows of the lookout towers a flintlock rifle could blaze away at an approaching enemy. In a land where families were often embroiled in long-running vendettas with their neighbors, even some houses had watchtowers.

Some older boys had climbed the crumbling wall beside the gate. "Hey, Ghaffar!" they called as the khan's son passed. He shot them a smile and watched them jump into the commons, where goats and a milk cow browsed the summer stubble.

Outside town the khan and his son followed the river. Two boys rinsing a water buffalo in knee-deep water paused long enough to wave. The rustle of poplar leaves in the slight breeze mingled with the distant murmur of the village muezzin, calling the faithful to prayer. "Allahu akbar!" came the liquid tone. "God is great!"

It was time for the midday prayers. "Go on ahead," the khan told his son. "I'll be home shortly." Stretching his prayer rug next to a poplar, he knelt and faced Mecca.

Ghaffar's father seldom missed the five daily periods of prayer, even when it meant stopping in his fields and spreading his prayer rug between two rows of sugar cane. He belonged to the clan of the Mohammedzais – "sons of Mohammed." To Behram Khan, this brought the responsibility to live in the light of the Prophet's word.

He was as blue-blooded a Pathan as lived in the valley, yet his villagers knew he had his own ways of living Pushtunwali, the unwritten Law of the Pathan. *Badal,* its strict code of revenge, obligated the Pathan to avenge the slightest insult. For centuries badal had set brother against brother, family against family, clan against clan. The Reverend T. L. Pennell, a respected physician who was running a missionary hospital in Bannu at the time of the Jubilee, wrote about how deeply badal had entered into the Pathan mentality. "Revenge is a word sweet to the Pathan ear," he explains, "and even a revenge satisfied by the culminating murder is the sweeter if the fatal blow, preferably on some dark night, is so managed that the murdered man has a few minutes of life in which to realize that he has been outwitted."

The Reverend Pennell describes one Waziri Pathan who had lost his sight at the hands of his enemies. He had come to the mission hospital and begged the doctor to restore his sight for just one day: "Oh, saheb, if you can give me some sight only just long enough to go and shoot my enemy, then I shall be satisfied to be blind all the rest of my life." When the doctor tried to talk to him of the "Gospel of goodwill and forgiveness," the Waziri "would shake his head and sigh: 'No, that teaching is not for us. What I want is revenge – revenge!'"

Once a bloodletting had set the wheel of vengeance in motion, only the annihilation of the other party could bring it to a stop, for obligations of badal passed from father to son. One vendetta in the province had claimed more than a hundred lives, yet no one could remember how it started.

There was no escape. If a man could not avenge an enemy's insult with his blood, what kind of a man was he? How could he face his clan or wife? To die seeking revenge was more honorable.

Behram Khan thought otherwise. He made no enemies; he avoided feuds. He did not like the taste of revenge. He was known throughout the district for a most un-Pathanlike quality: forgiveness. He had received his share of insults, and there were those who had taken advantage of his trusting nature. But honor, he believed, could be gained in ways more enduring and more pleasing in the eyes of God. He chose to forgive rather than seek revenge – a decision that must have deeply influenced the character and career of his youngest son.

Behram Khan perplexed the tribesmen of his villages – what kind of a khan was this? – but they knew instinctively that he was a man to trust. At the harvest, villagers handed over their savings to him for safekeeping and did not ask for any assurance.

Even the British liked this khan who bore no grudges. He had never given them service, as had most of the other khans of the area, but he was honest and he respected them. They sought his advice on delicate matters, and they did not complain when he confused such exotic names as O'Malley and Warburton and Short. They assumed – and they were right – that this khan would not intend an insult.

His prayers finished, Behram Khan walked to the farmhouse. His wife and youngest son were in the courtyard.

"Here, Ghaffar, today's dodai.*"*

Ghaffar's mother handed the boy two flat chunks of bread. He sat down cross-legged on a small pillow, scooping smooth green dal – cooked split peas – into his mouth with his right hand.

As the boys and their father ate, Ghaffar's mother sat to one side asking about the village. Purdah, the isolation of women from male society, was strict among the Pathan gentry. Ghaffar did not like his mother's isolation, and he made a point of remembering bits of news he gleaned in the village. Today, however, it was his father who did the talking. His mother's face turned ashen at the news of another rising. She had seen firsthand the dreadful costs of war. Every Pathan had.

Ghaffar's mother was a pious woman whose daily prayers, even as a girl, often turned into long periods of silent prayer. It was not her dark beauty alone that had drawn young Behram Khan to her; her vein of piety was a treasure he wanted his children to have. He did not pretend to understand her moods of prayer, but he had come to look upon them with awe. Sometimes Ghaffar would rest his hand on her shoulder until its warmth brought her back, eyes wide and wet, as though returning from a long, winged flight.

Perhaps because he was her youngest, Ghaffar and his mother had formed a deep attachment. She knew he had a temper – he was a Pathan! – but he was a pure, truthful boy. No one understood as she did the solemn moods that would steal over him while sitting under the shishim *tree, saying nothing, or peering into the flames of the cooking fire until it cooled to ashes.*

Even Behram Khan did not understand this independent, abstracted boy who preferred the company of sweepers and spent too much time along the river. But whenever his patience wore thin, his wife always reassured him. "He is a strong boy," she would say confidently. "He is a badshah, *a king."*

"Lord, Lord," Behram Khan would mutter, tugging at his beard. But if his wife said so, the boy would turn out all right.

Later that afternoon, or perhaps not until evening, word would have reached Behram Khan that the trouble in the north had already begun the day before. The first reports were clouded but encouraging: an enormous force of Pathans was attacking the British forts at Chakdarra and Malakand and slaughtering the armies of the Queen. The small contingents of soldiers could not possibly hold out. Mullah Mastun had apparently been right: the day of their deliverance had come.

The Tirah (Mela Ram)

CHAPTER THREE : JULY–DECEMBER, 1897

The Vale of Tirah

Our fault is that our province is the gateway of India. We were born in the Frontier Province. This is why we were doomed.

"IN THE SMALL HOURS" of July 27th, a Frontier war correspondent wrote to his London readers, "the officers of the 11th Bengal Lancers at Nowshera were aroused by a frantic telegraph operator who was astounded by the news his machine was clicking out. This man in his shirt sleeves, with a wild eye, and holding an unloaded revolver by the muzzle, ran round waking everyone. The whole country was up. The Malakand garrison was being overwhelmed by thousands of tribesmen. All the troops were to march at once."

Winston Churchill was twenty-three and a First Lieutenant of the Fourth Hussars in India at the time he wrote this account of the beginning of the Frontier War of 1897. He had joined the Malakand Field Force under General Sir Bindon Blood as a war correspondent when it was ordered into the field to exact "massive retaliation" against the rebellious tribes. "Like most young fools," he wrote, "I was looking for trouble."

Churchill's dispatches give a stirring, if transparent, account of imperial warfare at the turn of the century. While tattered swarms of tribesmen flung themselves against the cannon fire of the Queen's armies, the young lieutenant wrote to the London *Daily Telegraph* readership of daring and adventure:

The tale I have to tell is one of frontier war. The fate of empires does not hang on the result. Yet the narrative may not be without interest, or material for reflection.

The rumors of coming war grew stronger and stronger. The bazaars of India, like the London coffee-houses of the last century, are always full of marvelous tales – the invention of fertile brains. A single unimportant fact is exaggerated, and distorted, till it becomes unrecognizable. From it, a thousand wild, illogical, and fantastic conclusions are drawn. These again are circulated as facts. So the game goes on.

But amid all this falsehood and idle report, there often lies important information. As July [1897] advanced, the bazaar at Malakand became full of tales of the Mad Fakir. His miracles passed from mouth to mouth with suitable additions.

A great day for Islam was at hand. A mighty man had arisen to lead them. The English would be swept away. By the time of the new moon, not one would remain. The Great Fakir had mighty armies concealed among the mountains. When the moment came these would sally forth – horse, foot and artillery – and destroy the infidel. . . .

It was understandable, nevertheless, that the young telegraph operator at the Nowshera garrison should have been "astounded" at the news. Since the Chitral uprising in 1895, the Pathans had been noticeably quiet. And only a month ago, he had read from the same wire a cordial message from Her Imperial Highness, the Queen, in whose Diamond Jubilee ceremonies at Chakdarra, Malakand, and Peshawar many Pathans had joined.

A more informed party, however, would not have been surprised at the outburst of Pathan violence that July evening. British policies on the Frontier had been inviting just such an attack for two decades. Ironically, these were policies aimed not at Pathans, but at an enemy whose armies had never set foot in the province – and never would.

Ever since 1807, when Napoleon met Czar Alexander I of Russia on a raft in the Tilsit River and proposed a combined Russian-French assault on India, the Russians had been making the British nervous. Their steady expansion eastward across the Central Asian plain made many in the British Foreign Office fear that Russia's ultimate destination was India. In 1865 the czar's armies annexed Tashkent, then Samarkand, and in 1868 they turned Bokhara into a Russian satellite. The "Great Game" of imperial intrigue between Russia and Great Britain had begun in earnest.

Since the disastrous retreat from Kabul in 1842, the British had been keeping a respectful distance from the Pathan tribes of the Afghan empire. The "Close Border School" in the Foreign Office had argued for decades – successfully – that the best way to deal with the Afghan tribes was to leave them alone. The high Afghan plain, awash in intrigue, was all the buffer the British needed between their Indian Empire and the Russian menace.

The "Forward School," the hawks of the Foreign Office, thought otherwise. They argued for an assertive policy that would keep Afghans under the British thumb and free of Russian intrigue. The risk of stirring up a little violence among the Pathan tribes of the Frontier was a small price to pay for the security of India.

When the Conservatives took office in 1874 under Disraeli, the Forward School was made official British policy. A new viceroy was appointed, Lord Lytton, who immediately began an aggressive expansionist program to extend the Indian frontier into Afghan territory up to the slopes of the Hindu Kush. Lytton ordered thirty thousand troops to march on Kabul, forcing the Afghan amir to cede the administration of the Khyber Pass and other strategic areas to Britain. He also placed a British envoy in Kabul to direct Afghan foreign policy. Despite fears of a repetition of the 1842 debacle, Sir Louis Cavagnari was stationed in Kabul in July 1879 with a guard of eighty-one troops. On September 3 the British Residency was stormed and all its occupants killed. A second British force occupied Kabul in October, and this time a pro-British amir was placed on the throne. Afghanistan became, in effect, an appendage of the Empire.

But this was not enough to placate the fears of the Forward School. The borders between Afghanistan and India were ill defined and not easily defended. When Russian troops clashed with the Afghans in 1885, the Conservatives insisted it was Britain's "bounden duty" to build a permanent buffer zone between British India and Imperial Russia along a secure border. The obvious location for the border was the range of mountains between Afghanistan and British India. High and rugged, their narrow passes were easily defended. The only problem was that this placed the buffer garrisons squarely within the homelands of the Pathans. Not even Forward School hawks were eager to arouse Pathan ire. But the protectors of the Empire felt they had no choice: India, Britain's prize possession, must be defended at all costs.

In the autumn of 1893 Lieutenant Henry Durand was sent to Kabul to negotiate a border between Afghanistan and British India that would effectively hand over to the British most of the Pathan homelands, historically part of the Afghan empire. The proposed border – the "Durand Line" – cut through the heart of the Pathan nation, leaving a third of all Pathans in Afghanistan.

The Afghan amir warned the British that they had more to lose from the settlement than he did. "If you should cut the Pathan tribes away from my domain," he wrote the viceroy in desperation,

> they will not be of any use either to you or to me. You will always be engaged in fighting them or be involved in some other trouble with them, and they will always go on plundering.

The British forced the issue. On November 12, 1893, they got the amir's signature to a treaty that brought under their dominion all the territory from the Hindu Kush to the westernmost limits of Baluchistan – and made inevitable a conflict with the Pathans that would last to the Empire's final days.

The British set out to forge a buffer zone that would permanently seal British India off from external threats. Pathans were divided into "settled" tribes of the lower valleys and "free" tribes of the hills. More forts were built and additional troops brought in to make certain their presence was felt. For the independent-spirited Pathans, the girdling of their hills with forts and garrisons and the insufferable imperial rule that followed simply could not be borne for long.

British expeditions had already been sent against the Akazais in the Black Mountains in 1891; in 1894 they went into Waziristan. In January 1895, Chitral exploded in the north and fifteen thousand troops had to be sent to restore order. Forts were built at Malakand and Chakdarra in Swat to prevent further outbreaks. But the area was British in name only. Independent tribesmen saw the new forts as portents of a permanent occupation.

For two years they simmered. Then, in the early summer months of 1897, Mullah Mastun began touring the villages of the north. He reminded the tribesmen of their humiliation and roused them to religious hysteria by proclaiming that the Prophet himself had given the word: the time had come for *jihad,* a holy war that would drive the British out of the province and reclaim the Delhi throne, after a lapse of three centuries, for Islam. He had found the thirteen-year-old heir to the Mogul dynasty and would place him on the throne himself. Within a month, Mullah Mastun – Churchill's "mad Fakir" – had raised an army of ten thousand seething Pathans.

*

The explosion came at ten o'clock on a moonless July night. Descending simultaneously on the forts at Malakand and Chakdarra, the Pathans stormed the outer garrisons with their swords, knives, and ancient rifles. Caught off guard – but only momentarily – British and Sikh troops fought back with land mines, cannon, and devastating fire from their breech-loading rifles. Throughout the night, wave after wave of tribesmen were repulsed – by massive firepower, discipline, and sheer pluck. If the Queen's troops could hold out, reinforcements could reach the forts from Nowshera and Mardan by noon.

To the Pathans who threw themselves into the teeth of the cannon and rifle fire, setbacks meant little. Time was with them – as was Allah. They knew they outnumbered the British. Hundreds of them died in the avalanche of bullets and the bursts of cannon and land mines. But what was death? Only a promise of paradise.

Morning came, and the forts still held. Bodies littered the rocky ground around the forts, but the Pathans kept up the attack. Their cause was invincible.

Then an astounding thing happened. From over the bare hills of the pass came a great body of the Raj's soldiers and cavalry, with their breechloaders firing and their lances ready. The tribesmen simply stared, unbelieving.

"It is no exaggeration," Churchill writes,

> to say that perhaps half the tribesmen who attacked the Malakand had thought that the soldiers there were the only troops that the Sirkar [the government] possessed.
>
> "Kill these," they had said, "and all is done."
>
> What did they know of the distant regiments which the telegraph wires were drawing from far down in the south of India? Little did they realize they had set the world humming; that military officers were hurrying seven thousand miles by sea and land from England, to the camps among the mountains; that long trains were carrying ammunition, material and supplies from distant depots to the front....
>
> These ignorant tribesmen had no conception of the sensitiveness of modern civilization, which thrills and quivers in every part of its vast and complex system at the slightest touch.
>
> They saw only the forts and camps on the Malakand Pass and the swinging bridge across the river.

The miscalculation was typical of these impulsive tribesmen – and fatal. Churchill continues:

> Sir Bindon Blood had with his staff ascended the Castle Rock, to superintend the operations generally. From this position the whole field was visible. On every side, and from every rock, the white figures of the enemy could be seen in full flight. The way was open. The passage was forced. Chakdarra was saved. A great and brilliant success had been obtained. A thrill of exultation convulsed everyone....
>
> The 11th Bengal Lancers, forming line across the plain, began a merciless pursuit up the valley. All among the rice fields and the rocks, the strong horsemen hunted the flying enemy. No quarter was asked or given, and every tribesman caught was speared or cut down at once. Their bodies lay thickly strewn about the fields, spotting with black and white patches the bright green of the rice crop. It was a terrible lesson and one which the inhabitants of Swat and Bajaur will never forget.

The victory was thorough, but – as usually the case on the Frontier – inconclusive. By the time the Malakand Field Force had blasted its way through the higher regions of Swat, the Afridis had entered the Khyber. Further south, Orakzais were sending assault parties into the Kurram Valley. By the end of August the Frontier was up in massive revolt, and the Khyber Pass itself – gateway to India – fell from British hands.

A force of thirty-five thousand men, including sixty field cannon, a machine gun detachment, and thirty thousand pack animals, took the field in response. It was aimed at the heart of the Afridi homeland, the Tirah, which no foreign army had ever penetrated. By mid-October, the Tirah Expeditionary Force had fought its way through the protective ring of the Samana range and entered the Valley of Tirah Maidan.

There, in the midst of barren, blistered peaks, the British found a paradise. The passes opened onto wide cultivated fans, terraced orchards of apricot and plum, apple, fig, and orange trees. The harvest was in; the storage sheds behind the farmhouses were brimful with corn and barley, beans, potatoes, onions, and walnuts. In the crisp October air, the valley looked as serene as an English landscape. "The autumn tints upon the trees are beautiful," wrote a British correspondent accompanying the expedition, "and carry one back to the mother country at once. One can well imagine that when the spring crops are in and the valley is green from end to end, this is the beautiful spot which has so inspired the Pathan poets."

But the point of a punitive campaign is to punish – to render the landscape so incapable of supporting life that its inhabitants will be forced to surrender. And the Afridis had made the job easier than anyone expected. They were gone – fled with their families and flocks to the bare ridges above the valley. From there they watched, silent and helpless, as the khaki-colored troops spread out across the valley.

They started with the stocks. Wagonfuls of beans and potatoes and nuts were carted out of the storehouses and the orchards were stripped, and the trees then felled with axes or ringed to die slowly. Standing crops were burned.

As they reached a village, soldiers would hurry to sack the houses of the khans. Carpets and silks, copperware, furniture, and ornaments were piled into long wagons and carted back to the camps. What was not worth carrying back – utensils, farm equipment, household items – was heaped into a pile in the center of the village and burned. Wagonfuls of granite boulders were drawn alongside the wells and heaved in to poison the water.

Sometimes soldiers ventured too close to the valley walls and fell victims to ambush. At night, a lighted cigarette might draw rifle fire from a nearby crag. There were casualties, but by and large the soldiers moved about unimpeded. Once a village had been cleared, demolition units laid dynamite charges along the walls and towers. By mid-November the Tirah Valley was close to being a desert, while high on the ridges, the tribal children began succumbing to the cold. Khans trickled into Expeditionary Force headquarters to accept the terms of peace: three hundred rifles and a fine of thirty thousand rupees.

In December, the British began a quick withdrawal and just managed to get through the Samanas before a howling winter storm slammed the passes shut. The Afridi families were less fortunate. With little shelter and virtually no food stocks, many of the youngest and oldest died.

The punitive campaign had met its objective. The Frontier tribes had been beaten back and the war ended. But the price was high. The Empire had collected a few thousand rusting rifles and enough in fines to cover the expenses of a marching column for perhaps a week. In the process it had guaranteed the enmity of the Frontier Pathans for the next fifty years.

Before a decade had passed, the British would have to face new uprisings of Waziris and Orakzais – and once again have to enter the Tirah. If Churchill's plucky prose stirred the British back home to feel the glamour and romance of the Frontier wars, other Englishmen came to assess the net effect of Frontier policy in more sobering terms. Some of them – like Annie Besant, an Englishwoman in India already agitating for Indian "home rule" – came close to matching Churchill's fire:

> We loudly proclaimed that we had no quarrel with the Pathan nation, yet we burnt their villages, destroyed their crops, stole

> their cattle, looted their homes, hanged their men as "rebels" if they resisted, while we drove out their women and children to perish in the snow.
>
> From out of the darkness, moans of suffering reach us, and we shrink in horror from the work which is being done in our names. These starved babes wail out our condemnation. These frozen women cry aloud against us. These stiffened corpses, these fire-blackened districts, these snow-covered, blood-stained plains appear to humanity to curse us.
>
> Englishmen, with wives nestled warm in your bosoms, remember these Pathan husbands, maddened by their wrongs. Englishwomen, with babes smiling on your breasts, think of these sister-women, bereft of their little ones. The Pathan loves wife and children as you do. He also is husband and father. To him also the home is happy, the hearth is sacred. To you he cries from his desolate fireside and from his ravaged land. In your hands is his cause.

But the British were helpless to change course. The Forward Policy had overextended them into territories they could not fully subjugate; permanent occupation of the Pathan hills would have been far too costly an enterprise. But neither could they ignore the tribes; the Pathans themselves would see to that. Thus they were reduced to vindictive campaigns whose excesses only inflamed the Pathans while offending liberal sensibilities at home. In a sense, the British had become prisoners of their own imperial designs.

Thus, within a few months of Victoria's Diamond Jubilee and its celebration of the "new imperialism," at least some British were beginning to have second thoughts. The glittering image of the Empire had a dark side which the resolute Pathan resistance had begun to unmask. Within two years the atrocities of the Boer War in South Africa would confirm the darker aspects of empire. One more year and Victoria herself would die, mercifully spared the spectacle of her "best and bravest" dying by the hundreds of thousands on the fields of Flanders and Verdun. The benign face of Pax Britannica, so shimmering during the Jubilee summer, would never smile as brightly again.

A British fort in Chitral, 1895 (Robertson)

CHAPTER FOUR : 1907–1909

The Guides

The Holy Prophet Mohammed came into this world and taught us: "That man is a Muslim who never hurts anyone by word or deed, but who works for the benefit and happiness of God's creatures. Belief in God is to love one's fellowmen."

THE REVEREND Mr. E. F. F. Wigram was headmaster of the Edwardes Memorial Mission High School in Peshawar. The Reverend Mr. Wigram and his younger brother, Dr. Wigram, represented a class of men and women – not uncommon during the days of the Raj – who genuinely accepted the burden of improving the welfare of the Empire's less fortunate subjects. The two brothers loved the Frontier and its people, with their soaring spirits and their stern, uncompromising codes of honor.

The mission schools trained young Pathans in English, science, and mechanics, mainly to prepare them for the matriculation examinations of the Punjab university. From there they could enter the Indian Government Service as clerks, the only form of occupation other than the army open to native graduates. Much to the dislike of the Muslim clergy, the mission schools also taught the Bible.

Dr. Wigram oversaw the mission hospital in Peshawar, while his brother oversaw the high school. Their family in England supported the work, to the extent of offering scholarships out of their own pockets to promising Pathan boys.

Ghaffar Khan was as quick and strong-willed as any other sixteen-year-old in the mission high school the spring of 1907. His elder brother, Abdul Jabar Khan, the first boy from Utmanzai to attend a British school, was now in Bombay preparing to study medicine at Edinburgh. Ghaffar was the second boy from the village to attend the school, and the mullahs of Utmanzai did not like it. They condemned British schools because they competed with their own *maktabs,* which taught only according to the words of the Prophet. There boys learned a doggerel which could be heard spilling out into the road in front of the mosque:

Those who learn in schools
Are none but money's tools.
In heaven they will never dwell;
They will surely go to hell.

At first the mullahs of Utmanzai had made a sweeping rule: parents sending their sons to the mission school would be excommunicated. Before Behram Khan, no villager had dared to risk the mullahs' censure, but the khan was too broad-minded to let them interfere with the education of his boys. The mullahs muttered imprecations behind the closed doors of the mosque, but publicly they rationalized their loss. The khan's boys were pious, and hadn't young Ghaffar learned the Koran by heart? There was nothing to fear. "Let the boys read English," they compromised, "so long as they do not read the Christian scriptures; for the Christians have tampered with these books and it is no longer lawful for Muslims to read them."

Ghaffar was happy to be part of the same school his elder brother had attended. He did not mind the mild indoctrination into Christianity and Western – especially British – culture that all the students received. One of the questions that regularly appeared on examinations was to list the benefits bestowed upon the people of India by the Raj: the roads the British had built, with their high iron bridges; the magical telegraph lines that hummed messages through the passes to Delhi and down to Madras; the schools, of course, even though they thought Pushto too coarse to teach the boys; the railways that climbed the high, bare passes like iron serpents; the hospitals; the soldiers that maintained the rule of British law and kept the marauding hill tribes from harassing its "settled" farmers. It did not occur to most British that Pathans would rather have had their freedom than telegraphs and iron bridges and the "rule of law." Most Pathans – as the Frontier War demonstrated – preferred privation and hardship to servitude.

Ghaffar never forgot the dark, drained faces of the villagers who had returned from fighting the British during that dreadful summer of the Frontier War. He had seen the fire beaten from their bright, burning eyes. After that it was not the same when his father took him to the village guest house. For a long time the men did not sing and there was no poetry. They drank tea and spoke bitterly of the English masters, and the boy heard hatred and fear in their voices.

But since then much had changed. The boy had grown into a muscular young man, over six feet tall, and had made a number of British friends in Peshawar. He had come to respect the teachers in his school, and he admired the poise and courage of the British soldiers. Ghaffar was a born warrior – every Pathan was – and he recognized the qualities of a good soldier when he saw them.

He also admired Reverend Wigram – almost as much, in fact, as his own father. The missionary was a strict but generous man, and Ghaffar saw that although he was a foreigner from across the seas, he was more concerned about the future of these Pathan boys than their own parents were. An idea began to form in Ghaffar's mind: why not stay on in the school and work for this good man?

But the Guides changed all of that.

The Guides, an elite corps of Pathan and Sikh infantry and cavalry stationed at Mardan, had a long history of distinguished service to the Empire. The sons of wealthy and influential Pathans and Sikhs were even given officers' commissions, which brought further prestige – and a chance for glory. A Guides officer was the equal of an Englishman! At least this was what Barani Kaka, one of Ghaffar's servants and a lifelong friend, had been telling Ghaffar for the past year. The khan's son was six foot three and weighed over two hundred pounds, Barani Kaka reasoned: the British would snap him up!

Ghaffar was in his tenth and final year at the high school. He was halfway through the matriculation examination of the university when he learned that he had been granted a commission and should present himself before the recruiting officer the following day. In his exultation, he walked away from the examination on the spot.

Barani Kaka was ecstatic, as was Ghaffar's aging father. Behram Khan wasted no time in spreading the news to the guest houses in every village between Peshawar and Tangi. Ghaffar had joined the Guides!

*

After their last class, Ghaffar and Barani Kaka walked down to the Qissa Khawani Bazaar to meet a former schoolmate.

Peshawar had long been the terminus of the great caravan roads leading from Iran and Central Asia to India, and the point of departure for passengers and freight sailing down the Indus River to the open seas. Its bazaar was a sprawl of narrow, curving streets of stalls spilling over with the wares of the Central Asian plains: silks, carpets, prayer rugs, precious stones, copper and brass ware, bright colored shoes with curving toes and silk brocade, great swaths of cloth in shimmering colors, entire armories of rifles and curved daggers. Every street – the Street of the Coppersmiths, the Shoemakers, the Clothiers, the Storytellers, the Weavers – had its specialty.

The two youths turned onto the Street of the Silversmiths and stopped in a small tea shop where they could see the pure white minarets of the Mahabat Khan mosque. From these towers the Sikhs, during their bloody reign, had hung Pathans – two every day – as a curb to intrigue. Crowds of turbaned men with beards were milling in front of the mosque or sitting in tea shops, sipping dark qahwa tea sweetened with sugar and buffalo milk and puffing contentedly from clay pipes.

From out of the crowd a tall, uniformed Pathan stepped up to their stall, his combed hair glistening, his smile wide. It was their old schoolmate, now with the Guides. Ghaffar, taking in the crisp khaki uniform and the close-cropped Western-style haircut, asked him to sit down. They ordered cups of tea and started to talk.

Before long they heard a sharp, nasal voice: "Well, I'll be damned!" Two English officers from the Guides were staring at Ghaffar's friend's hair. "Really!" one of them snorted contemptuously. "Why, you damn 'Sardar Sahib' – you fake Englishman! So you want to be an Englishman, do you?"

Ghaffar's hand leaped toward his friend's to check the attack. No Pathan would let such an insult go unanswered.

But his friend did not move. The English officers turned away without waiting for a reply.

Ghaffar looked at his friend. His head was lowered. What could he have said? No Guides officer could speak to an Englishman with disrespect – not, that is, if he valued his commission.

Ghaffar turned on Barani Kaka, trembling with anger. "You told me that a Pathan Guide is the Englishman's equal!"

Barani Kaka tried to calm the young khan, but to no avail.

Shortly after, Ghaffar refused his commission. He had the feeling that he had rid himself of a curse – and just in time.

At home, however, Behram Khan fumed. Ghaffar had thrown away an opportunity denied to all but the most capable Pathan boys. Well, he decided, the boy would rejoin. Not even his wife could persuade him that his son had acted from deep principle. This time Behram Khan would not listen – his son would rejoin.

Pressed, Ghaffar wrote his brother in England. The choice, he explained, had been obvious. He could not serve the British government because it turned brave Pathans into slaves – and offered the risk of getting insulted into the bargain.

Khan Saheb had always admired the courage of his younger brother. He would not have done the same thing himself, but they were different. He wrote their father that Ghaffar had done right: no man should be made to suffer dishonor and disrespect. It was reasoning that any Pathan could appreciate. Behram Khan relented. How could he hold out against the pleadings of his wife, the thick-headed righteousness of his youngest son, and now the polished arguments of his eldest? Ghaffar could go on with his studies.

*

Ghaffar Khan began the next term at an Islamic school in Campbellpur, on the other side of the Indus river. He wanted to learn Arabic. But the dry, hot climate of the Punjab did not suit him. He left Campbellpur and enrolled in a mission school at Aligarh, in the center of northern India.

Near the end of the term, he received a letter from his father. The Reverend Wigram had persuaded Behram Khan that Ghaffar should follow his brother to England. He was a good student of geometry; he could live with Khan Saheb and study engineering. The Reverend would make all the arrangements.

England! The boy could not believe his eyes. And to live with his brother! His father sent him three thousand rupees to get himself ready to go. His passage was booked on a P. & O. liner that would leave in a few weeks.

Ghaffar hurried home. In the prescribed manner, he went to his mother to ask her permission to go. But at the first words, he saw her hands clench and her eyes fill with tears. "Not my last boy!" she said in a whisper. No.

Ghaffar argued with her. "Look at our country, Ma. Innocent people are dragged to the courts and men who have committed no crime are put to death. Nobody's life is safe here. In England I can learn ways to challenge these bad laws."

No. *Not the last son. The mullahs had told her that a person who goes to a foreign land never returns to his native home.*

"But it will be only two years – and I'll be living with my brother!" No. *One son, the mullahs said, had already gone from her to the unbelievers' land, and he would never return.*

"Ma, I won't come to any good if I stay here."

No. *They said he would marry an English girl, as his brother had, and become a Christian, a stranger to his own people.*

No.

Khan's strong shoulders slumped. The stricken face of this woman, who was closer to him than any other person on earth – who knew him better than he knew himself – was enough. "All right, Ma."

He could not build his future on his mother's sorrow. "All right. I'll stay."

The Malakand Pass, 1895 (National Army Museum, London)

CHAPTER FIVE : 1909–1913

Islam!

It is my inmost conviction that Islam is amal, yakeen, muhabat [work, faith, and love] and without these the name "Muslim" is sounding brass and tinkling cymbal. The Koran makes it absolutely clear that faith in One God without a second, and good works, are enough to secure a man his salvation.

IT HAD LONG BEEN insinuated by the rugged tribes of the hills that the settled Pathans of the Peshawar and Kurram valleys had grown soft. They loved their land more than they loved battle. Certainly most of the Mohammedzais – including Behram Khan – would have pleaded guilty to the charge.

When Ghaffar's plans for England collapsed, therefore, it was natural for him to take to farming his father's lands. He began to work the rich fields along the Swat with his usual energy.

But he felt restless. As he talked with the peasants of the district, he became painfully aware of the state into which most of his people had fallen. He looked at the poverty, the ignorance, the apathy and violence all around him, and he wanted to do something about it.

At first he did not understand these feelings. Social reform was not characteristic of the Pathans; it was a British notion. Although the mullahs railed at the sinful, decadent foreigners, they remained firmly in their grip: the Raj protected the iron rule of the mullahs over the villagers, and in return the mullahs discouraged any social or political reform.

Young Khan knew all this. He knew that any attempt to improve the lot of his people would be discouraged, even harassed. In the moral life of the Pathan, the world belonged to those who were strong enough to take what they could hold: mercy and generosity were left to Allah. But although he wondered where it came from, the twenty-year-old farmer felt the need to serve.

One afternoon, working in the fields behind the farmhouse, Ghaffar Khan was thinking about the Reverend Wigram, his old schoolmaster. In the silence of the summer air, an ancient proverb chimed. Kharbuza ra kharbuza dida rang me girad: *"When a melon sees another melon, it takes on its color." Ghaffar had spent years watching the unassuming brothers at the Mission. The color of their love and generosity must have rubbed off, he decided – the melon will take its color as it will. Very well, then: he would serve.*

But how? And where? Certainly no help would come from the mullahs. Who was he – a twenty-year-old Mohammedzai farm boy, not even matriculated from high school – to uplift an ancient, noble people?

Well, he was just that, a Mohammedzai – a child of the Prophet himself. What more did he need? He could read. He could write. He knew farming. All right, then, he would start a school.

*

"I know these men," wrote George Nathaniel Curzon of Kedleston:

> They are brave as lions, wild as cats, docile as children. . . . It is with a sense of pride that one receives the honest homage of these magnificent Samsons, gigantic, bearded, instinct with loyalty, often stained with crime.

Lord Curzon meant every word he wrote about the Pathans. He admired them, but he had no illusions about them. In 1899 he was appointed viceroy of India precisely because he knew more about the Pathans than any other man in England – and because he had a plan to Pathan-proof the Frontier. Between the risings of 1897, when the Tirah was devastated, and 1910, when Ghaffar Khan started his first school, much had changed on the Frontier, and most of the changes were due to the plans of the energetic and resolute Curzon.

The savage outburst of the Frontier wars of the 1890s made it clear to the British that they were sitting atop a powder keg that threatened to explode at the very gateway to the Indian Empire. As long as the Frontier could erupt in violence at the whim of any crazed mullah, it would be vulnerable to Russian intrigue. The Forward Policy had checked external threats, but internally the Frontier was still vulnerable. India's security was at stake. As viceroy, Curzon knew that the security of the Indian Empire was his paramount duty, and he intended to let nothing – not even his admiration for "magnificent Samsons" – stand in its way.

Curzon's plan put the Frontier directly under the control of the viceroy in Delhi. Crucial decisions could be made swiftly at the least sign of disturbance. The hill tribes remained isolated from the settled districts; settled Pathans like Ghaffar Khan could not even enter the tribal areas without permission. Vivisection of the Pathan nation was complete.

Included in Curzon's plan was a standing army of ten thousand men that girded the province along a two-hundred-mile perimeter, from the Malakand in the north to the southern tip of Waziristan on the Iranian border. More forts were built and railways and roads laid down to move army units quickly to any trouble spot. A six-thousand-man police force maintained peace. The province was declared to be "a sealed book, a hunting-ground for the officers of the Political Department and the military."

Lord Curzon also enacted a series of restrictive laws known as the Frontier Crimes Regulation. A man could be "transported" – sent to a foreign penal colony – for life without counsel or trial. Justice was in the hands of the political agent or pro-British landlords called in to hear cases. The most elementary rights extended to Her Majesty's subjects throughout the Empire were denied the Pathans. All this only confirmed what the Pathans had long suspected: the imperial powers in Delhi and London regarded them as savages.

On November 9, 1901, the North-West Frontier Province came into being. It was in fact an armed garrison, a police state. These were the conditions when Ghaffar Khan opened his school in Utmanzai. Neither he nor Curzon could have imagined that someday the small school would help to undermine the viceroy's plans.

*

For several years the Haji Abdul Wahid Saheb of Tarangzai had been working in the villages of Mardan, near Utmanzai, giving religious instruction. He was the Frontier's first social reformer. Pathans throughout the district knew him as Haji Saheb and regarded him as a saint. He had attracted a dedicated band of young volunteers, and when he heard that a young Mohammedzai had started a school in Utmanzai, he was naturally interested. He guessed that he would find a kindred spirit and invited Khan to come to Mardan.

Ghaffar's school had been an instant success. The mullahs had always urged villagers to boycott the British schools, but they had offered no real alternative. The more liberal Pathans began to take notice of the school in Utmanzai. Khan and a co-worker, Abdul Aziz, started several more like it in surrounding villages, and in a short time they had enrolled a large number of students.

Less sympathetic interests took notice too. Khan's fledgling schools caught the ever-watchful eye of the British, who did not want an awakened peasantry on the Frontier. In addition, the mullahs saw him as a competitor. If villagers became too educated, they might stop giving alms.

Khan tried to reason with them. "Mullah Saheb," he once pleaded with a priest at Murree as they walked down the main street, "look at that bungalow. What do you think of it?"

"It is very beautiful," the mullah replied. "I like it."

"Do you know who the man is who lives there?"

"No, who is he?"

"He is an English mullah. If a country prospers and its people progress, then the priests can also live well. But if we remain ignorant, then you will have to go begging from door to door for your stipend."

The mullah was not impressed.

"Compare your life to the life of the English priest," Khan suggested. "What a difference!" The priest shrugged. His income was meager, but at least it was certain. Who knew what would happen if too much education were given out?

"My words were wasted on the mullah," Khan told Abdul Aziz later. "If God Himself could not make him understand, what could I do?"

When the Haji Saheb invited Khan to meet him in Mardan, he asked him to start a school for older boys at Gaddai, in the north. Khan accepted at once.

Ghaffar Khan liked the village, and he liked contact with the Haji's circle of young liberals. Under their influence he began to read more widely. He subscribed to progressive Muslim periodicals like *Zamindar* and *Al-Hilal* that were just beginning to appear. A Muslim renaissance was in the making, and its fresh, vigorous breezes were just beginning to stir Muslims in India.

The British on the Frontier were feeling the breeze too. They blacklisted anyone who read *Al-Hilal.* Under the Frontier Crimes Act public meetings were illegal except in mosques, so Khan and the Haji Saheb's co-workers were forced to move about the province secretly.

All this activity was making Behram Khan uneasy. His two daughters were well married; his eldest son was learning medicine in England. But his youngest son had resigned a commission in the Guides and was spreading education. The old khan worried. Too many brave young Pathans had been jailed for lesser offenses, or deported to prison camps on the Andamans in the Indian Ocean – or simply hanged.

Behram Khan's wife tempered his concern. Ghaffar, she said, was a responsible boy who knew what he was doing. Behram Khan yielded. If his pious wife approved of the boy's activities, who was he to stand in the way? Still, he decided, life would look different to the boy if he were married and settled. He arranged a marriage to a girl who had caught Ghaffar's interest, gave them a village to manage, and hoped for the best.

Ghaffar adored his beautiful wife, and in 1913 a son, Ghani, was born. The young khan began to think that he might enjoy the more regular life of a landlord.

But the restlessness persisted. Holding his infant son in his arms in front of the evening fire, he often felt something stir within him. His thoughts would drift to the impoverished, ignorant villagers of the province. His wife could not understand the long silences and grew to fear these moods. But what could she say?

Abruptly, disaster struck Ghaffar Khan's dreams. The Haji Saheb decided to fight the British openly. He tried to rally the villagers of Buner to drive the foreigners from their hills. But the Frontier War was still too fresh in their minds, and the Haji Saheb found himself caught between the mullahs, who intrigued against him, and the alarmed British. When his arrest appeared imminent, the Haji fled one night to the remoter territories of the Mohmands. He never returned.

For years after, the British would say that their biggest mistake on the Frontier was letting the Haji Saheb slip away. But they were not about to risk another full-scale war with the Mohmands to get him back.

*

The Haji's flight was a catastrophe for twenty-four-year-old Ghaffar Khan. Now only brave young men like him were left to carry on. Who would lead them?

Khan decided to look for help. In 1913 he attended a conference of progressive Muslims at Agra, once the center of Mogul India and still a symbol of the most enlightened aspect of Islamic civilization. There he met Muslim leaders like Maulana Azad who were engaged in the social, educational, and political uplift of backward Muslim populations all over the Indian subcontinent. A year later, at another conference at Deoband, they suggested that Ghaffar Khan try to work among the "free" tribes of the hills, where the need for education was greatest.

The hills? Ghaffar explained to these cultured Muslims from Delhi and Lahore that the Frontier Regulations prohibited settled Pathans like himself from even talking with the hill tribes. Nevertheless, he agreed, the idea was compelling, and worth a try.

He decided to visit Bajaur, the mountainous district to the north where fifteen years earlier the tribesmen of Mullah Mastun had started the Great Frontier War. The British had not forgotten. They had made the Malakand – like other trouble spots on the Frontier – a "Political Agency," something of a political no-man's-land. It came under the absolute control of the local political agent, whose word was law – and the British in Delhi made sure that his word would be harsh. Only the most hardened administrators were sent out to the Agencies.

The political agent of the Malakand was a notorious man named Cab. By his ordinance, Pathans had to bow low before any passing Englishman. Any Pathan who failed to do so was locked in stocks in the commons, his head and feet sticking out through the holes. The entire district was ruled like a feudal fiefdom.

One winter morning, Khan left for Bajaur with a Mohmand colleague. They reached the Malakand Pass at dusk. Police were searching anyone who looked suspicious, and Khan knew he would be stopped and perhaps arrested. He lay down in the back of a horse carriage and covered himself with his long cotton cloth.

It must have been dark, or perhaps the guard was tired. The tonga driver told him there was no one in the back. He peered for an endless moment at the pile of cotton on the carriage bottom and let it through. Khan's friend, being a Mohmand, walked right in.

Once they were past the Chakdarra checkpoint, the two left the main road and climbed steep trails toward Bajaur. They walked through cedar forests, then into pines. Friends of the Haji Saheb gave them food and rooms to sleep in – at Chamarkand, a small cottage on the edge of the forest, with hives of honey bees droning in the morning sun. Following the creeks of the Panjkora for another day, they reached Bajaur.

Itinerant travelers were not unusual sights, even to these remote, high-country villagers. Wandering mendicants often set themselves up near the village mosques to read the scriptures and tell stories about the saints and seers. But this was no mendicant. It was difficult not to notice him.

Ghaffar thought the small village of Zagai would make a good place to start work. It was remote enough, he thought, to escape undue attention, and the villagers seemed to like him. He sent a message to the plains for other workers to join him. Then he waited.

From near the mosque, one could look out over the pine and cedar forests and into the valleys of Bajaur. There the British watched everyone and everything that passed through. After a few days of waiting, Ghaffar began to wonder if something had happened to his friends. Had they even received his message?

Another day passed. And another.

In the seclusion of the woods, the reality of his situation bore down upon Ghaffar Khan. He did not like hiding from the authorities. How could he work under such conditions, when even students were paid by the British to inform on their teachers?

Alone and perplexed, young Ghaffar Khan fell back upon his instincts. He decided to perform a *chilla,* a fast. If he could not find help outside, he would seek it within himself. He found a small mosque and told his Mohmand friend to wait for him. No, he explained, he did not know what he was going to do. He hoped to find out.

Khan stayed in the small, dim room for several days, eating nothing. At night he sipped creek water. And he prayed. When his knees tired of kneeling, he sat cross-legged on the prayer carpet.

He sought answers. Should he stay and risk capture? Should he return to the relative safety of Utmanzai? What should he do? Finding no help, he entered into the depths of his consciousness, until the questions stopped.

*

Francis Bernardone of Assisi was a year older than Ghaffar Khan when, seven hundred years earlier, he entered the broken, deserted church of San Damiano to pray and heard a bold, clear voice command him: "Francis, rebuild my church!" Obediently he walked out into the countryside to collect some stones and start the repair.

That the impetuous Francis took the command too literally – that "church," in fact, was meant to indicate an institution far beyond the four walls of that broken structure – did not matter.

Francis mistook the call, but he did not mistake his calling. He knew, however dimly, that the hand of God had rested on his bare shoulder, and that it was lifting him up to a great task.

Laying those undressed stones along the broken wall of San Damiano started Francis of Assisi on a mission that utterly changed the course of his life. Ghaffar Khan was even more reticent about his inner life than Francis was, and in an immediate sense, to judge from his own terse references, his chilla in the mosque at Zagai was clouded and inconclusive. But it can be observed from that point on that his activities and words are stamped with a singleness of purpose – the service of God – that does not alter over the course of eight decades.

It was early morning when Ghaffar Khan ended his fast. He folded his prayer rug under his arm and walked out with the vague but powerful awareness that he was not the same man who had entered the mosque a few days before. He had not received the direct answers he had sought – he still did not know what to do. But he felt a strength he had not known before. And he understood, dimly, that it was the strength of God.

Islam! *Inside him, the word began to explode with meaning.* Islam! *Submit! Surrender to the Lord and know His strength! Ghaffar felt swelling within him the desire to serve this great God. And since He needed no service, Ghaffar would serve His creatures instead – the tattered villagers who were too ignorant and too steeped in violence to help themselves.*

Ghaffar looked down into the valley. There were the British with their stern tyranny, the entrenched khans, the overly conservative priests. He saw before him only pain and unending labor. But he felt buoyed. Like Francis, he did not fully understand the nature of his calling; but he knew he had been called. He would submit and he would not seek rest in this life.

He swung his prayer carpet over his shoulder and started down the footpath, dodging the broken, peppered granite in his way.

Ghaffar Khan could hardly have suspected that his life now moved along a path taken a decade earlier by another subject of the Indian

Empire, Mohandas Gandhi. By the time Khan had returned to his village and set about reopening the schools closed by the British after the flight of the Haji Saheb, a steamship was carrying Gandhi away from South Africa, where the forty-five-year-old barrister had concluded history's first successful nonviolent struggle against imperialism. In South Africa, Gandhi had undergone a transformation of character that utterly altered his life's purpose. For a decade he had been systematically reforming his lifestyle to transform himself from an affluent lawyer into a disciplined seeker of God. He had thrown all the forces of his powerful personality into the task of reducing every ego-centered drive in him "to zero." Walking the dry hills of Natal as a stretcher bearer during the Zulu "rebellion" of 1906 – another notorious British punitive expedition – he had heard within him the call to selfless service and felt the surge of power that follows the surrender of the human will to an overriding cause.

Gandhi returned from his ambulance service acutely aware of a new strength, but still unaware of what he was to do. Within weeks he found himself at the head of a wholly new kind of campaign – systematic, nonviolent resistance to discriminatory legislation. Through trial and error, sometimes supported by thousands of Indian laborers, at times only by a handful of friends, Gandhi finally succeeded in winning the basic rights denied his people by the government. In the summer of 1914, confident of the power of his new way of fighting, Gandhi left South Africa to return to India.

The forces released in the Hindu barrister and the Muslim reformer were slowly converging – and they were unlike anything the statesmen and generals of the Raj had ever faced. The British, masters of the arts of diplomacy and war, had conquered a quarter of the earth's people. But the forces of history were now moving to pit them against something altogether new: *satyagraha,* "soul force," power unleashed from the depths of the human spirit.

India seemed supremely secure that summer of 1914. Most British would have scoffed at the notion that the Raj would collapse in just three decades. Ghaffar Khan would probably have scoffed along with them. Like Gandhi, he had chosen to serve. He did not question the future.

Part Two

Badshah Khan at 35 (Nehru Memorial Library)
Previous pages: Pathan tribesmen in jirgah (council) (Yunus)

CHAPTER SIX : 1914–1921

Badshah Khan

I have one great dream, one great longing.

Like flowers in the desert, my people are born, bloom for a while with nobody to look after them, wither, and return to the dust they came from.

I want to see them share each other's sorrow and happiness. I want to see them work together as equal partners. I want to see them play their national role and take their rightful place among the nations of the world, for the service of God and humanity.

AUGUST 1914, with its heat and dust, brought the crisis of World War to the Indian subcontinent. The British, hinting at political reforms and perhaps even dominion status for India when the crisis was over, encouraged Indians to join the war effort. Over half a million swelled the fighting forces in France, Germany, Turkey, Syria, and North Africa, and much Indian blood was shed in defense of the Empire.

In India, however, conditions were even harsher than before. Wartime restrictions censored newspapers and curtailed political meetings, and the merest suggestion of anti-British sentiment was suppressed. Secret military tribunals sent a number of Indian leaders to prison.

In the Frontier, Ghaffar Khan worked with new certitude, stepping into the leadership role vacated by the Haji Saheb. He stormed the Pathan villages, reopening schools, starting new ones, and urging villagers to improve their lot.

At every turn he found opposition. The political agent Cab, who still ruled the Malakand Agency with an iron grip, either threatened Khan's workers openly or managed to subvert their work. One day he called the nawab of Dir to his office to express his feelings about the district's only school. "Look here," he declared, "all this education is creating endless trouble for us. If you want to avoid getting yourself into difficulties, you'd better see that this school is destroyed as soon as possible."

The nawab had the school demolished.

In December 1915 an influenza epidemic swept the province, and Ghaffar Khan's two-year-old son, Ghani, fell dangerously ill. One cold afternoon Khan had spread his prayer rug alongside the cot of the unconscious child. After prayers, he looked up to see his young wife enter the room. She walked solemnly around the cot and stopped at the child's head. "O Allah!" she cried, her arms stretched out over the small figure. "Spare my boy's life. Give his sickness to me."

Walking around the cot once more, she repeated the prayer: "Lord, take this illness away from my innocent child and let me suffer in his place."

As the first gray light brightened the room, the boy stirred and moaned softly. His fever had broken. But by then his mother was lying in bed next to the cot. Her body shook with fever throughout the afternoon and evening. By the next morning she had died.

Khan had his wife's body taken to the burial ground dressed in her wedding robe and covered with flowers. Grief-stricken, he left his two boys with his mother and buried his sorrow in his work, touring the villages, teaching agriculture and sanitation, and starting more schools. He found solace in the faces of the poor and ragged villagers he loved to serve.

*

Gradually Khan had been enlarging his contacts with Muslim thinkers throughout the subcontinent. Now he began to hear about Gandhi and the nonviolent campaigns that were beginning to rouse the whole of India. He responded immediately to Gandhi's simple lifestyle and his insistence upon truth and nonviolence in all of life's affairs. And he recognized in Gandhi – the Mahatma, the "great soul" – a kindred spirit, a seeker who was attempting to serve God by serving the poorest of his creation.

As Gandhi's work and ideas spread, Khan's attempts at reforming and educating the Pathans took on new meaning: this was not only uplift, it was also the path to freedom. Buoyed, Khan redoubled his efforts. Between 1915 and 1918 he visited every one of the five hundred villages in the settled districts of the Frontier. He sat with the men in the guest houses and spoke of sacrifice and work and forgiveness, and in the evenings he laughed with their children around the cooking fires. The villagers loved but did not quite understand this gentle giant of a man. He was not a mendicant – he did not take alms. And he was not a renouncing fakir – didn't he own a village? Well then, what was he?

One afternoon in the mosque at Hastanagar a group of khans from Charsadda finished their meeting with Ghaffar Khan in a high pitch of excitement. He had roused them and they felt grateful. Someone in the back stood up on the low wall and shouted into the din: *Badshah Khan!* The others heard it and picked up the call. Badshah Khan – the khan's khan! That's what this brave young reformer had become. The whole group of bearded faces took up the cry and let it thunder over the high walls of the mosque into the countryside. *Badshah Khan!* The king of khans.

The name spread. If the khans called him their badshah, there would be no arguments from the villagers. Ghaffar had to swallow his fate and bear this new title as Gandhi bore being called Mahatma. From now on, when he entered villages from Mardan to Kohat, he would be met by the cry: "Badshah Khan is coming! The badshah is here!"

The Pathans had their leader – and they had found him just in time. For the Frontier was about to erupt in the greatest explosion since the Frontier War of 1897.

*

This time the explosion was triggered not by enraged Pathans but by a slight, soft-spoken Indian. Neither British nor Indians had seen anything quite like Gandhi. This once-dapper lawyer now dressed like a Gujarati peasant, ate like an ascetic, and talked at least as much about sanitary measures as he did about British exploitation. Millions followed him, but no one – not Indians, certainly not the British – claimed to understand him.

At the heart of Gandhi's movement – and the source of much of the misunderstanding – was his notion of nonviolent resistance.

In countless speeches and articles, Gandhi instructed Indians in his bold, revolutionary approach. Nonviolence was not passive, he insisted: "Nonviolence in its dynamic condition means conscious suffering. It does not mean meek submission to the will of the evil-doer, but it means the pitting of one's whole soul against the will of the tyrant."

Dissatisfied with phrases like "passive resistance," Gandhi coined his own term: *satyagraha.* The word combines *satya,* truth, with *agraha,* firmness. "Truth," Gandhi explained, "implies love, and firmness engenders force. I thus began to call the Indian movement 'satyagraha'; that is to say, the force which is born of truth and love or nonviolence."

Far from a passive submission to evil, satyagraha implied a dynamic resistance to personal, social, economic, and political exploitation. But it used the weapon of love. "Satyagraha is soul-force, pure and simple," Gandhi said. And one who practices satyagraha – a *satyagrahi* – arms himself or herself with an "indomitable will," the capacity to accept suffering, and the determination never to inflict suffering on an opponent. "It seeks to liquidate antagonisms," Gandhi wrote, "but not the antagonists themselves." Yet it must never give way in the face of tyranny or exploitation.

"There is no time-limit for a satyagrahi nor is there a limit to his capacity for suffering," Gandhi concluded. "Hence there is no such thing as defeat in satyagraha."

At the war's end, Gandhi had been back in India only three years. Yet he had already captured leadership of the Indian National Congress party, transforming it from a debating society for urban intellectuals to an active political movement with mass support. Now, in the early months of 1919, Gandhi was about to lead the country into its first revolt against British rule in fifty years – and it was to be conducted without violence.

The British, fearing unrest, had failed to remove wartime restrictions when the war was over. Instead, in March 1919, Parliament passed the Rowlatt Acts, making wartime emergency restrictions the law of the land. After shedding their blood to save the Empire, Indians found themselves thanked by the most repressive laws since the so-called Mutiny of 1857.

Gandhi called for a *hartal* – a day of complete fasting and prayer. The whole country responded. Buses and trains stopped running. Shops, government offices, and factories did not open. Whole cities closed down.

On the Frontier, Peshawar was virtually deserted while thousands of Pathans gathered in Utmanzai. Even Behram Khan was drawn in. It was the first political meeting he had attended in his life, and he listened with pleasure as his son urged the great gathering to resist British tyranny.

The British listened too. The Frontier government declared martial law, arrested Ghaffar Khan, and sentenced him – without a trial – to six months in prison. They kept his feet shackled in a pair of irons too small for his great legs, cutting the ankles to the bone and scarring them permanently.

At Utmanzai the government left a different kind of scar. Troops surrounded the village, herded the villagers at gunpoint – men, women, and children – into the compound of Khan's school, and ordered them to sit down. Machine guns were mounted on the ground and loaded. While the villagers prayed, soldiers aimed the guns at their front ranks and waited. The commanding officer raised his arm. "Prepare to fire!" Shrieks filled the air.

But the guns did not fire. Instead the troops rushed at the dazed villagers, stripped them of their valuables, and then sacked their homes. Everything that could be carried was loaded onto wagons and driven away.

While the soldiers worked, the British commissioner lectured the villagers. In broken, stumbling Pushto he told them their rebellion would cost the village thirty thousand rupees. Seventy hostages – including Behram Khan – were escorted to the Peshawar prison, to be released only when the fine was paid in full.

Ghaffar Khan must have been pleased but puzzled to look up and see his formerly apolitical father walking over to him in the prison yard. For his own part, Behram Khan was overjoyed. He thought they had hanged his youngest son – but here he was! The old khan's three months' stay in prison was an unintended gift, he chortled: how else would he have seen his boy?

Released at the end of six months, Khan discovered that his parents had found him another bride. He was surprised; he had not thought to remarry. Dutifully he started for Peshawar to buy some wedding clothes. But he was a badshah now, and thus never far from the Frontier officials' minds. Before he could reach Peshawar he was arrested again and locked in a small cell, with two lice-infested blankets for protection against the severe autumn cold.

At the end of a week he was released. "Why did you arrest me?" Khan asked the British commissioner.

"I was investigating your case," the commissioner replied briefly. He was writing a report and did not bother to look up.

Khan persisted. "Why didn't you investigate my case *before* you had me arrested?"

"I decide whether to investigate first or to arrest first."

"But I am a human being," objected Badshah Khan. "Think of my position. You put me to great trouble for no reason."

The Englishman's hand stopped writing. His eyes turned up and for a long, tense moment he looked at the tall figure spotted with grime, noting the fringe of dark hair along the jaw and the bare, cold feet tinged with blue.

The commissioner's face relaxed. He turned back to his writing. "What's all this talk of your *position?*"

*

Remarried and settled again with his wife and boys, Khan next guided the creation of the Anjuman-e Islah ul-Afaghena, a non-political missionary organization that encouraged economic, social, and educational improvements in the Frontier. He particularly stressed Pathans' taking to professions other than agriculture, since there was not enough land to support them all as farmers. He even opened a shop at Utmanzai to set an example to fellow tribesmen.

In 1920, Muslims throughout India protested British policies toward the Turkish caliph by emigrating en masse to Afghanistan. Thousands of Pathans joined the vast pilgrimage and Khan went with them. Soon, however, it became apparent that exile would be a mistake. He returned to the Frontier to continue his reform work.

The schools caught on. He was ready now to expand the Azad school at Utmanzai to include secondary students, and he found eager, bright young Pathans for teachers.

In 1920 the Indian National Congress party met at Nagpur and, for the first time, openly resolved to fight – nonviolently – for complete self-rule. Khan attended the historic session, his first Congress meeting, and felt deeply attracted to Gandhi. But his diffidence kept him in the background. Politics did not attract Badshah Khan. The endless discussions, the displays of temper and ego, only repelled him. He preferred quiet work in the villages.

As his success among the villagers increased, his disfavor with the British grew. Sensing a momentum building among the Pathans, they harassed some of Khan's teachers with threats of jail and offered others higher-paying jobs in British schools. Many quit. Activities and ideas which could be tolerated and even encouraged in greater India alarmed the military officials of the Frontier. As the Frontier went, its officials argued, so did India.

Chief Commissioner Sir John Maffey knew Behram Khan. He asked him to come to his office in Peshawar. "I have noticed," he said, "that your son is touring the villages and opening schools." He knew Behram Khan to be a cautious man. "I have also noticed that other people stay quietly at home and don't bother about these things."

True enough, the old man observed. He himself couldn't understand the boy's ways.

"Would you kindly ask your boy to give up these activities? Tell him to stay at home like other people."

Behram Khan agreed. Straightaway he confronted his youngest child. Why couldn't he stay at home like everyone else? He had a beautiful new wife and two strong boys. He had his village to oversee. Why all this *activity?*

Ghaffar knew his father better than the old khan knew himself. "Father," he began, "if everybody else stopped doing *lemundz* – the daily prayers – would you advise me to follow their example?"

"God forbid!" the old man said. "*Lemundz* is a sacred duty."

"To my mind," Badshah Khan said, "educating the people and serving the nation is as sacred a duty as prayer."

Pathan honor had been stirred. Behram Khan felt the full weight of his son's conviction. Honor could not be trifled with. "Son," he said with gravity, "if it is so sacred a duty, you must never give it up!"

Behram Khan sent his regrets to Chief Commissioner Maffey in Peshawar. Pathans could not possibly give up their religion and sacred duties for his sake.

But the commissioner was not one to be put off. He sent for Ghaffar. "What guarantee is there that your organization will not be used against the government and its interest?" he said bluntly.

"You must trust me," Khan rejoined.

"No," the commissioner shot back. "You must apologize and give a bond that you will not do it again."

Khan stiffened. "Give a security that I shall cease to love and serve my people?"

"This is not service," came the reply. "This is rebellion."

A few days later Khan was arrested – for spreading education among impoverished and illiterate people. He writes:

> When I was arrested, I was not put in a lock-up, as is usual when one is awaiting sentence, but I was put in the criminal's cell. When the door was opened a most odious smell met my nostrils. The source of it was a clay chamberpot full of the last occupant's excrement lying in a corner. I told the prison officer that I could not stay in such a dirty cell, but he said coldly: "You are in prison, you know!" and pushed me inside.
>
> My cell was bitterly cold because it faced the north and never got any sun. I was given three blankets and a piece of gunny sacking which were no protection against the cold.
>
> After I was put in prison my friends were also arrested. We were kept locked up day and night. Our food was shoved in through a barred opening in the door. The result of this cruel treatment was that most of my colleagues decided to furnish security. But Abdul-ul-Qayyum and I refused to do that.

After ten days, Khan was taken before the deputy commissioner and locked inside a docket with iron bars. Looking at the tall, muscular Pathan, the Englishman expressed his disbelief about Khan's professed nonviolence. Khan told him it was because of Gandhi.

"And what would you have done," the deputy commissioner prodded, "if you hadn't heard of Gandhi?"

Khan placed his large hands around two of the bars and slowly pulled them apart. "That is what I would have done to you," he said without a smile.

The deputy commissioner was not amused. He asked the attending policeman what offense the prisoner from Utmanzai had committed. "He has opened his own schools," came the reply, "and gone on pilgrimage to Afghanistan."

The deputy commissioner exploded. "He left the country? And you allowed him to return?"

Before the policeman could explain, Khan cut him off. "First you take our country from us and now you won't even let us live in it?"

Such impudence from a Pathan, before an official representative of His Majesty's justice, was too much to be borne. "Take him out of my sight," the deputy commissioner answered. "I'm sentencing him to three years' imprisonment."

He looked up. Khan stood immobile, his eyes fixed on the Englishman. "At hard labor," the deputy commissioner added.

With Pathan villagers (National Gandhi Museum)

CHAPTER SEVEN : 1921–1924

O Pathans!

One learns a good deal in the school of suffering. I wonder what would have happened to me if I had had an easy life, and had not had the privilege of tasting the joys of jail and all it means.

THE BRITISH DID NOT want to punish Khan, they said. They merely wanted to persuade him to their point of view. Yet they classed him as a criminal rather than as a political prisoner, and began his prison term with two months in solitary confinement.

When he returned to his regular cell, Khan found his brother waiting to see him. The two men fell into each other's arms. Dr. Khan Saheb, as he was now universally known, had just returned from England, having served as a medical officer in the British Army in Europe. Transferred to the Frontier, he was ordered to join an expedition against the Waziris – and promptly resigned.

The two chatted, then embraced again. Dr. Khan Saheb handed over a note from the chief commissioner. He bore Ghaffar Khan no ill will, it said, and was ready to commute his sentence. He could go free. He would even be allowed to run his schools. But he could not tour the villages. If he agreed to this one condition, he could walk out with his brother that very afternoon.

Khan read the note. He looked at Khan Saheb, then back at the note. Abruptly he tore the paper into small pieces and dropped them on the ground.

Dr. Khan, the physician, looked at his younger brother. The pale cheeks were already sunken, the eyes dark-ringed. Signs of scurvy showed in the skin. He tried to reason with him, but Ghaffar only shook his great bearded head.

The next week Khan's hands and feet were shackled, an iron ring was locked around his neck, and he was transferred to the prison for habitual criminals in Dera Ismail Khan. Since he was not prepared to cooperate with His Majesty's government, he would be treated accordingly: as a dangerous criminal. From the iron ring hung a small identity disk with his name and sentence stamped upon it, and his crime – sedition.

At Dera Ismail Khan he was again placed in solitary confinement – and given forty pounds of corn a day to grind.

It was an offense to keep food in one's cell, but a fellow Pathan from Utmanzai slipped Khan a few pieces of *gur,* sugar candy, as a gesture of fellowship. Khan was looking at the gur when the guard told him the superintendent was coming.

What should he do with the gur? He didn't have time to eat it. Hastily he slipped it under his blanket. But what if the superintendent inspected his bed? Where could he hide anything?

The superintendent entered, talked with him for a moment, then left. As the door slammed closed, Khan reached for the gur and threw it out the window. He resolved on the spot that he would never break the regulations again. Subterfuge created fear – and fear made a prisoner hostage. He had seen it happen to fellow prisoners too many times: they broke the rules, then had to bribe the jailer to escape punishment. It cost them their self-respect. Khan made up his mind that it would not happen to him.

The jail at Dera Ismail Khan was a nightmare of corruption. The British superintendent spoke only English, so the prison had fallen under the control of his deputy jailer, a petty tyrant named Gangaram who had turned the institution into an efficient machine for making money. A prisoner's treatment depended solely on his ability – and willingness – to bribe the deputy jailer. If a prisoner was to survive his sentence, privileges must be purchased.

Khan refused to pay. "Give him the money," one of Gangaram's agents implored, "and he will get you out of solitary."

Khan shook his head.

"Your fellow Peshawaris are ashamed to have you in solitary grinding corn like a murderer. They'll pay the money for you."

"I was sent here in the first place," Khan said, "because I refused to pay the security. Why should I bribe Gangaram to secure good treatment, if by bribing the British I could walk right out?"

The agent shook his head. Even honor could be carried too far. He too was a Peshawari; he did not want to see the badshah suffer.

Yet Khan's example touched both the prisoners and the guards, who had succumbed to the poisoned atmosphere. One day he was grinding his allotment of corn when a guard told him he could stop.

"You are the only one in this prison who is here on behalf of God. How could I justify myself before Him if I made you grind corn?"

Khan stopped grinding, but when the guard left he resumed. The guard was watching him through the slot in the door and came back into the cell. "I allowed you to stop," he said, somewhat indignant. "Why are you still grinding?"

Khan pointed to the prisoner in the next cell. "Do you see that man? He is a robber and murderer and you have him grinding corn. Why should I mind grinding for my cause, which is pure and holy?"

The guard shook his head.

"You are a good man," Khan said. "Why have you become part of this evil system?"

"I must feed my children."

Khan went back to grinding the corn. A few days later he found he had a different guard. The first man, he was told, had found another job.

Since most of the prisoners were Pathans, they could not avoid being moved by the refusal of their badshah to become corrupt. Those who had avoided the crushing prison work through bribes stopped their payments at Khan's urging and accepted the work as honorable penance for their crimes. Most of the quarreling among them stopped.

Seeing his income dwindle, Gangaram complained to the superintendent. This badshah was causing trouble in the workshop, and Gangaram would not be responsible for discipline as long as he remained. "The superintendent," Khan recalls, "was convinced that Gangaram was lying. But an Englishman can be persuaded to do anything for the sake of preserving discipline. Gangaram, after all, had not failed him in preserving law and order."

Without his knowing it, Gangaram's interference probably saved Khan's life. "It was by the grace of God," he remarked later, "that I was transferred to Dera Ghazi Khan. Otherwise I might not have survived." The four months in solitary had broken his health. He had lost fifty pounds and contracted scurvy and pyorrhea.

The prison at Dera Ghazi Khan, almost three hundred miles south of Peshawar, was a detention center for political prisoners from the Punjab, a state with a history of active resistance to British rule. There Khan came in contact with many of the leaders of India's independence movement. Hindus, Christians, and Muslims held discussions and studied each other's scriptures. It proved an unexpected and rich education for the young badshah. In addition, both the climate and the food were better, and the superintendent was a good Muslim who respected Khan's mission. A dentist was brought in to extract Khan's diseased teeth and refused payment. "You are jailed because of your love for our country," he explained. "I cannot match your sacrifice. Let me do this much."

In 1923, while Khan was still in prison, he learned that his mother had died. No one had told him; he came across the news in the paper. It was a terrible blow. "She had been most keen on visiting me in jail," Khan wrote,

> but she was very old, and Dera Ghazi Khan was far away and the Indus lay between us. To spare her discomfort and trouble, I always entreated her not to come for the interview. But, alas, I did not know that the Almighty was soon to take her away from me! . . .
>
> When I went to my village on my release, my sister told me that my mother spoke of me when she breathed her last: "Where is Ghaffar?" With my name on her lips, she passed away.

*

During Khan's three years in prison, India underwent great struggles. Gandhi's noncooperation movement, launched in earnest at the Nagpur session of Congress in 1920, gained momentum rapidly. Indian lawyers abandoned their practices in the British courts, students left English-run schools and universities, prominent Indians returned their honorary medals and titles, and villagers even refused to pay taxes. The movement swept the country like a grass fire in a dry wind. By January 1922, thirty thousand Indians had been jailed. Even conservative Indians began to reflect that Gandhi had been right: nonviolence could bring them complete independence.

Not all Indians, however, remained nonviolent. In some cities telegraph wires were cut, British buildings burnt, officials assaulted. On February 5, 1922, an Indian crowd went out of control in the small village of Chauri Chaura and killed a dozen policemen.

Gandhi stopped the movement. He embarked on a fast and ordered all noncooperation to cease.

The Indians were stunned. They had come so close, it seemed; victory was so near. But Gandhi was adamant. He did not want victory through violence. "It is better to be charged with cowardice and weakness," he wrote, "than to be guilty of denial of our oath and to sin against God. It is a million times better to appear untrue before the world than to be untrue to ourselves."

The British, gladly accepting the windfall, had Gandhi arrested. This time he was accorded a trial, in which he enthusiastically pled guilty to all charges of sedition and tendered a bitter appraisal of the results of British rule – serving notice, in effect, on the British Empire. He was sentenced to six years in prison – and the first Indian civil resistance movement collapsed. With Gandhi in jail, India quieted down again. But her people had not lost faith in their leader. They were waiting.

Ghaffar Khan was released from prison in 1924 and immediately went home. He found to his delight that his imprisonment and suffering had actually strengthened his movement and fired the hearts of his people. His Azad school in Utmanzai had flourished and his service organization was as active as ever. Teachers and students had used immunity in the mosques to talk to the Pathan villagers. Even Khan's nine-year-old son, Ghani, had joined in. "O people!" he would cry out. "Go and ask this government why they are keeping my father a prisoner! Go and ask them what crime he has committed!" At Utmanzai a meeting was called and thousands of Pathans gathered to welcome their badshah back. There were people from Mardan, Kohat, and Peshawar, and some Swatis from the north. Even a few Mohmands had slipped down from Bajaur to see their badshah again. Aged Behram Khan, congenial and peppery, poured out buckets of tea spiced with crushed cardamom seeds. The huge crowd whooped and chortled. How had their badshah escaped the gallows? God himself must watch after him!

Even with sunken cheeks and thin shoulders, Khan was still a regal figure. His people wanted him to speak. Khan protested: this was a celebration, not a rally. But the gathering would not be denied. A speech!

The tall khan rose and looked out over the bobbing, bearded faces. Hoots and whistles! Thunder! He felt the glow from a thousand grizzled faces and watched the bluster melt from their eyes. He told a story:

> One day a lioness attacked a flock of sheep. She was pregnant, and during the attack she gave birth to a cub. In the course of birth the lioness died, and her cub was left to grow up with the flock of sheep. It learned to graze and even bleat.
> One day a lion from the forest attacked the flock and was surprised to see a lion cub running away from him, terrified and bleating like the sheep. Outraged, he managed to catch the cub and draw it away from the flock, down to a nearby river.
>
> "Look in the water!" he commanded the cub. "You are not a sheep; you are a lion! You have nothing to fear. Stop bleating like a sheep and roar!"

Khan waited. The gathering was still. He felt his strength again. "O Pathans!" he boomed, "so also I say to you. You are lions, but you have been brought up in slavery. Stop bleating like sheep. Roar like lions!"

The Pathans roared. They roared again. The sprawling crowd sent up a thunderclap that exploded over the valley and broke against the ridges of the Khyber. These Pathans were happy. As the sun fell beyond the bare hills they returned to their villages full of spiced tea and laughter. Their badshah had returned – and with him, the promise of better days.

Badshah Khan (D.G. Tendulkar)

CHAPTER EIGHT : 1925

The Pathan Mystique

Is not the Pathan amenable to love and reason? He will go with you to hell if you can win his heart, but you cannot force him even to go to heaven. Such is the power of love over the Pathan.

BRITISH REPRESSION notwithstanding, the greatest obstacle in Badshah Khan's path was still the cult of revenge and violence that pervaded Pathan society. The power of this centuries-old code of honor made it almost impossible for a man to allow insults or wrongs to go unanswered, regardless of the suffering that followed.

And suffering followed for everyone. Families were left fatherless; neighbors lived in fear of each other; life itself was shot through with uncertainty. Yet the mystique of the avenging hero remained the primary source of Pathan romance, poetry, and even status, though it wedded Pathans to unending tragedy.

No one felt these contradictions more strongly than Badshah Khan, and no one was more aware of the price Pathans were paying for their infatuation with violence. They had been dispossessed of their freedom, he held, only because of their own self-destructive tendencies.

The contradictions of the Pathan mystique are almost impossible for an outsider to comprehend, although they touch everything that makes up life on the Frontier – custom, values, the daily round. "The Pathan is not easy to love," wrote Badshah Khan's eldest son, Ghani. "He takes a lot of knowing. He loves fighting – but hates to be a soldier. He has great ambition and no patience – that is why he usually dies young."

To illustrate the depth to which revenge and violence have penetrated Pathan culture, Ghani tells a story from his youth which shows that not even Badshah Khan's family was immune to the glamour of badal or revenge. The story conveys better than any cold analysis can the tangle of values and emotions that makes up the Pathan mystique.

It begins one morning in 1925, when the body of a local outlaw-hero was found next to Behram Khan's water mill outside Utmanzai. The body was that of Atta Khan, a notorious renegade whom the village boys had lionized. He had been shot twice by his best friend, Murtaza.

Ghani was only twelve years old at the time, but he recalls being pleased to hear about Atta's death. "I had always hated Atta," he writes,

> in spite of his fine looks and the stories of superhuman daring that were told about him, because he had killed a dear old man, the father of one of my school friends. I was too young to know then that the dear kind old man owed a debt of blood from the days of his youth. He sowed in youth and Atta grew up to make him reap in his old age. For the blood of a Pathan cannot be paid for except with blood.
>
> This dear old man was young and reckless once and had trampled underfoot the rights of some weaklings. But the weaklings produced Atta. He grew up. He saw his mother hang down her head in shame, he saw his brothers look at the ground when certain things and people were mentioned. He understood that he must kill the dear old man. He was too young, too handsome, and too strong for shame.
>
> So Atta picked up his gun and blasted that shame out of this world and thus established his right to be taken notice of and respected.

Now the wheel of badal had turned again, and it was Atta who paid.

It took several platoons of police and a hundred villagers to capture Murtaza, Atta's murderer, and his gang in the hills. Bullets zinged from the rock walls and everyone ducked for cover. Finally

Murtaza ran out of ammunition. He stood up, threw his rifle into the well, and stepped out into the sunlight – hands high and grinning.

Late that afternoon, Ghani recalls, a squad of policemen escorted Murtaza back into Utmanzai. The village exploded. Now that Atta was dead, Murtaza was the new hero. After all, Atta had killed a lot of good khans. What did it matter if Murtaza was a robber? Wasn't he brave? With Atta dead, the villagers who had worshipped him for so long now remembered all his crimes and – with typical Pathan volatility – turned their adoration on the man who had killed him.

Ghani watched Murtaza enter Utmanzai surrounded by a score of policemen, his hands and feet manacled, a bandage around his forehead where a bullet had grazed it. Still grinning, Murtaza walked with the swagger of a war hero. He laughed, winked at his admirers, and cracked jokes. This was his hour.

At one point, Murtaza stopped the whole parade with a raised palm and barked out orders: cold drinks for everyone! The villagers cheered. Even the police relaxed while they sipped their drinks.

And Ghani beamed. Wasn't Murtaza his relative? "I was proud to tell the other village boys that he was a distant cousin of mine."

Finally the cloud of admiring villagers, police, horses, and captives spilled out onto the main road and headed for the jail. Ghani joined the mob to escort the new hero to his future – a sentence of twenty years in prison.

One winter night, many years after the murder at the mill, Ghani was sitting before a fire when he heard a whisper at his door. "Where are you, friend?"

Ghani opened the door. It was Murtaza Khan – dust-caked, ragged, a gun slung over his shoulder. "You would never think of letting him into your room," Ghani writes, "but I opened the door and my heart to him because I knew him and his father knew my father and his grandfather my grandfather."

There, by the fire, he ventured the question he had wanted to ask for many years: "Murtaza, Atta was your best friend. What made you kill him?"

"It was my uncle," Murtaza replied – "the one I hated and still do. I was an outlaw with a band of brave followers. I was his pet. He feasted me and supported me because I intimidated his powerful rivals for him and added to his importance in the eyes of the English rulers. I thought he loved me because I was his flesh and blood, the son of his brother – and I returned his love with sincere respect and devotion.

"One evening he sent for me. Out of my hideout in the bitter cold I went to the warmth of my grandmother's hearth. He came – my uncle – and related a long story of how Atta had conspired with his enemies to murder him. He held my feet and wept. He implored me to save him and the family honor. I refused.

"Then my aunt joined in. She looked at me with deep sorrowful eyes and asked if I would stand by and see my father's brother killed. 'He is old and gray,' she said, 'and you are young and strong. Do you owe nothing to the family that brought you into the world and gave you its name and prestige? Your father, Abdullah, never shirked a nasty job. He was born a khan and lived like a khan and died like a khan.'

"That finished me," said Murtaza. "I promised to do it."

"Were you afraid of him?" asked Ghani.

"My friend," Murtaza said coldly, "I have never feared anything except death by disease. But an outlaw is always afraid. There are too many enemies who will pay for his death.

"Anyway, I hated killing Atta, and I hated my uncle for making it impossible for me to do otherwise."

He shivered, and a look of agony came into his brown eyes. "I wanted to put the world between him and me but I have never succeeded. He is always with me, the living Atta. He talks and laughs, bravely and recklessly. . . .

"I tried to shoot that uncle of mine to pay for it," Murtaza added, "but I could not. So my uncle had a long life, and I a sad conscience." He smiled bitterly and shrugged his shoulders: "Atta was going to kill my uncle if I had not killed him first. But come, my friend," he said to Ghani, "play us a tune."

Ghani picked up his sitar and played something sorrowful. "We both looked at the flames and said no more. There was no need to. I knew. I too was a Pathan."

*

Beneath the blustery surface of the Pathan lies a proud nature and simple need. Too often impoverished, Ghani writes,

> he would rather steal than beg, because he is a man and not a worm. He looks at the torn clothes of his beautiful young wife and the hungry eyes of his child. He picks up his rifle. . . . He would rather face the anger of God and man than the shame and disgrace of poverty. That is why I love him in spite of his thick head and vain heart.

Ghani's sharp eye catches both the splendor and the tragedy of the Pathan spirit: "His violent nature, strong body and tender heart make a very unstable combination for living, but an ideal one for poetry and color." He goes on:

> Let us go to his valley in Dir. There he is – walking towards us, of medium height and sensitive build. He has long locks, neatly oiled and combed, wrapped in a red silk kerchief which is twisted round the head like the crown of Caesar. He wears a flower in his hair and collyrium in his eye. His lips are dyed red with walnut bark. He carries his sitar in his hand and his rifle at his shoulder. You would think he is very effeminate until you looked at his eyes. They are clear, manly and bold. They do not know fear. . . .
>
> This son of the bravest tribe of Pathans never takes cover in a fight and laughs and sings when he is frightened. He will soon die fighting, for he knows only how to love and laugh and fight and nothing else.
>
> "The coward dies," the boy's mother tells him, "but his shrieks live long after." So the boy learns not to shriek. He is shown dozens of things dearer than life so that he will not mind either dying or killing. He is forbidden colorful clothes or exotic music, for they weaken the arm and soften the eye. He is taught to look at the hawk and forget the nightingale. It is a perpetual surrender – an eternal giving up of man to man and to their wise follies.

The Pathan learns to surrender himself to the will of the tribe in an act that will, most probably, demand total self-effacement. This is how he learns the two supreme arts of Pathan life: how to kill and how to die. Through these he becomes most fully a Pathan. Thus a violent death is almost assured – and, in a way, sought. For this is the surest path to Paradise: dying with his rifle smoking and, if he can manage it, a smile on his face. He does not ask for more. "One day he goes out," Ghani says,

> and never comes back. He has laughed his way into a bullet that was fired by another of his own blood and race. His wife inherits from him a moment of joy, two sons, and a lifetime of sorrow. She hangs up his rifle and sitar for his sons. She learns to hide her tears when she hears a love song in the evening. She worships her elder son because he looks like his father, and the younger one because he smiles like him. "What was our father like?" the boys ask. She cannot tell them that he was a great doctor, or a philosopher or a priest. She says he was a great man and a great fighter and she sings to them the song that was made about that fight, the fight in which their father died with his three brothers and five cousins:
>
> It was a cursed day, bleak and cold,
> It was the last day of spring. . . .

"He must shoot," Ghani writes of the Pathan whose honor has been violated. "He has no alternative. If he does not, his brothers will look down upon him, his father will sneer at him, his sister will avoid his eyes, his wife will be insolent and his friends will cut him off. *He must shoot.* Atta had to kill his people's tormentor. Murtaza had to kill Atta, his best friend. "Revenge and Death," Ghani concludes. "Death and Revenge – always and forever."

The Pathan was not a wanton killer but a victim of his own distorted sense of honor. That made him easy prey for subversion – and no one knew it better than the British. One strand of the Raj's Forward Policy was to divide the Pathans against themselves. "The sole role of the political department of the Government of India," Ghani argues,

> was to try to teach the hawks of the Khyber the wretched ways of the crow and the vulture. It seduced the lowest and the

greediest of the tribes and gave them importance and brought them influence....

The British succeeded beautifully. The Pathans were too busy cutting one another's throat to think of anything else. There was blood and darkness everywhere. The Empire was safe and the Pathan damned.

But then, as Ghani says, something happened – something not unlike a miracle in that tangled, centuries-old net of death and revenge. The miracle was Ghani's father. The genius of Badshah Khan saw Pathan violence for what it was – a consequence not of bloodlust but of ignorance, superstition, and the crushing weight of custom. Beneath the violence and ignorance, Khan saw men and women capable of extraordinary self-effacement, endurance, and courage. He knew his task: to educate, to enlighten, to lift up, to inspire. With understanding, he saw, the violence and venality would fall from the Pathan character like dead limbs from a tree. It was his job to wield the axe.

"Badshah Khan is really the politics of the Pathans," Ghani concludes:

> He understands the Pathans and the Pathans understand him – and you cannot understand either unless you are a Pathan. When you see him next, look into his kind brown eyes and you will know more about Pathan politics than I could tell you in a thousand chapters. For the holiest and the finest in a man is as inexpressible as stardust and moonlight.
>
> Badshah Khan has discovered that love can create more in a second than bombs can destroy in a century; that the kindest strength is the greatest strength; that the only way to be truly brave is to be in the right; that a clean dream is dearer than life itself. These are the things he has taught the Pathan.

With officers of the Khudai Khidmatgars (Nehru Memorial Library)

CHAPTER NINE : 1926–1929

The Servants of God

There is nothing surprising in a Muslim or a Pathan like me subscribing to the creed of nonviolence. It is not a new creed. It was followed fourteen hundred years ago by the Prophet all the time he was in Mecca, and it has since been followed by all those who wanted to throw off an oppressor's yoke. But we had so far forgotten it that when Gandhiji placed it before us, we thought he was sponsoring a novel creed.

IN 1926 BEHRAM KHAN died. No one knew exactly how old he was, but his clear recollection of the 1857 "Mutiny" placed him over eighty.

Pathan custom decrees that alms be distributed at the funeral of a great khan, so a crowd of mullahs flocked to Behram Khan's funeral with open palms. This was no halfpenny khan who had died.

Ghaffar Khan declared that he would give away two thousand rupees in memory of his father. He would let the gathering of sorrowing villagers decide whether he should give it to the mullahs or bestow it on the school.

"Give it to the school!" they cried.

After his father's death, Badshah Khan, his sister, and his wife decided to go to Mecca on *haj*, pilgrimage – the most sacred act an orthodox Muslim can perform. Always as practical as he was devout, Khan timed his visit to coincide with a conference of Islamic nations in Mecca. He enjoyed encountering men representing so many different facets of Islam, but the constant bickering over fine theological points disillusioned him.

Once again tragedy struck: Khan's wife fell from a high flight of stairs in Jerusalem and was killed. This time he vowed not to remarry. "Henceforth," he said, "there would be no room for another marriage in my life of dedication to the service of my country." In the moral world of the Pathan, this was tantamount to a vow of celibacy.

Khan kept the vow. Like Gandhi, he learned to harness his deep passions to the task of liberating his people and raising them to their rightful place in history.

On his way back to India, Khan visited Palestine, Lebanon, Syria, and Iran. He felt a surge of energy in the Islamic countries that were undergoing modernizing reforms. Islam was in the midst of a renaissance, and Khan became aware for the first time how much nationalist movements in Muslim countries looked to India for inspiration. India was the cornerstone of the British Empire; if that stone were removed, British power in the Middle East might topple – and that of the French could follow.

On his return from the Middle East, fresh with new ideas, Khan formed the Pushtun Jirgah, the Pathan Youth League, which drew its members from the growing number of graduates of his Azad schools. With the Youth League he launched a new program of educational, social, and political reforms.

One of his first concerns was the role of women. Badshah Khan had long lamented the traditional system of purdah, which restricts Muslim women from participating fully in society. He encouraged them to come out from behind the veil, as the women in his own family had done. His sisters became increasingly active in his movement, until by 1930 they were touring the districts of the Frontier and giving speeches – activities which would have required courage even in the cosmopolitan capitals of Islam, but which in the conservative Frontier showed truly extraordinary daring.

Gandhi too believed that an active women's movement was essential to gaining freedom through nonviolence. In December 1925 he had handed over the presidency of the Congress party to Mrs. Sarojini Naidu, a poet with a remarkable gift for leadership. Her example galvanized Indian women and demonstrated their capacities for political activity.

To help spread these ideas, Khan had been thinking for some time about starting a journal written in Pushto. He knew that

Pathans who emigrated to other parts of the world were quick to adopt the local language and drop their mother tongue, and even in the Frontier, educated Pathans had abandoned Pushto in favor of English and Urdu. This saddened Khan. He loved the rolling rhythms of his language and its rich body of folklore, epics, and lyrics, which included some of the finest mystical poetry on the subcontinent. A journal in Pushto could restore the Pathans' pride in their own language, and at the same time carry the message of reform to all Pathans.

Pushtun, "The Pathan," was an instant success, not only in the Frontier but elsewhere – even as far away as the United States, where many Pathans still live. Educated Pathans were delighted to find Pushtunwali, the way of the Pathan, celebrated: they were a noble, daring, effervescent race. And they enjoyed, almost as much, the steady barrage of criticism from the editor's pen. The title page carried a poem by – who else? – fifteen-year-old Ghani Khan, already an aspiring and impassioned writer:

If I a slave lie buried in a grave
under a dazzling tombstone,
respect it not; spit on it!
O mother, with what face will you wail for me
if I am not torn to pieces by British guns?
Either I turn this wretched land of mine
into a Garden of Eden
or I wipe out the lanes and homes of Pathans!

Pushtun contained articles on hygiene, social issues, and Islamic law. It openly and repeatedly questioned purdah. "In the Pathan land, whose beautiful daughters gather fuel in the hills and carry it on their heads, reap the harvest and walk through the battlefield," one author wrote, "there is no place for purdah. The purdah did not exist in the past, it does not exist today [except by custom] and it will never be there in the future." One Pathan "sister," Nagiria, exclaimed, "Except for the Pathan, the women have no enemy. He is clever but is ardent in suppressing women. . . . O Pathan, when you demand your freedom, why do you deny it to women?"

*

All this time, in the rest of the subcontinent, tension between Indians and British was swelling. The new viceroy, Lord Irwin, had answered Indian demands for self-government by declining to meet with Gandhi or any other representative of the people. Instead, with what one English biographer has called "a deplorable lack of tact," Irwin invited a special commission to advise him on the fate of India – a commission composed entirely of British lords and members of Parliament.

Without significant exception, the Simon Commission met with a complete boycott when its members arrived in February 1928, and throughout that year there were huge demonstrations that were sometimes violently broken up by the police. The Punjab, neighbor state of the Frontier, was particularly restive. Its sixty-four-year-old leader Lajput Rai was struck by a policeman in Lahore and died soon after; within weeks, in December 1928, the assistant police chief of Lahore was assassinated. In Bengal, another perpetual hotbed of resistance, Subhas Chandra Bose was agitating for violent revolution.

In this turbulent setting, that same December, Muslim leaders convened a conference in Calcutta, the capital of Bengal. Khan attended and was disturbed by the tenor of the gathering. In an opening address the president of the conference attacked and ridiculed the Hindus. Later, when the man was hotly criticized by a speaker from the Punjab, he lost his temper and began hurling abuse back. Another Punjabi on the speaker's platform stood up and drew a knife, and the meeting broke into chaos.

None of this embodied Islam to Khan – nor, it must be added, to some of the other Muslim leaders. Finding that the Indian National Congress was meeting in Calcutta at the same time, Khan decided to attend and, if possible, see Gandhi.

He found him addressing a committee meeting, where a young man in the audience kept heckling him. Gandhi did not get angry; he just laughed and went on talking. His patient good humor made a deep impression on Khan. When he went back to his own conference, he told its president privately that he thought the movement would be stronger if its leadership embodied a little more tolerance and self-restraint. The man lost his temper again.

"So," he said, "the wild Pathans have come to teach about tolerance!" The words stung.

Khan left the conference and went home, but the example of Gandhi remained with him. It was becoming more and more clear that violence and quarreling only kept his people divided.

A few months later, at another Congress meeting in Lucknow, Khan met Gandhi. He also met Jawaharlal Nehru, the brilliant young leader of the Indian nationalist movement, who had been a friend of his brother's when they were students together in England. Khan was able to discuss Pathan affairs with the man who would become India's first prime minister – the beginning of a deep bond between two men of kindred spirit, never to be broken even when their lives diverged.

From Lucknow, Khan went straight on to Delhi and met with other nationalist leaders. Everywhere he encountered a fierce sense of urgency. Since their near-victory over the Raj in 1922, Indians had been warning the British that unless they were granted some form of self-government, another clash was inevitable. The British remained aloof. Indians were becoming restless. They wanted freedom, and they were willing to fight for it.

Young leaders like Nehru and Subhas Chandra Bose were arguing that the time had come for an all-out battle with the Raj. Gandhi, always cautious, asked them to wait and give the British time to demonstrate their intentions. Besides, he urged, India was not ready for battle. Give the British a year. If they did not grant concessions by then, the impatient young Indians could have their fight – and it would be to the finish.

Khan imbibed this new urgency and returned to the Frontier determined to sweep Pathans into the mainstream of Indian affairs. He spent the summer on a grueling tour through hot, dust-choked villages, trying to stir provincial people to see beyond their own fields and families. By the end of the summer he was drained and impatient. Something more was needed.

*

The world, once weak with summer's heat,
Grows strong again.

For the poet Khushal Khan, as for all Pathans, autumn rather than spring brings renewal. Then the sun dips south toward the Arabian Sea, the air from the passes cools, wedges of geese float over from the Central Asian plateau, the poplars and willows turn amber – and Pathan blood stirs.

September of 1929 brought cooling winds to the Peshawar valley. Khan felt ready to do battle again – not with the British yet, but with his Pathans. He felt a great moment approaching and he was determined that his people would be fit for it.

At a boisterous gathering in Utmanzai one afternoon, Khan stood up and unveiled his feelings. He began by outlining the petty vices that had crippled his people. These hardy Pathans, whom no one could beat in an open, fair fight, were helpless before the clever British, he declared. And they had no one to blame but themselves.

"There are two ways to national progress," he told them:

> one is the path of religion, and the other is the road of patriotism. . . . You have all heard of America and Europe. The people in those countries may not be very religious, but they have a sense of patriotism, love for their nation, and social consciousness.
>
> And look at the progress that has been made there. Then take a look at ourselves! We have hardly learned to stand on our own feet yet. Look at their standard of living and then take a look at ours.

Thousands of proud Pathan eyes looked around – at the tattered rags, the hide-bare burros and thin goats browsing the stubble, the gaunt faces . . .

> If we are on the road to ruin, it is because we have neither the true spirit of religion, nor the true spirit of patriotism nor love for our nation. . . . A great revolution is coming and you haven't even heard about it!
>
> During my recent visit to the subcontinent, I noticed that men and women were fully prepared to serve the nation. And here? Leave alone your women, even your men do not show any

desire to serve. They hardly seem to understand the meaning of the word "nation"!

Khan looked around, his dark eyes blazing. The edge in his voice had brought the milling mass to silence. Bearded, turbaned heads did not move. Two goats shuffled behind the raised platform but no one noticed. Khan continued to hammer:

A revolution is like a flood! A nation can prosper by it, and it can perish by it as well. A nation that is wide awake, that cultivates brotherhood and national spirit, is sure to benefit through revolution. If the people are vigilant they will be ready for the flood. When it comes the whole nation will move along with it.

But if the people are asleep! If they are indifferent to each other and indifferent to the country, the whole nation will be swept away by the flood when the revolution comes.

Khan paused again and took a deep breath. "O Pathans!" he thundered:

Take a look at the developed countries of the world. Do you think their prosperity has just dropped from the sky? It has not, no more than our prosperity will drop from heaven!

The secret of their prosperity is that they have men and women who sacrifice their luxuries, their pleasures, and their comfort for the sake of the prosperity of the nation.

We do not have such men among us. We look only to our self-interest and let the country go to the devil! In other countries, people have learnt that no man is an island. But in our country everyone lives in a dream world of his own – like the animals. Any animal can find a place to live, find a mate, rear its young. Can we call ourselves the crown of creation if we do just that and nothing more?

Rarely had a Pathan spoken to fellow Pathans with words so plainspoken:

Please remember this. If the nation prospers, it will affect everyone. Every man, woman, and child will benefit. Do not think that by acquiring riches for yourselves your country will become prosperous. It will not. If you want your country and your people to prosper you must stop living for yourselves alone. You must start living for the community. That is the only way to prosperity and progress.

He had finished. Pathan vows filled the air, invoking the name of Allah, and men spoke with steel in their voices. The badshah's words had cut their Pathan pride like a razor-sharp *tulwar*, but they were not bitter. They knew that the tulwar had been hurled from love – to rescue the honor of their nation.

*

For one young Pathan, Khan's words cut deep enough to keep him awake the whole night. The badshah had spoken nothing but the hard truth. Much had been promised by the gathering; a thousand oaths had been sworn. But was that enough? The flood was already near.

The next morning, before the muezzin had called out the time for morning prayer, this young man was banging on the gate of Khan's courtyard, rattling a dozen chickens out of their roosts. He poured out his heart. Something had to be done. What about an organization, he argued, one whose members would swear on Allah's name to give their lives for their country? Not the Youth League – that was for organizers and social workers. What the country needed was men ready to die for it. It needed . . . soldiers!

Khan liked the fire in this Pathan's voice. "Sit down. Let's talk." Tea was brought, salted and hot, with a platter of fresh bread. The sun was still below the horizon.

Soldiers! Khan liked the idea. Plenty of Pathans were fighters, but those who actually went to join an army fought only for the Raj. Perhaps they did need soldiers – but certainly not more violence.

An idea slipped out, as formless at first as the faint shadows of the courtyard around them in the early rays of dawn. An army of nonviolent soldiers, drilled and disciplined, with officers, cadres, uniforms, a flag – perhaps even a drum and bagpipe corps like the Guides! And pledged to fight: not with guns but with their lives.

As far as Khan knew, it had never been done. An army of trained professional nonviolent soldiers was something new.

The young man looked at the badshah. But Pathans? An army of unarmed Pathans?

"Who else?" Khan shot back. Who else but a Pathan would be reckless enough to try it? What could possibly take more bravado than facing an enemy in a righteous cause without weapons, neither retreating nor retaliating? It was the loftiest kind of honor.

Khan called for more tea. True, he admitted, Pathans would see it as a disfigurement of badal – at first. The code of revenge seemed in their blood from birth. But then, hadn't Gandhi been talking for a decade about "the nonviolence of the strong"? He had argued that it was meant especially for the undaunted, for those who were not afraid to fight whatever the cost. A nation that was unfit to fight, he had said, could not prove the virtue of not fighting. Well, Pathans were ahead there! All they needed was the understanding. If he could persuade half a dozen to try it . . .

*

They called themselves Khudai Khidmatgars, "Servants of God." Their motto was freedom, their aim, service. Since God himself needed no service, they would serve his people.

The Khudai Khidmatgars, under the leadership of Abdul Ghaffar Khan, became history's first professional nonviolent army – and its most improbable. Any Pathan could join, provided he took the army's oath:

> I am a Khudai Khidmatgar; and as God needs no service, but serving his creation is serving him, I promise to serve humanity in the name of God.
>
> I promise to refrain from violence and from taking revenge. I promise to forgive those who oppress me or treat me with cruelty.
>
> I promise to refrain from taking part in feuds and quarrels and from creating enmity.

I promise to treat every Pathan as my brother and friend.

I promise to refrain from antisocial customs and practices.

I promise to live a simple life, to practice virtue and to refrain from evil.

I promise to practice good manners and good behavior and not to lead a life of idleness. I promise to devote at least two hours a day to social work.

For a Pathan, an oath is not a small matter. He does not enter into a vow easily because once given, a Pathan's word cannot be broken. Even his enemy can count on him to keep his word at the risk of his own life. Nonviolence was the heart of the oath and of the organization. It was directed not only against the violence of British rule but against the pervasive violence of Pathan life. With it they could win their freedom and much more: prosperity, dignity, self-respect.

Khan drew his first recruits from the young men who had graduated from his schools. They flocked to him. Trained and uniformed, they snapped in behind their officers and filed out into the villages to seek recruits. They began by wearing a simple white overshirt, but the white was soon dirtied. A couple of men had their shirts dyed at the local tannery, and the brick-red color proved a breakthrough. It did not dirty easily, the dye was cheap, and – best of luck – it had style. Villagers dropped their plows to see who these glowing figures were.

Recruits did not come easily, but Khan and his eager young volunteers persisted. Within a few months they had five hundred recruits – not enough for a Raj-shattering holy war, but a beginning. Volunteers who took the oath formed platoons with commanding officers and learned basic army discipline – everything that did not require the use of arms. They had drills, badges, a tricolor flag, the entire military hierarchy of rank – and a bagpipe corps.

Khan set up a network of committees called *jirgahs,* named and modeled after the traditional tribal councils that had maintained Pathan law for centuries. Villages were grouped into larger groups, responsible to district-wide committees. The Provincial Jirgah was the ultimate authority. Since all the committees were filled by elected officers, the Provincial Jirgah became a kind of unofficial parliament of Pathans.

Officers in the ranks were not elected, since Khan wanted to avoid infighting. He appointed a *salar-e-azam* or commander-in-chief, who in turn appointed officers to serve under him. The army was completely voluntary; even the officers gave their services free. Women were recruited too, and played an important role in the struggles to come.

Volunteers went to the villages and opened schools, helped on work projects, and maintained order at public gatherings. From time to time they drilled in work camps and took long military-style marches into the hills. As they marched, they sang:

> We are the army of God,
> By death or wealth unmoved.
> We march, our leader and we,
> Ready to die.
>
> We serve and we love
> Our people and our cause.
> Freedom is our goal,
> Our lives the price we pay.

Watching the narrow columns threading a curving mountain pass, one could easily imagine that some angry mullah was unleashing another holy war against the foreigners. But these Pathans, who for years had carried rifles and tucked small armories of revolvers and knives inside their waistbands, now carried only a stick for walking. They armed themselves only with their discipline, their faith, and their native mettle.

Part Three

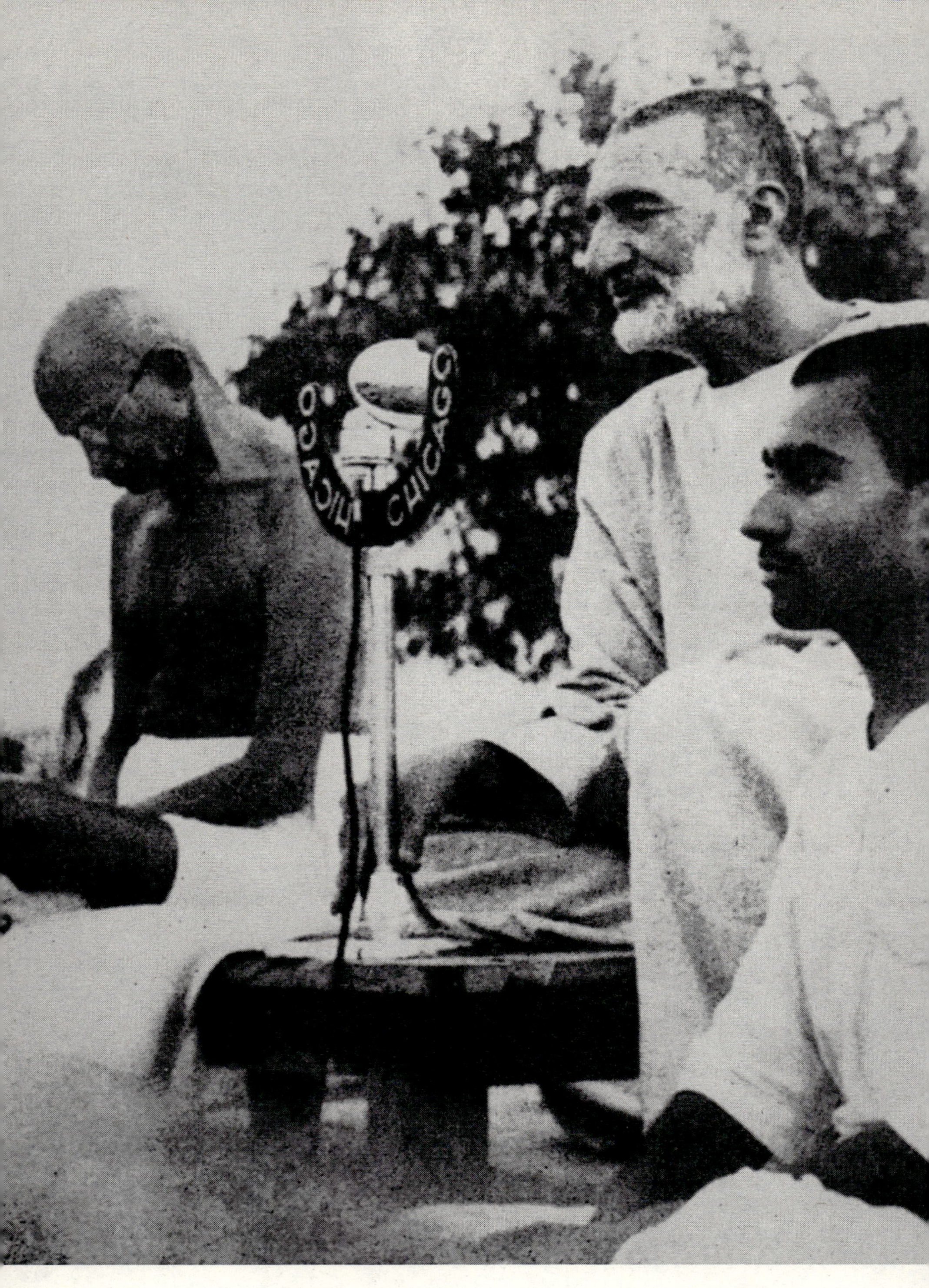

With Gandhi at a prayer meeting (Govt. of India)
Previous pages: First meeting of the Khudai Khidmatgars, April 1930 (Nehru Memorial Library)

CHAPTER TEN : 1930–1931

The Weapon of the Prophet

I am going to give you such a weapon that the police and the army will not be able to stand against it. It is the weapon of the Prophet, but you are not aware of it. That weapon is patience and righteousness. No power on earth can stand against it.

When you go back to your villages, tell your brethren that there is an army of God and its weapon is patience. Ask your brethren to join the army of God. Endure all hardships. If you exercise patience, victory will be yours.

ON THE STROKE OF MIDNIGHT, December 31, 1929, a deafening roar swelled over the ancient city of Lahore and spilled into the dark Indian countryside. It was the cry of freedom. Five thousand Congress delegates, closely watched by some twenty-five thousand sympathetic onlookers, had spent the previous week arguing India's future. Should they demand independence outright – and unleash a revolution – or go on reasoning and pleading with the British? On close examination, there was no argument. The British had been given a year to think the matter over and their purposeful silence was answer enough. India, in their eyes, would remain British indefinitely.

Thus the cry. The five thousand delegates decided to declare themselves and all Indians free men and women, henceforth and forever. Their declaration echoed the small band of American colonials at Philadelphia in July of 1776:

> We believe that it is the inalienable right of the Indian people, as of any other people, to have freedom and to enjoy the fruits of their toil and have the necessities of life so that they may have full opportunities of growth. We believe also that if any government deprives a people of these rights and oppresses

> them, the people have a further right to alter it or to abolish it. The British Government in India has not only deprived the Indian people of their freedom, but has based itself on the exploitation of the masses and has mined India economically, politically, culturally and spiritually. We believe, therefore, that India must sever the British connection and attain complete independence. We hold it to be a crime against man and God to submit any longer to a rule that has caused this fourfold disaster to our country.

The young Jefferson could not have phrased the words with cleaner accuracy. No doubt the image of the American colonials must have loomed in the minds of many under the sprawling pavilion – as did images of the American Revolution itself.

Yet there was a difference. This was the Indian Revolution, not the American, and the words were Gandhi's. The end was the same, but the means would be utterly, startlingly different. The resolution went on:

> We recognize, however, that the most effective way of gaining our freedom is not through violence. We will prepare ourselves by withdrawing, so far as we can, all voluntary association from the British government, and will prepare for civil disobedience, including the nonpayment of taxes. We are convinced that if we can but withdraw our voluntary help, stop payment of the taxes, without doing violence even under provocation, the end of this inhuman rule is assured.

The Indian tricolor was raised and the gathering exploded in celebration. Two hundred Pathans led the way, locking their arms in a great circle. Their drums thumped and the circle swayed in one of the wild Pathan dances so reminiscent of the Cossacks. Even Nehru put on a Pathan turban and kicked up his patrician heels. India was free! All she had to do now was prove it to the British.

That was Gandhi's job. He would choose the day and the issue on which India would begin satyagraha – nonviolent resistance.

Gandhi told Indians to prepare themselves for the final plunge while he waited for the inner voice. When the call came he would know it – and give the signal.

India waited and simmered. Like monsoon clouds boiling on the horizon, the whole country of three hundred million waited for the storm to break. January passed, then February. There was no word from Gandhi. The British murmured in their offices and clubs about the storm brewing – and waited. They were not about to make something out of nothing. Let Gandhi show himself.

On March 2, 1930, Gandhi sent the viceroy what has been described as "the strangest communication the head of a government ever received." After a detailed, reasoned review of why he "regarded British rule as a curse," he informed Lord Irwin respectfully that unless he "opened a way for a real conference between equals," nationwide civil disobedience would begin in nine days. He did not say what would happen or where.

Irwin acknowledged receipt of the letter.

On March 12, Gandhi left his ashram on the Sabarmati River and began a twenty-four-day march to the seaside village of Dandi. On the morning of April 6, with thousands of cheering Indians surrounding him, he picked up a pinch of sea salt from the Dandi beach and broke the law restricting the making and selling of salt to the government monopoly. The great Salt Satyagraha had begun.

A pinch was sufficient. Gandhi's act signaled Indians across the country to break the salt law, one of the more onerous forms of exploitation in a tropical land where salt is as essential as water.

The law not only monopolized the market for salt but levied a tax on it which, until recently, had been the government's second largest source of revenue. Everyone in India, rich or poor, had to use salt. Everyone was touched by the salt law. Therefore, Gandhi reasoned, everyone was in a position to break it. The salt law was a perfect symbol of colonial tyranny, which the simplest Indian peasant could understand.

A monsoon of resistance broke over the country. In open defiance, Indians by the millions made, sold, and bought millions of pounds of illegal salt. It was the unmistakable gesture of a people who had declared themselves free and were now beginning to act like it.

By the end of the month, India was convulsed by revolution. The British had never seen anything like this – no government had in all of history. Their armies and police beat down the unarmed crowds with *lathis* (steel-tipped staffs), raided Congress offices, confiscated property, and eventually arrested every major political leader except Gandhi, assuming that the movement would collapse from under him. Meetings were banned and newspapers shut down. One hundred thousand people ended up in jail.

But the storm only grew. Every arrest or beating only brought forth new resisters. Finally, unable to bear the mounting criticism from London, the viceroy arrested Gandhi on May 4. Gandhi went with one simple message for his countrymen: to carry on the struggle with complete nonviolence. Memories of the aborted movement of a decade ago, called off by Gandhi because some policemen had been killed by demonstrators, were still fresh in Indian minds. This time they would not try their Mahatma's patience. In spite of intense repression, there was no violence on the part of Indians.

On the Frontier, repression reached another order of magnitude. After the first week of April, no reporters were allowed in or out of the province, and local newspaper reports came out heavily censored. Rumors of firings on unarmed crowds, beatings, and humiliations ran rampant; no one on the outside could sort out the truth. Congress appointed an inquiry committee under Vithalbhai Patel, who had just resigned as speaker of the Legislative Assembly, to visit the Frontier and come up with an accurate account of events. The government countered with its own Suleiman Inquiry Committee – and turned the Congress representatives back at the border. Patel and his colleagues stayed in Rawalpindi, just outside the Frontier, and opened their inquiry there. After interviewing seventy-nine witnesses, they released a three-hundred-fifty-page report which the government promptly banned. It told a chilling story of brutality on a scale Indians had never seen before. But along with the brutal details, contraband copies brought to the rest of India a first heartening glimpse of the heroism that is possible when the strong and fearless renounce arms and use love and nonviolence as their only weapons.

*

The story of the Peshawar "disturbances" begins, appropriately, with Badshah Khan.

On January 1, 1930, the declaration of independence at Lahore had been repeated in mass meetings all over India, including several locations in the Frontier. Khan and his red-shirted Servants of God immediately embarked on an intensive campaign of education and organization, touring villages throughout the Frontier. The British, apprehensive but unwilling to provoke the Pathans, stalled. Then the chief commissioner of Peshawar ordered Khan in to see him and told him to stop what he was doing.

"This is basically a social movement," Khan replied, "not a political movement. Indeed, the government itself should have launched it. I am doing your work; you should extend your help and cooperation."

The commissioner did not take Khan's advice, nor did Khan take his. He told the Khudai Khidmatgars to continue their organizing in the villages. A few weeks later Gandhi arrived at the seashore of Dandi and picked up his historic pinch of salt. Within days, it has been estimated, almost the entire population of Peshawar had broken the salt laws. Throughout the Frontier, the British felt hopelessly outnumbered among an alien people they feared and could not control. In their minds it was all too likely that – as in the past – the Frontier would erupt in violence.

On April 23, 1930, Khan rose before a mass meeting in Utmanzai and exhorted his people to join in civil resistance. He then set out for Peshawar to make a similar appeal and was arrested in a town called Naki. The townspeople, true Pathans, promptly declared themselves all Khudai Khidmatgars from that time on. Word of Khan's arrest spread rapidly, and soon thousands of demonstrators had gathered and surrounded the jail. Khan's elder brother, Dr. Khan Saheb, arrived in time to remind the crowd to remain nonviolent, while Badshah Khan and four of his co-workers were taken out of the Frontier without incident and sentenced to three years' imprisonment.

Meanwhile, the Frontier was exploding – nonviolently. In Peshawar other Khudai Khidmatgar leaders had been arrested in the early hours of that same day, and by mid-morning a spontaneous general strike was in effect all over the city. A large crowd gathered in Qissa Khawani Bazaar to protest the arrests. Troops were called in from the nearby army base and arrived with three armored cars. By that time all the arrests had been concluded peacefully, and the subinspector of police commanded the crowd to remain nonviolent and go home. They had begun to do so, the Congress Inquiry Committee report relates in its matter-of-fact way, when "all of a sudden two or three armored cars came at great speed from behind without giving warning of their approach and drove into the crowd. Several people were run over, of whom some were injured and a few killed on the spot. The people were not armed – [not even with] stones or bricks. The crowd behaved with great restraint, collecting the wounded and dead."

More people collected. The troops were ordered to fire. "Several people were killed and wounded," the report continues,

> and the crowd was pushed back some distance. At about half past eleven, endeavors were made by one or two outsiders to persuade the crowd to disperse and the authorities to remove the troops and the armored cars. The crowds were willing to disperse if they were allowed to remove the dead and the injured and if the armored cars and the troops were removed. The authorities, on the other hand, expressed their determination not to remove the armored cars and the troops. The result was that the people did not disperse and were prepared to receive the bullets and lay down their lives. The second firing then began and, off and on, lasted for more than three hours. . . .

In his study of nonviolent movements, Gene Sharp of Harvard includes a description of the firing in Qissa Khawani Bazaar:

When those in front fell down wounded by the shots, those behind came forward with their breasts bared and exposed themselves to the fire, so much so that some people got as many as 21 bullet wounds in their bodies, and all the people stood their ground without getting into a panic. A young Sikh boy came and stood in front of a soldier and asked him to fire at him, which the soldier unhesitatingly did, killing him. The crowd kept standing at the spot facing the soldiers and were fired at from time to time, until there were heaps of wounded and dying lying about.

The Anglo-Indian paper of Lahore, which represents the official view, itself wrote to the effect that the people came forward one after another to face the firing and when they fell wounded they were dragged back and others came forward to be shot at. This state of things continued from 11 till 5 o'clock in the evening. When the number of corpses became too many the ambulance cars of the government took them away [and burned them].

Throughout the afternoon the government troops chased unarmed Pathans through the bazaar and down the Streets of the Storytellers and the Silversmiths, shooting on sight. The Congress report estimated that two to three hundred were killed and many more wounded.

At one point the government ordered its crack Garhwal Rifles to fire on the crowds. Faced with unarmed men, women, and children lying down to be slaughtered, the Garhwalis refused. "You may blow us from your guns, if you like," they told their officers. (Indians in the "Mutiny of 1857" had been shot from cannon as punishment.) "We will not shoot our unarmed brethren."

When word of the Garhwalis' heroism got out, it moved all India. The soldiers paid a high price for it. The whole platoon was arrested, and seventeen men were court-martialed and sentenced: one to banishment in an overseas penal colony for life, another to fifteen years' imprisonment, and the rest to rigorous prison terms.

This was one of the most famous regiments in the world,

known for their loyalty as well as their courage, and their refusal to obey orders gave the British a chilling reminder of the "Great Mutiny." They were determined to check it. Even after an eventual truce freed all of the one hundred thousand political prisoners of the Salt Satyagraha, the Garhwalis were exempted from the general amnesty and served their full terms.

Peshawar itself fell into chaos, as the troops and police tried to quell the demonstrations. For the next two days, the committee reports, "Peshawar became a hell to live in, owing to the atrocities of the British troops." Then, on the night of the twenty-fifth, both the military and the police evacuated the city, leaving it in the hands of the Khudai Khidmatgar volunteers. A few days later the police and military reappeared and took control of the city again. One of their first acts was to declare the Khudai Khidmatgars illegal and close down their office, scattering all their papers and removing their cash. "From that day onward," the Congress report concluded,

> the city has been for all practical purposes under martial law. Life, liberty or property of no one in Peshawar is safe. . . .
>
> The province has become a forbidden land to the outside world. It is isolated from the rest of India and no public leader is allowed to step in there. . . . In spite of all this the spirit of the people has remained unbroken and strict nonviolence has been observed.

That same day repression began also in Khan's village. Dr. Khan Saheb, after dispersing the crowds that had surrounded his brother's jail in Peshawar, heard that a mass meeting had been called in Utmanzai and rushed to the scene to help. "Here," says the man who was later to be elected prime minister of his province, "I made my first political speech in a public place." Dr. Khan spoke for nonviolence. As he concluded his speech, the Guides cavalry arrived.

The Guides commander announced that his men were going to open fire and ordered the crowd to disperse. When no one heeded him, he appealed to Dr. Khan for help. "The best thing for you to do," Dr. Khan told him, "is to go back and let us march to our destination. But if you want to do any shooting, you must start now, because once we leave the place, shooting would not be a very brave thing." After some bluffing the cavalry left, and the Khudai Khidmatgars proceeded to march. On the road they were attacked by cavalry. "The officials lost their heads," Dr. Khan reported tersely, "and repression was intense. But the Khudai Khidmatgars stood their ground without retaliating, and "the result," he concludes, "was that by the end of September we had over eighty thousand volunteers."

*

What alarmed the British – and stunned and inspired Indians – was the nonviolence of the Pathans. No one expected it, and the British were clearly unnerved. "The British feared a nonviolent Pathan more than a violent one," Khan wrote later. "All the horrors the British perpetrated on the Pathans had only one purpose: to provoke them to violence." Much of the government's extreme behavior during the months that followed can be understood only as attempts to goad the Pathans into breaking their nonviolent vow. If they broke down and retaliated, the British would be back on familiar ground.

Here British ingenuity came to the fore. They knew on what fine points a Pathan's honor turned, and they bent themselves to pushing the Khudai Khidmatgars to the breaking point. Government troops returned to Utmanzai before dawn on the morning of May 13, 1930. Eight hundred British troops, a regiment of Indian cavalry, and a special corps of shock troops with four Lewis field cannon "and numerous other guns" surrounded the village under cover of darkness. (Utmanzai at that time probably numbered no more than five thousand inhabitants all told.) At dawn the troops entered the village and surrounded the little shop over which Khudai Khidmatgar headquarters was located. Unable to break in the front gate, they scaled the walls and posted themselves around the balcony. Inside, Rabnawaz Khan, the Khudai Khidmatgar commander, told all the volunteers in the building – including Khan's fourteen-year-old son, Wali – to remember their vow of nonviolence. The British deputy commissioner – apparently the same man who had ordered his men to open fire in Qissa Khawani

Bazaar – commanded the Pathans to go down into the street and take off their red uniforms. They refused. The deputy commissioner drew his revolver and held it to the chest of one of the Pathans. Remove your clothes!"

"Saheb, it is impossible," replied the Khudai Khidmatgar. "The trousers of a Pathan cannot be taken off as long as he is alive."

A rifle struck him across the head and he fell unconscious. His clothes were stripped from his body and he was beaten.

A man named Faiz Mohammed was next. He too refused, and the soldiers started to strip him forcibly. The man was tall and powerfully built, and although he did not fight back, he did not cooperate. Eight or nine men were required to strip him, and even then he too had to be beaten into unconsciousness.

One by one, other volunteers received the same treatment. Some were pushed from the second-story balcony into the street. None fought back – nor did they run away.

The soldiers came to Mohammed Naquib Khan, a Khudai Khidmatgar captain. He too was beaten mercilessly, and they finally succeeded in taking off his shirt. But when he was ordered again to take off his trousers, something snapped. The blood drained from the Pathan's face. Badshah Khan had said they must be prepared to face death, and the captain was willing – but this was worse than death. He turned to run for a gun. He would die fighting – like a Pathan!

"Mohammed Naquib!" boomed the voice of his commander. "Is your patience exhausted so soon? You swore to remain nonviolent until death!"

Mohammed Naquib was proud and volatile even for a Pathan. His commission as a captain in the district's volunteer corps might well have raised eyebrows: virtually every man in the corps had a history of violence, and was accustomed to dishing out punishment rather than receiving it. Now his eyes burned as his position became clear to him. He turned back toward the waiting soldiers. They were not smiling. Across the face of the captain appeared a trace of a grin. It was the defiant smile of the Pathan warrior – caught in open cross-fire, knowing his defeat is imminent, taunting his pursuers that though they may have conquered his body, his Pathan spirit is winging its way to Paradise. The shaggy head reared back and Mohammed Naquib Khan started to walk slowly, with majestic Pathan swagger, back to the English officer.

Young Wali Khan was standing in uniform when the commissioner got to him. "Who are you?" the Englishman demanded. "I am the son of Khan Abdul Ghaffar Khan!" Wali answered, in a voice meant to be heard across the street. The commissioner began to abuse him, and a British soldier threatened him with his bayonet. One of the Indian soldiers, a Muslim, could not stand by any longer. He stepped forward and pushed the bayonet away, and in the confusion a Pathan named Hassan Khan grabbed Wali, jumped with him from the balcony, and took him to refuge in the mosque.

The soldiers then set to work. They burnt the office building to the ground and looted the village. Villagers could not go out of their homes to farm or graze their cattle or even to answer calls of nature. Cows seen outside their compound were shot or bayoneted. Anyone with a red shirt was stripped, beaten, and taken to jail.

Finally the village was cleared. No volunteers were left to arrest. "Any more Red Shirts?" bellowed the commissioner provocatively.

It was too much for one old villager named Abbas Khan. He was not a Red Shirt. What had he to do with these radical reformers? But arrogance like this could not be borne.

He went to his home, doused a shirt in some red fluid, put it on – still wet – and ran back into the street. "Here is a Red Shirt!" the old man barked into the face of the British commissioner.

Pathan pride will out. Abbas Khan was the rule rather than the exception. Where Khan had been able to recruit only a thousand or so Khudai Khidmatgars, British repression and effrontery converted eighty thousand men and women to the movement by the end of the summer.

Undaunted, the government tried other methods. Martial law was declared in August and the province was placed completely in the hands of the military. Khudai Khidmatgars were stripped and flogged and made to run the gauntlet through cordons of soldiers who prodded them with rifles and bayonets as they passed. One enterprising assistant superintendent, a Mr. Jameson, had volunteers stripped and physically humiliated in public, then thrown into nearby cesspools. For some the strain was too great. They chose suicide rather than break their vow of nonviolence.

The British also tried to subvert the movement by insinuating a Bolshevik influence among the Red Shirts. An order was sent from the British commissioner to all the village chiefs:

> You must prevent Congress volunteers wearing red jackets from entering your villages. They call themselves Khudai Khidmatgars (Servants of God). But in reality they are the servants of Gandhi. They wear the dress of Bolsheviks. They will create the same atmosphere as you have heard of in the Bolshevik dominion.

"The two years that followed," says a Pathan writer, Mohammed Yunus,

> formed an astounding period of darkness for the province. Shootings, beatings and other acts of provocation were perpetrated against these people, who had never suffered before without avenging themselves. "Gunning the Red Shirts" was a popular sport and pastime of the British forces in the province, observed an American tourist.
>
> At Kohat, in the bitter cold of the winter, our men were beaten up and later thrown into the icy stream running through the city. It was the same story at Bannu [where the British made an unsuccessful blockade to starve the villagers into submission] and Dera Ismail Khan. The residents of Swabi saw their fields destroyed, their wheat stocks ruined by oil poured upon them.
>
> But the Pathans, notwithstanding the fact that they had been brought up in an atmosphere of violence and bloodshed, stood unmoved by such provocations and died peacefully in large numbers for the attainment of their goal.

*

This time, nothing – not even jailing Gandhi – worked for the British. Leaders came from nowhere, and the movement surged with invisible momentum. All across the subcontinent, strikes, picketing, meetings, parades, and innumerable acts of open disregard for British rule continued throughout the fall and winter of 1930. And Indians remained nonviolent.

At the end of the year Lord Irwin invited Gandhi to Delhi to discuss a truce. It was the first time the British had officially recognized Gandhi and his movement. They knew they had no choice.

After several days of negotiations Gandhi and Irwin signed an accord – as equals. Civil disobedience was suspended, and throughout India all political prisoners were released. On the Frontier, Khan's movement finally won long-sought concessions from the government. Even the unsympathetic conceded that it was "thanks largely to earlier Congress–Red Shirt pressure" that the Frontier "now became a full-fledged governor's province with an appointed indigenous minister at the head of local government. . . . At long last, the Pathans had achieved political parity with the rest of British India."

But the terms of the Gandhi-Irwin truce satisfied no one. For politicians in London, too many concessions had been granted; for Indians who had expected freedom, far too few. But two men understood the watershed that the truce represented: Gandhi, who knew that India's freedom had been granted in principle if not in fact; and Churchill, imperial to the marrow, who seethed over "the nauseating and humiliating spectacle of this one-time Inner Temple lawyer, now seditious fakir, striding half-naked up the steps of the viceroy's palace, there to negotiate and to parley on equal terms with the representative of the King-Emperor." Inconclusive as it appeared at the moment, the Gandhi-Irwin Pact marked the beginning of the end of imperialism. Churchill, who knew his history better than most, heard the death rattle.

Badshah Khan at 74 (National Gandhi Museum)

CHAPTER ELEVEN : 1931–1934

The Frontier Gandhi

I have but one standard of measure and that is the measure of one's surrender to God.

A SIMPLE BUT passionate faith in God underlies every aspect of the Pathan's life. As with all devout Muslims, his day is fixed by the five moments of prayer. He stops, bows low toward Mecca, and prays. He looks to the village priest for guidance; hence the mullah is usually the true power center of a tribe. Though the Pathans' battles are carried out by warriors, they are inspired by priests – Mullah Mastun, Churchill's "Mad Fakir," being just one example.

Lacking theology, the Pathan seeks spirituality in the lives of the truly devout. The Pathan hills are spotted with the shrines and tombs of holy *pirs* and fakirs. In a sense these are the real power centers, for no tribe is without at least one tomb-shrine of a great saint. Upon these rock clusters, lodged often on an almost inaccessible crag, the Pathan takes his most solemn oaths.

Much to his discomfort, Khan quickly found himself cast as a saint. After his return to the Frontier in March 1931, following the Gandhi-Irwin truce, Khan found himself besieged by villagers who believed that his touch could heal. When he dug a well, the water was emptied – wasn't it holy? Moreover, in the rest of India, Khan's pure faith and austere ways had made him known as the Frontier Gandhi.

He did not like it. "Do not add the name of Gandhi to my name," he told an audience of students. "I am not fit for the praise you have showered on me. The praise is due to the nonviolent method, which has changed the nature of our people." Playing the curmudgeon, Khan told the Pathan villagers in plain words that their hard work was a hundred times more pleasing to him than their veneration. Nor did he like this "badshah" – he was a servant of the people, not their king. But all this was no use. The badshah could say what he liked; these people knew a true saint when they saw one.

His actions did not help to dispel the notion, either. He had given up eating meat and – unheard-of for a Pathan – stopped drinking tea. He ate little and wore homespun clothes. And shortly he would make the supreme sacrifice for a Pathan: renounce his land, turning ownership over to his three sons. A Pathan without land loses his right to vote in the jirgah and thus, in a sense, no longer counts as a Pathan: he is literally a fakir, landless. The Pathans were uneducated, but even the simplest could recognize this austere, self-effacing, and landless khan for what he was: a spiritual lamp.

Khan's touring of the villages was almost incessant now, and lined with difficulties. Twice he was nearly assassinated. Resistance rose up not only from the British and the mullahs but from wealthy khans who saw reforms as a threat to their interests. The British carefully protected the privileges of such people, using them as levers against popular unrest. Khan found himself in a triple cross-fire. Illiteracy was so high among the villagers that only constant personal contact could keep them inspired and committed. Khan tried to visit every village in the province. Carrying only a bundle of extra clothing and a few other necessities, he often covered as much as twenty-five miles a day, stopping at three or four villages and speaking for an hour at each one. Sometimes he and his volunteers staged dramas that instructed the villagers in nonviolence.

When he reached the last village of the day, his first task was to go to the mosque – often just a low room of undressed rock and mortar – and sweep it clean. He especially liked to stay with the village poor. With a child or two draped across his shoulders he would chat with the tribesmen, exhorting them to be cleaner, stronger, more loving. In the derahs at night, in the mosques during the day, Khan never let up. "There are two objects in view," he repeated everywhere, "to liberate the country and to feed the starving and clothe the naked."

Khan's sister addressed meetings throughout the Frontier. With Gandhi's example before him, Khan had begun to waken Pathan women, and almost overnight they stepped from the medieval world behind the veil to open leadership. Khan loved it. "My sisters," he told a large gathering at Bhaizai,

> I am feeling a peculiar sort of pleasure, because wherever I went in India and saw the nationwide awakening of the Hindu and Parsi women, I would say to myself, "Would such a time come when our Pathan women would also awaken? . . ." I had cherished this longing ever since. Thank God, today, I see my desire being fulfilled.
>
> God makes no distinction between men and women. If someone can surpass another, it is only through good deeds and morals. If you study history, you will see that there were many scholars and poets amongst women. It is a grave mistake we have made in degrading women. . . .
>
> If we achieve success and liberate the motherland, we solemnly promise you that you will get your rights. In the Holy Koran, you have an equal share with men. You are today oppressed because we men have ignored the commands of God and the Prophet. Today we are the followers of custom and we oppress you. But thank God that we have realized that our gain and loss, progress and downfall, are common.

The British wanted Khan's touring stopped. The Frontier government informed the viceroy that they intended to arrest Khan unless he quit. Gandhi protested that Khan's arrest would snap the truce, and asked to visit the Frontier himself to study the government's complaints. He was refused, but his son Devadas was allowed in and reported that the Frontier government was alarmed only because Khan was continuing to rouse the politically dormant Pathans. "At the end of my six days' wanderings," Devadas wrote,

> I have realized more than ever before the power and inspiration of the personality of Khan Saheb [i.e., Abdul Ghaffar]. The one central and unquestionable fact that emerges was . . . that Khan Saheb himself is held in great esteem by all, not excluding the critics of the Red Shirt movement.
>
> Large numbers of Pathans have come under the influence of Khan Saheb, whose personality seems to act like magic among them. He gives himself no rest. He moves about from place to place and mixes freely among the villagers, living exactly as they do.
>
> The simplicity of his character, and the deep sympathy he evinces for the poor and the oppressed, have created for him an abiding place in the hearts of the people.

The government banned meetings within four miles of any road, and had Khan followed day and night by British intelligence officers. Often he was the target of distortions in the British press. "Holy war threat in India started by Abdul Ghaffar Khan," accused the *Daily Express* – a classic British fear to play on, for Mullah Mastun had not been the only fiery priest to arise in the Muslim corners of the Empire. The *Daily Mail* was predictably even more colorful. It called the Frontier "an outpost of the Soviet Republic," claimed it was "the spearhead of an attack on India," and spoke of "Russian gold pouring in across the Khyber Pass" and "Muslims being armed with the Russian weapons." "Their leader," it concluded, "is the terrible Abdul Ghaffar Khan, a jailbird and relentless enemy of the British."

In spite of the calumnies and obstruction, however, Khan refused to stop touring. The village of Rustam had been placed under a prohibitory order, Section 144 of the Criminal Code, which forbade public gatherings. Khan urged the villagers to defy the order which, he felt, was a breach of the truce. "Do not fear death," he told them.

> Section 144 is your test. If you cannot oppose this order, how can you come out to the battlefield? Pay no attention to the order. Be ready and come out to the nonviolent battlefield.

> Nonviolent war means a kind of war your ancestors fought fourteen hundred years ago. Show the people you are their descendents. . . .
>
> Rule yourselves, and as long as you live, do not submit to the rule of anybody else. Be prepared and free yourselves from this oppressive rule. If you perish on the battlefield, what does it matter? Everyone must die.

Tensions on the Frontier mounted. On December 22, 1931, the chief commissioner of the Frontier, Sir Ralph Griffith, invited Khan to attend a reception. Khan refused. As long as the government was suppressing the Khudai Khidmatgars, he could not socialize with it.

Griffith was undeterred. He had a policeman bring Khan to him. "I am a plain man," Khan told the commissioner. "I like a straight talk. Don't try to be diplomatic with me."

"Politics," the commissioner answered, "is a chess game with moves and countermoves. I checkmate you and you checkmate me – if you can."

"Then I am not the man for you," Khan answered, and rose to leave.

"Wait," the commissioner replied, seeing his error. "Look at all those people out there." He waved his hand towards the waiting room benches, lined with khans and villagers. "They wait for an interview with me for days together – but even then I don't meet with them. Yet in spite of my repeated requests to meet you, you don't want to oblige me."

Khan laughed. He liked this candor. "Those people all want something from you," he said, taking his seat again. "I don't want anything. Why should I tire myself out waiting?"

Sir Ralph's big fist banged the desk in front of him. "An unfortunate government it is from which the honest people keep away and which surrounds itself with the dishonest. It is destined to be doomed!"

Khan and the chief commissioner discussed their differences. Like Gandhi, Khan spoke plainly. If "half the money spent in ruination and the killing of tribesmen" were used to develop cottage industries and schools, he said, the British would have no need to be afraid of the Pathans; they would be their lifelong friends. And as far as protecting India from Soviet invasion went, the best way for the British to achieve that was to allow the Pathans to be masters in their own land. "No one can dominate us," he said flatly. "If anyone thinks of waging a war against us, we are willing to sacrifice everything for the protection of our country."

When Khan rose to go, Sir Ralph expressed the hope that they would meet again. Khan could not resist a parting gesture. "Surely," he said, heading toward the door. "But you'll have to send another policeman for me."

At their best, whatever charges might be leveled against them, the chief administrators of the Frontier knew whom to respect. The courage and candor of these Pathan tribesmen won their sincere admiration. But it did not stop them from discharging their imperial duties. Sir Ralph Griffith bid goodbye to Khan, left for Delhi and a visit to the viceroy, and returned on December 24 to have Khan arrested. Dr. Khan Saheb and Ghaffar Khan's sons, Wali, Ghani, and Ali, were arrested too. Within two weeks, in fact, every major political leader in India would be in prison.

The truce was over. On Christmas Day, 1931, six columns of British troops occupied Peshawar. Things would be different this time; there would be no "half-measures" as before. A new, tougher viceroy had replaced the accommodating Irwin, with instructions from London to give no quarter. On the Frontier, the order went out: crush the Red Shirts.

*

Gandhi was arrested around midnight on January 4, 1932. One of his parting instructions was to ask an Englishman, Verrier Elwin, to get into the Frontier and supply the rest of India with reliable information on what was happening there. Elwin managed to cross the border and quickly dispatched a grim twenty-page report:

> Since December 25th, the chief activity of the Red Shirts has been to send the volunteers for picketing from the villages to

Peshawar. The police take down the names and addresses of these picketers, which are always – it is their rule – faithfully given. Then a column of troops goes out by night to raid the village from which the picketers come.

The column normally arrives at about three in the morning. The village is surrounded. The leading men are ordered to produce Red Shirts. If they refuse, they are severely beaten. If any Red Shirts are found, they are arrested, beaten, and their uniforms removed and burnt.

The local Khudai Khidmatgar office is burnt to the ground. Police raid the houses and take whatever they can. No one knows if he is safe.

The authorities mistook Elwin for a trader, so he was able to spend a week in the Frontier interviewing both Indians and British. He had no trouble confirming, from the mouths of British soldiers themselves, the worst of the rumors that had been reaching India.

What had changed things was the truce itself. Hardened career officers and soldiers of the Frontier had seen the truce as a stinging defeat – and had been waiting to even the score. The breakdown in the truce gave them their chance. "This Red Shirt business must be smashed," one official told Elwin, "and we are determined to do it." Elwin was told of mass firings on crowds, beatings, public floggings, wholesale confiscation of property, and the sacking of whole villages to recover fines. "The soldiers collect money as if they were Moguls," one policeman gloated.

Thirty-five hundred people had been arrested in Peshawar alone. By the time Elwin reached the city, on January 11, there was not a Red Shirt to be seen. Government officials spoke openly and without compunction. "This is the Frontier," one of them told Elwin. "You 'down-country' people [in the rest of India] don't understand."

Elwin replied that even "down-country" people understood that inhumanity is inhumanity.

In a small village "under the great hills of the north" Elwin talked with the tribesmen, "splendid men with finely molded features and kind eyes."

"What is going to happen?" I asked.

"That is hard to say," was the reply. "We shall do everything we can, even to the giving of our lives, but to bear this *zulum* [tyranny] without retaliation is indeed hard."

"But will violence help you?"

"Certainly not."

"Do you then believe in nonviolence?"

"With all our hearts."

What can account for such impassioned commitment to nonviolence on the part of these uneducated, provincial villagers? An overwhelming love for their badshah, surely; they knew he was giving his life for them. And the sheer challenge of it must have appealed to the Pathan bravado. But for so many to stand so much without Khan's constant inspiration – he was usually in jail – these rough Pathan villagers must also have grasped something at the very heart of nonviolence: that it works. "To gain independence," Khan once explained,

> two types of movements were launched in our province.... The violent movement [the uprisings before 1919] created hatred in the heads of the people against violence. But the nonviolent movement won love, affection and sympathy of the people.... If a Britisher was killed [during the violent uprisings] not only the culprit was punished, but the whole village and entire region suffered for it. The people held the violence and its doer responsible for repression. In the nonviolent movement we courted self-suffering.... Thus, it won love and sympathy of the people.

True to Gandhi's insistence on scrupulous accuracy in his reports, Elwin was careful to inquire whether the Red Shirts themselves had resorted to violence. There were instances, he found, though often not involving Khudai Khidmatgars but other aroused village Pathans. Policemen had been insulted, spat at by children, and occasionally attacked with stones. "But even so," Elwin wrote, "instances of this kind are rare and cannot possibly be used to justify the policy of terrorization on which the authorities have embarked" – a chilling litany of systematic beatings, torture, and reprisals.

Elwin heard varied accounts of Khan. "He is an old rascal," one official remarked. "He's no good; he can't shoot," said an Afridi tribesman. "He is a Christ," said a British woman who had lived with his family.

Elwin wrote for an interview with Commissioner Griffith to hear the government's point of view. Griffith responded by having Elwin arrested and sent out of the province on the first available train. Elwin concluded that the government had succeeded in creating a kind of peace, but it was the "peace of the dead. It has managed to make life unpleasant for a large number of our brothers and sisters in the north, but it has not crushed their spirit and it will never do so."

Khan was removed from the Frontier Province and placed in solitary confinement in a prison in Bihar, in northeastern India. He was denied newspapers and letters and was not allowed contact with anyone. Other prisoners could not even cross the footpath in front of his cell.

In April 1934 Gandhi suspended the civil disobedience movement, which had lost its momentum, and threw himself and his co-workers into the uplift of village India to ready the nation for the final drive to freedom. Most political prisoners were released, but not Khan. His physical condition continued to deteriorate. Finally, after a visit from an understanding official, he was given a cell mate: Dr. Khan Saheb was transported to Bihar to stay with his brother. Badshah Khan never was sentenced; the government simply held him, at its pleasure, for three years. But at least it gave the brothers a chance to be together.

With Gandhi and Dr. Khan Saheb at Wardha (Nehru Memorial Library)

CHAPTER TWELVE : 1934

Men of the Book

As a young boy, I had had violent tendencies; the hot blood of the Pathans was in my veins. But in jail I had nothing to do except read the Koran. I read about the Prophet Mohammed in Mecca, about his patience, his suffering, his dedication. I had read it all before, as a child, but now I read it in the light of what I was hearing all around me about Gandhiji's struggle against the British Raj. . . . When I finally met Gandhiji, I learned all about his ideas of nonviolence and his Constructive Program. They changed my life forever.

BRITISH OFFICIALS on the Frontier were caught in a dilemma. They did not want Khan back in the province, but they did not know how to keep him in prison any longer. During the summer of 1934, they found a solution and informed the government in Delhi:

> The political atmosphere is charged with rumors that Mahatma Gandhi will visit Peshawar after concluding his self-imposed fast in August. It is believed that he will refuse to obey any prohibitory order and thus focus attention on Abdul Ghaffar Khan's release. . . .
>
> In order to ease the situation as far as possible and in order to deprive him of an excuse for hunger-strike which might commend itself to public opinion, both in India and other countries, the Government of India may think it advisable to release Abdul Ghaffar Khan and Khan Saheb . . . provided neither of them is allowed to enter the Punjab, Kashmir or the North-West Frontier Province. . . .
>
> Abdul Ghaffar has established such a strong and superstitious hold over the masses and can so easily by his speeches

> work them up into a state of ferment that he could not be allowed under anything like the present conditions to return to the Frontier.

Ghaffar Khan and his brother were released from the Hazaribagh Central Jail on August 27, 1934, and banned from the Frontier. The banishment turned out to be an opportunity. Since they could not return to their home, the brothers accepted an invitation from Gandhi to live at his new ashram in Central India. Though Khan had met Gandhi a number of times, he had never had the chance to spend time with him. Work, jail, and the demands of the movement had so far kept India's two leading advocates of nonviolence from coming to know each other.

Khan was a popular figure now, and crowds besieged him everywhere. Khan did not like the attention now any more than before. "Please do not call me the Frontier Gandhi," he pleaded with his audiences. "There should be only one Gandhi. Mahatma Gandhi is our general and there should be one general only."

Since the Salt Satyagraha, Gandhi had become a world-famous figure. He had moved to the remote, scorching plain of Central India to escape the firestorm of politics, settling down near one of the poorest villages in the area. He wanted to concentrate on his Constructive Program: the uplift of India's ravaged villages. Gandhi had taught Indians how to fight and die nonviolently; now he faced the more challenging task of showing them how to live nonviolently. That was the purpose of the ashram that came to be called Sevagram.

The two brothers reached the ashram in September and quickly settled in with the menagerie of devotees, children, and goats, mingling with the pilgrims who came in an unbroken stream from all over the world to see the Mahatma in person.

Life there was simple and hard. The brothers loved it. They shared the plain food and work and visited surrounding villages with Gandhi to teach basic hygiene. Dr. Khan opened a small clinic and regularly walked out into the villages to give medical care. Khan taught himself how to spin.

Their childlike candor charmed the whole ashram, especially Gandhiji. He asked his secretary, Mahadev Desai, to talk with them and prepare a biography called *Two Servants of God.* "The more I knew" of the Khan brothers, Gandhi wrote in the foreword,

> the more attracted I felt towards them. I was struck by their transparent sincerity, frankness and utmost simplicity. I observed too that they had come to believe in truth and non-violence not as a policy but as a creed. The younger brother, I found, was consumed with deep religious fervor. His was not a narrow creed. I found him to be a universalist. His politics, if he had any, were derived from his religion.

Desai describes Khan's spiritual temperament:

> The greatest thing in him is, to my mind, his spirituality – or better still, the true spirit of Islam – submission to God. He has measured Gandhiji's life all through with this yardstick and his clinging to Gandhiji can be explained on no other ground. It is not Gandhiji's name and fame that have attracted him to Gandhiji, nor his political work, nor his spirit of rebellion and revolution. It is his pure and ascetic life and his insistence on self-purification that have had the greatest appeal for him, and his whole life since 1919 onwards has been one sustained effort for self-purification.

In the afternoons the conversation would often turn to the valleys and fields the Khan brothers had not seen for three years. They wanted Gandhi to visit the Frontier, to stay on their farms and walk along the river where they had built a small retreat. "You can have your ashram there, Mahatmaji," Khan pleaded. "There is no more lovely spot on the face of the earth. The whole Peshawar valley abounds in fruit and grain. You will put on pounds of weight there, with the rest and good food we could give you."

Gandhi must have smiled at the thought. For some time he had wanted to visit the Frontier and talk with the Khudai Khidmatgars and spend long hours with these big-hearted brothers whose warmth had already buoyed the Mahatma's spirits. "The brothers' friendship seems to me to be a gift from God," Gandhi wrote. "To be with them more, is to love them more. . . . They are so nice, so simple, and yet so penetrative. They do not beat about the bush."

In the evenings, residents and visitors of the ashram used to gather around a neem tree for a prayer meeting. Hymns were sung and prayers from different scriptures read. Khan sat next to Gandhi and read from the Koran, sometimes borrowing Gandhi's glasses when he had forgotten to bring his own. While the sun dropped behind the great plain, Gandhi's eyes would close as he became lost in the holy words.

The brothers provided an interesting contrast. Dr. Khan was outgoing; his years in Europe had made his temperament more elastic. Where Khan viewed life as essentially religious, Dr. Khan saw it in a more worldly light. Khan was austere and almost naturally disciplined; Dr. Khan had indulged himself without regret. "Ghaffar offers the *namaz* for both of us," he liked to joke.

While Dr. Khan could meet patiently with even his bitterest enemies, the more volatile Khan found it difficult to bear the hauteur of the British. Thus, when the Frontier was asked to send its first representative to the Central Legislative Assembly in Delhi, it was the older brother who agreed to run. They both were Khudai Khidmatgars, and their differing natures simply meant that they would serve differently. Desai writes:

> It is these brothers that are bracketed today with India's "public enemies." They have made unparalleled sacrifices. They have gone through suffering which few have experienced. . . . The secret of their hold on their people lies certainly in their sacrifices and their suffering, but more in their daily life. While the younger brother is a man of God, the elder is a knight *sans peur et sans reproche.* All untruth, unreality, show and glamour produce in them nothing but loathing. Born aristocrats, they have taken to a life the simplicity of which it is difficult to surpass.

More often than not, the brothers and their host did not talk politics. Gandhi wanted to learn more about the Khudai Khidmatgars. How deep was their nonviolence? And he was intrigued by Ghaffar Khan's devout yet broad-minded Islam. Once he asked Khan about Dr. Khan Saheb's English wife. Was she a convert to Islam? "You will be surprised that I cannot say whether she is a Muslim or Christian," Khan replied. Even Gandhi must have been impressed by such detachment on a point that would seem fundamental to more orthodox Muslims. "She was never converted – that much I know – and she is completely at liberty to follow her own faith. I have never asked her about it. Why should I? Why should not a husband and wife adhere each to their respective faiths? Why should marriage alter one's faith?"

"I agree," said Gandhi. "But would most Muslims?"

"No, I know that they would not. But for that matter, not one in a hundred thousand knows the true spirit of Islam. I think at the back of our quarrels is the failure to recognize that all faiths contain enough inspiration for their adherents. The Holy Koran says in so many words that God sends messengers for all nations and peoples. All of them are Ahle Kitab – 'Men of the Book' – and the Hindus are no less Ahle Kitab than Jews and Christians."

Ghaffar Khan sent for his daughter, Mehar Taj, who was fourteen, to come to Wardha from England to join the school at the ashram. She arrived in November. Ghani arrived not long after, having had to conclude his university studies in the United States because of lack of funds. Khan's other sons, Wali and twelve-year-old Ali, also joined him. Wardha became the scene of a Khan family reunion, the first time they had been together since the Christmas arrests three years before.

Khan received word that the Muslims of Bengal wanted him to come to talk with them. Gandhi was wary. The government would not want the fiery Pathan let loose on the quiescent Muslim populations of northern India. It would find ways to interfere — perhaps by arresting him. Khan left with detailed instructions from Gandhi about what to say and what not to say. This was not a time to court imprisonment, he instructed, but to show Indians the other face of the revolution, the constructive side.

Khan spoke in Calcutta and urged Bengali youths to form their own Khudai Khidmatgar movement. During his tour he saw the real significance of Gandhi's insistence on spinning. Where villagers spun, they had enough to eat; where they did not, they starved. He appealed to urban Bengalis in Calcutta to turn their attention to the impoverished villages he had visited.

When he finished his tour, Khan promised the Bengalis that he would return in early December and stay. If he could not be in the Frontier – he was still banned from entering the province – then he felt that his place was with the impoverished Muslims of northern India. He needed to serve – and he needed to serve with his own hands.

In October 1934, Khan went with Gandhi to the annual Congress session in Bombay. To his discomfort, he found himself a celebrated hero. The main pavilion was named after him, and he was asked to accept the presidency of the Congress. He declined. "I appreciate the friends who have started this move," he explained, "but let me declare, as I have done over and over again, that I am only a humble soldier and it is my ambition to end my days not as a general but as a soldier."

Gandhi, meanwhile, resigned from the Congress to devote himself entirely to his Constructive Program. He explained to the assembly that he wanted to go to the Frontier:

> I would like to bury myself in an Indian village, preferably in a Frontier village. If the Khudai Khidmatgars are truly nonviolent, they will contribute the largest share to the promotion of the nonviolent spirit. . . . I am yearning to test the truth for myself of the claim that they have imbibed the spirit of nonviolence and they are believers, in the heart, of unity of Hindus [and] Muslims.

Asked about Gandhi's unexpected retirement, Khan said it did not surprise him:

> I have never found it easy to question his decisions, for he refers all his problems to God and always listens to His commands. Every great reformer has been like that and there always comes

> a stage in every reformer's life when he must take leave of his following and soar on ample pinion, untrammeled by their limitations and weaknesses. But he does not, by doing so, limit – but instead increases – the reach and sweep of his services.

During his stay in Bombay, Khan spoke on several occasions. On October 27, 1934, he told the Indian Christian Association the story of the Khudai Khidmatgars. As the story of the savage repression unfolded, Khan's emotions surged and he unveiled his deepest feelings. "What is our fault?" he asked rhetorically:

> Our fault is that our province is the gateway of India. Because we live there, the government calls us the gatekeepers and openly tells us, "How can we give reforms to the gatekeepers? If we give them anything, India will go out of our hands." The Britishers regard it as dangerous and think that they will not be able to rule India if the gatekeepers join hands with the Indians. It was for this very reason that our movement was crushed at the very outset....
>
> We started our own schools, but the government, under some pretext or the other, cleverly ruined the educational institutions of our little children.
>
> We were born in the Frontier Province and this is why we were doomed. This is our great crime, that we wanted to see the people of the villages civilized in that very Frontier Province which is called the gateway of India, while they wanted that these people should go on fighting among themselves and remain in need of them and remain in a ruined and destroyed condition so that they might rule our country without feeling any anxiety.

On his last day in Bombay Khan spoke to the Women's Unity Club, praising the sacrifices made by the thousands of women who had joined the freedom struggle. If the women of India were awakened, he said, it was not possible for any power on earth to keep India in slavery.

Then he returned to Wardha. Joined by his family, he entered again into the ashram routine. Long hours were spent with Gandhi, mapping out a program of reform for the Muslims of Bengal. Khan could not wait to get back; it had been too long since he had had a chance to work with the poor. He would leave on December 8.

But he did not get the chance. Bengal, like the Punjab, had always been a volatile province for the British to govern, and they could not have looked with much favor on Khan's plan to settle down with the Bengali Muslims. They took their usual recourse. On December 7, one hundred days after Khan had been released from prison, the district superintendent of police came for him at the ashram and placed him under arrest again for "seditious" remarks he had made in Bombay.

Gandhi read out the warrant and asked the superintendent to give Khan time to take leave of his family. "This time," he added, "we are going to offer a defense."

Khan stopped. A defense? Satyagrahis never defended themselves in court.

"This is different," Gandhi countered. "We are not offering satyagraha just now and we do not want to go to jail if we can help it."

"As you wish," Khan replied.

The children were stricken. Once again they were going to lose their father – for how long? There were tears, but Khan himself did not cry. He had steeled himself too many times against these scenes. With the more emotional Dr. Khan Saheb it was different. He had grown deeply attached to his younger brother during these three years. How many times would they go through this scene before freedom was won?

What saddened Ghaffar Khan most was that he could not fulfill his promise to the Muslims of Bengal. "I had promised to live and work among them," he told Gandhi, "and I may not now do even that little service."

Khan looked around at the children holding his arms, Dr. Khan looking at the floor, Gandhi talking to the superintendent. He turned to Gandhi. "I am quite certain that it is all God's doing. He kept me out of prison just for the time he wanted to use me outside. Now it is his will that I must serve from inside. What pleases him, pleases me."

With Gandhi on their evening walk (J.V. Mehta)

CHAPTER THIRTEEN : 1934–1938

The Two Gandhis

Whenever Gandhiji takes an important decision, I instinctively say to myself, "This is the decision of one who has surrendered himself to God, and God never guideth ill."

TO APOLOGIZE TO A BRITISH court for his statements in Bombay was a bitter pill for Ghaffar Khan. He did as Gandhi asked – but he was prepared, he stated in court, to defend the truth of every word he had said. "And indeed," his lawyer said later, "it amazed an honest Pathan to be told that he could not defend his words – that they might bring the Government into contempt and ridicule if he told the truth." But Gandhi did not want him in jail, and to Khan, Gandhi's word was law. He swallowed hard and apologized:

> I am a loyal Congressman and have accepted its policy of not seeking arrest and imprisonment at the present moment.
>
> I had, therefore, no desire whatsoever to utter words of sedition. I am, therefore, sorry that I made the statements in the speech, however unwittingly, which are open to exception from the prosecution's point of view.
>
> At the same time I would like to state that in describing the movement of the Khudai Khidmatgars, which I did at the instance of my Christian friends who had invited me to speak to them, I felt bound to state what I believed was the truth about the movement. I had no intention of wounding anybody's susceptibilities.

It wasn't enough. The British wanted him out of the way, and they did not mind offending the "susceptibilities" of Indians – and some British – who could not understand the severity of his sentence after his public apology. Khan's words were deemed "deliberate and grave, serious and reckless" by the presiding magistrate, H. P. Dastur. Khan, he said, was "a man of great influence and his words would have a greater effect than that of an ordinary person."

Since Khan had offered no defense, the magistrate based his judgment on the text of his Bombay speech. Particular attention was given to the report Khan had given to the Indian Christian Association in Bombay of the shootings at Qissa Khawani Bazaar. The story, the magistrate explained, "amounts to a very serious charge against the Government, namely, that it will not hesitate to butcher or kill in cold blood two hundred to two hundred fifty innocent persons. . . ." Such words, he concluded soberly, "would undoubtedly create resentment and disaffection in the minds of his hearers. . . ."

On December 15, 1934, Khan was sentenced to two years' rigorous imprisonment and sent to His Majesty's House of Correction at Byculla in Bombay. From there he went to Sabarmati Central Prison, where he was placed in solitary in a cell with two blankets and no bed. He slept on the concrete floor. Even the guards were forbidden to speak to him.

The hot climate was hard on him. He lost his appetite and contracted a severe case of influenza. By March, his once-robust 200-pound constitution had been reduced to 149 pounds. The government, worried about possible public reaction, requested that he be transferred to the Central Provinces where the climate was more congenial. The notion did not electrify the local officials, already feeling burdened by Gandhi's presence there. They begged off:

> The province has already had the presence of Mr. Gandhi thrust upon it for an apparently indefinite period. His residence at Wardha is the haunt of every leading Congressman in India, and if political troubles were to arise, [his residence here] would at once become a center of disaffection. . . .
>
> To put it bluntly, the farther Mr. Gandhi's Frontier confrere

> is kept away from Mr. Gandhi's residence, the better will it be for our peace of mind.

"With considerable difficulty and reluctance," however, local officials finally agreed to the move, and Khan was transferred to Almora – to the very cell from which Jawaharlal Nehru had recently been released. He worked in the little garden Nehru had begun. During this period of political quiescence, when no other major Indian political figure was imprisoned, Khan spent another eighteen months in jail.

On his release in July 1936, Khan went straight back to Gandhi. His ashram friends eagerly went to meet him at the train depot at Wardha. They found him in a third-class compartment with his legs dangling over the end of a bench and a gunny sack for a pillow. The aristocratic all-India hero could have been mistaken for a wandering mendicant. He looked up from the bench and smiled. "So this is the brotherhood of Congress!"

The British, still wary, extended Khan's ban from the Frontier for another year. The ban would have continued indefinitely had not fate – or at least Dr. Khan – intervened. The first elections for India's newly-formed legislative councils took place in January 1937. Dr. Khan ran for a seat in the Frontier legislature from a thousand miles away – he too was still banned from the province – and won. In July he became prime minister of the Frontier, and in his first official act he removed the ban on his brother.

Thus, at the end of August, Khan returned to his homeland for the first time in six years. His Pathan biographer, Mohammed Yunus, describes his return:

> At long last, after six weary years in jails and exile, 1937 saw the national hero of a grim tragedy welcomed back to his fatherland amidst scenes of great enthusiasm. It is difficult to forget that wild and passionate reception, a welcome springing spontaneously out of the intense affection in the hearts of his people.
>
> Ghaffar Khan was there, but in his face one could see traces of the deep and excruciating misery inflicted upon him during

those years. He had come to steer the ship once again through the turbulent currents. The general elections had taken place, and his lieutenants had been called upon to form the government of the North-West Frontier Province. That was surely his hour of triumph. After twenty-five years of endless labor and suffering, during which he had worked day and night, Fakhr-i-Afghan, "The Pride of the Pathans," was witnessing his party occupying places of partial authority. It was his courage, determination, skill, and judgment that had inspired his underfed, ill-equipped and rugged Khudai Khidmatgars to challenge the might of the British Empire and wrest some share in the government for themselves.

In October and again in the following January, Nehru visited the Frontier and toured most of the districts with Khan by his side. And finally, in May 1938, Gandhi came, fulfilling a long-held dream. The Indian political scene was quiet, so the viceroy let him go.

Khan was jubilant. He met Gandhi at Nowshera and took him to Dr. Khan's residence in Peshawar. Great crowds of Pathans, silent and still, lined the streets to greet them. Gandhi was delighted. For decades he had endured the unbridled affection of Indians cheering in his ears and rushing to touch his feet. It had been one of his greatest trials. These Pathans had been trained to demonstrate their devotion with discipline. At Utmanzai and surrounding villages, Gandhi found the same reception: thousands of Khudai Khidmatgars standing along the roadsides in their red-shirted uniforms, erect, smiling, still.

Khan beamed. He was proud of his ragged, determined people and he did not try to conceal it. At each stop villagers came up to their badshah as if he were a brother-in-law, chatting, joking, looking for advice. The water rates had been raised; should they boycott? No longer afraid of either the British or their mercenary landlords, these simple villagers had found their strength. Gandhi could not miss the bond between them and their leader. "I noticed wherever I went," he wrote later,

> that every man, woman, and child knew him and loved him. They greeted him most familiarly. His touch seemed to soothe them. [He] was most gentle to whomever approached him. All this has filled me with boundless joy. A general merits such obedience. But [Ghaffar Khan] has it by right of love, unlike the ordinary general who exacts obedience through fear.

Khan had made it clear that the spirit and inspiration of the revolution was Gandhi. At each stop some Pathan would stand before the assembly, red-shirted and eager, and tell the Mahatma what he meant to the Pathan nation. "We can never forget the debt we owe to you," one burly Pathan said at Mardan, "for having stood with us in our stricken plight. We are ignorant, we are poor – but we lack nothing because you have taught us the lesson of nonviolence."

Gandhi cut short his visit because of health problems, promising to return at the end of the summer for an extended stay. He wanted to study the Khudai Khidmatgars in detail. Their fearlessness and discipline could well become an object lesson to all of India. "I congratulate you," he said, departing. "I shall conclude with the prayer that the Frontier Pathans may not make only India free, but teach the world . . . the priceless lesson of nonviolence."

*

Gandhi returned in October. He wanted to talk with Khudai Khidmatgars, especially officers, personally and at length. He felt their nonviolence was sincere but incomplete. Like most of his followers on the subcontinent, they understood the notion of nonviolent resistance but had yet to understand nonviolence as a tool for building a just and productive society.

First Gandhi rested at Khan's farm in Utmanzai. Overwork had sapped his health to the point where he had suspended public speaking. Now, however, the long hours walking through fields of cane and cotton and fruit orchards along the river proved a perfect tonic. After a week, Gandhi and Khan sat in the open courtyard of the farmhouse with a dozen officers from the Charsadda district and talked. While an autumn breeze cooled the air around them, the Red Shirts explained to the Mahatma that their nonviolence was absolute. Unbending.

Gandhi looked skeptical. Didn't their nonviolence depend upon Badshah Khan?

No. Even if Khan himself – God forbid – should renounce nonviolence, they would adhere.

Gandhi smiled. He liked their childlike bluster. Weren't they being overbold? But he answered himself before they could respond. "No, I will take you at your word."

The real question on his mind was whether they fully understood what nonviolence meant. It was relatively easy, he said, to maintain a passive nonviolence when you were faced with a fully armed opponent. You had no choice – you simply resisted. That was nonviolence of the weak.

The officers looked to Khan, puzzled. Had Gandhiji heard about Qissa Khawani Bazaar and the Kohat shootings and the raid on Utmanzai . . . ? "What about nonviolence among yourselves?" Gandhi went on, before anyone else could speak. "What about among your own weak villagers when there is nothing to check your force except your own discipline and will?"

The bearded heads were still. Finally one officer said he did not understand what Gandhi meant by nonviolence of the strong.

"I mean," Gandhi said, "that you feel stronger – not weaker – for having renounced your knives and rifles." If they did not feel stronger, he added, then it was better that they take up their rifles again and fight like the brave soldiers he knew them to be.

"A charge has been often leveled against me and Badshah Khan," he explained: "that we are rendering India and Islam a disservice by presenting the gospel of nonviolence to the brave and warlike people of the Frontier. They say that I have come here to sap your strength. The Frontier Province, they say, is the bastion of Islam in India. The Pathans are past masters in the use of the sword and the rifle, and mine is an attempt to emasculate them by making them renounce their arms and thus undermine the citadel of the strength and security of Islam."

The officers snorted, whispering curses to themselves. What did outsiders know about the Khudai Khidmatgars, who had withstood the bayonets and bullets and tortures rained upon them during the last satyagraha?

"I repudiate the charge," Gandhi said, answering his own question. "My faith is that by adopting nonviolence you will in fact be rendering a lasting service to India and to Islam itself. Yours will be the spiritual strength with which you can not only protect Islam but even other religions."

He stopped and looked at the serious faces. A gust of wind stirred some dust and the robes of the soldiers fluttered. Gandhi implored them: "If you have not understood the secret of this strength, if as a result of giving up your rifles you feel weaker instead of stronger than before, it would be better for you to give up the profession of nonviolence. I cannot bear to see even a single Pathan turn weak or cowardly under my influence."

He paused. "I would rather that you returned to your arms with a vengeance."

Gandhi's hands fluttered in the air as he spoke. The depth of his conviction riveted them. They understood that their nonviolence did not approach the ideal Gandhi carried in his heart, and they wanted to hear more.

"Today a force of 178,060 government soldiers is able to rule over us," Gandhi continued. "If the Khudai Khidmatgars really felt within themselves an upsurge of soul force as a sequel to their renouncing arms, not even 17,000 would be needed to win India her independence . . . because they would have the strength of God behind them.

"But if one million of them professed nonviolence, while violence still lurked in their hearts, then they would count as nothing. . . . It may even prove dangerous."

"What does it mean to remove violence from one's heart?" asked a captain from Charsadda.

"It is not just the ability to control one's anger," Gandhi cautioned; "it is the complete eradication of anger from the heart. If an attacker inspires anger or fear in my heart, it means that I have not purged myself of violence. To realize nonviolence means to feel within you its strength – soul force – to know God. A person who has known God will be incapable of harboring anger or fear within him, no matter how overpowering the cause for it may be."

As the afternoon light dimmed and the shadows of the poplars stretched across to the guest house, Gandhi talked about the implications of being a true Khudai Khidmatgar – a servant of God. A Khudai Khidmatgar had first to be a man of God, he explained, which would demand purity and industry. He should learn a craft which he could practice in his home, since a man who has renounced the sword dare not remain idle. He should learn to spin and master the rudiments of sanitation and first aid. And he should repeat the name of God. A person who has renounced violence, Gandhi said with passion in his voice, will take the name of God with every breath. He had done just that for more than two decades, so that now the name of God would repeat itself even in his sleep.

"It is not wearing the red shirt that makes one a Khudai Khidmatgar," Gandhi concluded, shading his eyes against the low sun, "nor is it standing in ranks. It is to feel within you the strength of God which is the opposite of the strength of arms. You have so far only arrived at the portal of nonviolence. Still," he added, looking into the rapt faces, "you have been able to achieve so much! How much greater your achievement will be when you have fully entered its holy edifice!"

*

By October 15 Gandhi's strength returned and he started with Khan on a tour of the southern districts. They traveled in a small van donated by Nehru, stopping to talk casually with volunteers. At one village Gandhi was presented with an armful of figs and melons. "We want you to settle in our midst," the khan of the village told him, "and make our province your home. After all, you kept our Badshah a prisoner in your part of the country for six years. We can keep you as a prisoner of love for at least six months!"

Through the sheer walls of the Kohat Pass and down into the Kurram valley they drove. Gandhi began to address the crowds; he could not resist their enthusiasm. The Pathan was "a bogeyman" in India, he told them; children in his home state of Gujarat turned pale at the very mention of their name. For them to renounce violence stood for much more in the eyes of the world than for a gentle Hindu to do it. "Even as the rose fills with its sweet fragrance all the air around," he told one group of volunteers, "when one hundred thousand Khudai Khidmatgars become truly nonviolent, their fragrance will permeate the entire length and breadth of the country and cure the evil of slavery with which we are afflicted."

The two Gandhis continued south into the dry, twisted landscape of the Dera Jat. Red-shirted Khudai Khidmatgars lined the road for miles, interspersed with bands of tall, white-turbaned Waziri and Orakzai tribesmen, down out of their strongholds to get a glimpse of the Mahatma and his foremost disciple. Standing gaunt against the barren landscape, flanked by their ponies and camels, rifles slung from their shoulders, they gave Gandhi a glimpse of why the British had come to call the Frontier "the Grim." Drumbeats and the high wail of surnais along the way made an odd combination of festivity and dirge.

On the twenty-fourth they reached the city of Bannu, still lying under the cloud of a recent raid by outlaw tribesmen from the hills. The police had stood helpless as two hundred Waziris stormed the city, killing some merchants and plundering their shops. Gandhi pointed out that the Waziris were humans who responded to the human touch. "If I had my way," he told a crowd in Bannu, "I would mix with the tribes and argue it out with them. I am certain they will not be impervious to the argument of love and reason."

At the end of the month, Khan and Gandhi turned back toward Utmanzai.

*

On Khan's farm many of the fruit trees had dropped their leaves, but the gold of the poplars still quivered in the wind. One morning Khan went with Gandhi for a walk along the river. They talked again about the Khudai Khidmatgars. How nonviolent *were* they?

"My impression," Khan offered, "is that – as they themselves admitted – they are raw recruits and fall short of the standard you speak of. There is violence in their hearts, which they have not been able altogether to cast out. But there is no doubt as to their sincerity, Gandhiji. Given a chance, they can be hammered into shape. I think the attempt is worthwhile."

But Pathans in general had a long way to go. Khan was still disturbed over the amount of feuding between tribes and families.

"Mahatmaji," he said after a while, "this land you see, so rich in fruit and grain, might well have been a smiling little Eden upon this earth. But it has fallen under a blight. Violence has been the real bane of us Pathans. It shattered our solidarity and tore us internally with feuds. The entire strength of the Pathan is spent on thinking how to cut the throat of his brother. To what use might this energy not be put if only we could be rid of this curse!"

Gandhi did not reply. He looked across the still river as Khan unburdened himself.

"I am firmly convinced that as far as the Frontier is concerned, the nonviolent movement is the greatest boon that God has sent us. There is no other way of salvation for the Pathans except through nonviolence. I say this from experience. We used to be so timid and indolent. The sight of an Englishman would frighten us. Now even the little children taunt the foreigners when they see them pass: "What! Are you still here?" Englishmen are afraid of our nonviolence. A nonviolent Pathan, they say, is more dangerous than a violent Pathan."

The two men turned along a row of willows, whose leaves brushed the still surface of the water.

Gandhi suggested that Khan begin to train the volunteers in the Constructive Program. He had seen little evidence of it in the province. Pathans knew how to fight nonviolently, Gandhi said; there was no doubt. Now Khan had to teach them how to live nonviolently – a more difficult task, because it lacked the glamour of fighting. Peace would always be less compelling than war. Perhaps that was why there was so little of it in the world.

The Khudai Khidmatgars should emphasize cottage industries, Gandhi said, like spinning and weaving. He had noticed that few of the volunteers wore handspun cloth, which in greater India was the unofficial uniform of the civil resistance movement. Khan agreed. He already had a plan to open a center near Utmanzai. His idea was to build a model village. "At the home of the Khudai Khidmatgars, we shall set before us the ideal of self-sufficiency: wear only the clothes that we ourselves produce, eat only fruits and vegetables that we raise there, and set up a small dairy to provide us with milk."

"And the Khudai Khidmatgars should take their share in the building of the huts as well!" Gandhi added quickly.

"That is our idea too."

Gandhi liked it. He suggested that Khan first send a group of Khudai Khidmatgars to Wardha, where they could learn spinning and weaving as well as first aid, hygiene, basic education, and – to promote unity – Hindustani, the nearest thing to a national language in a country with some fifteen major tongues.

Khan's face took on a glow at the thought.

"But your work will not make headway," Gandhi cautioned, "unless you take the lead and yourself become an adept in all these things."

The copper-colored sun rested on the ridge of the Safed Koh to the west. The air was cooling quickly. They turned back toward the farmhouse.

"Throwing away one's weapons is not enough," Gandhi emphasized. "Nonviolence is an active principle of the highest order. It is soul force, the power of Godhead within us." He stepped quickly across the furrows of the cotton field. "We become Godlike to the extent we realize nonviolence. Even a tiny grain of true nonviolence acts in a silent, subtle and unseen way, and leavens the whole society."

As they reached the edge of the plum orchard, Gandhi stopped. "Do you see?" he said with quiet passion, looking into the face of his devoted disciple. "If you can set things right in Utmanzai, your whole problem of violence would be solved. The basic principle on which nonviolence rests is that what holds good in respect of yourself, holds good equally in respect of the whole universe. Even our relations with the English will be transformed if we can show to them that we do not stand in need of the protection for which their police and army are ostensibly kept."

As darkness fell over the valley, Gandhi and Khan ate a frugal meal and talked of their plans to lose themselves together one day in a remote village somewhere in the high hills. "You should see Swat," Khan said to him, remembering his own apprenticeship years ago in the pine forests of the north. "It is Paradise."

On November 11, Gandhi got ready to leave the Frontier for northern India. He told the volunteers in Peshawar, "The Khudai Khidmatgars have set a brilliant example in the practice of nonviolence to the extent to which they have understood it. But they now have to move a step further. Their conception of nonviolence has to be broadened and their practice of it, especially in its positive aspects, made fuller and deeper. But with all that the result is sufficiently striking to encourage me to carry on with the experiment with the Khudai Khidmatgars. God willing, it will succeed."

At Taxila, on the very edge of the Pathan homeland, Gandhi boarded the train for Wardha. The two dogged freedom fighters looked long into each other's eyes before they parted. As the train carried him across the wide plain of the Punjab, Gandhi jotted down his thoughts about the companion he had left behind in the Frontier:

> Whatever the Khudai Khidmatgars may ultimately turn out to be, there can be no doubt about what their leader is. He is unquestionably a man of God. He believes in His living presence and knows that his movement will prosper only if God wills it. Having put his whole soul into his cause, he remains indifferent as to what happens.
>
> When we parted at Taxila, our eyes were wet. The Frontier Province must remain a place of frequent pilgrimage for me. For though the rest of India may fail to show true nonviolence, there seems to be good ground for hoping that the Frontier Province will pass through the fiery ordeal.
>
> The reason is simple. Badshah Khan commands willing obedience from his adherents. He has but to say the word, and it is carried out. [His] nonviolence is no lip service. His whole heart

is in it. Let the doubters live with him as I have all these precious five weeks and their doubt will be dissolved like mist before the morning sun.

With Nehru at the Simla conference, 1945 (Nehru Memorial Library)

CHAPTER FOURTEEN : 1939–1947

The Fire of Freedom

The Prophet faced many handicaps, but he never gave up hope, and finally triumphed. He has left that lesson behind, and if we face our difficulties in the same spirit, I do not see why we should ever fail. The cause of freedom is always just and the fight against slavery is always noble.

ON SEPTEMBER 1, 1939, the armies of Nazi Germany rolled across the Polish borders. The next day the British government in London declared war on Germany – as did Lord Linlithgow, the viceroy, in Delhi. Without their consent or even consultation, three hundred million Indians woke up that September morning to find themselves at war on the other side of the world.

Two weeks later the Congress Working Committee declared that while it condemned fascist aggression, the Congress would assist the British war effort only on one condition: "A free democratic India will gladly associate herself with other free nations for mutual defense against aggression." India had to be free before it would fight for the Empire. What did the British intend to do?

They could not say, Linlithgow answered, at least not until the war was over. There would be time enough then to discuss India's future. For now, the government said, fight with us – for the Empire.

Six days later the Congress Working Committee voted not to aid the British unless they made their plans for India clear. They instructed all the Congress ministers, including Dr. Khan in the Frontier, to resign in protest. After seven years of peace between Congress and the Raj, battle lines were being drawn.

Meanwhile, another and more intractable battle line had been cutting through the heart of practically every village and province in the subcontinent. It was between India's two largest religious populations, the Hindus and the Muslims. After centuries of living together in relative peace, the two communities were feeling the effects of the long-held British policy of Divide and Rule.

As early as 1859 Mountstuart Elphinstone, Governor of Bombay, had instructed his subordinates: "*Divide et Impera* was the old Roman motto, and it should be ours." In spite of many differences of custom and manners, Hindus and Muslims in India had shared a common history for more than five centuries. Within a given province like Bengal they dressed the same and shared a common language. To an untrained eye, they seemed indistinguishable. But to the British rulers, their differences were an irresistible weak point to exploit.

The Muslim League had been formed in 1909 and gained strength during the Muslim renaissance that followed World War I. After working together during the noncooperation movement of 1920, the League and Congress had become political rivals – Congress advocating independence and noncooperation with the British, the League opting for dominion status within the Empire and the support of the Crown. Khan's Khudai Khidmatgars was the only major Muslim organization to oppose British rule after 1920.

In the late thirties, as independence began to look inevitable, the idea of a separate Muslim nation gained momentum. In March 1940, at Lahore, the Muslim League officially demanded a Muslim state, "autonomous and sovereign." The League's president, Mohammed Ali Jinnah, declared that the Muslims were a nation unto themselves and that they must have "their homelands, their territory and their state." The proposed Pakistan would be made up of the provinces in the north where Muslims formed a majority: Bengal, Kashmir, Assam, the Punjab, Sind, Baluchistan, and the North-West Frontier Province. The League asked Khan and his Khudai Khidmatgars to join them in their fight against what they called "Hindu rule."

Khan refused. He argued that the real enemy of Muslims was not the Hindus but the British. After the British left, he countered,

Muslims and Hindus could continue to live together in a united India as they had for so many centuries. He asked the League to join the Congress in its fight against British tyranny.

The offer was rejected. The League would have nothing to do with the Hindu-dominated Congress. It began to call Khan a Hindu. The rift between the Congress and the League, between Hindus and Muslims, widened.

In June 1940, France fell to the Germans. Britain would be next. The Congress Working Committee debated how India should respond in the event of an attack. Should their defense be nonviolent or not?

Gandhi and Khan argued that there was no issue. Nonviolence was not an expedient that could be dropped once a goal had been reached; it was a way of life, a code of conduct. It had to be consistent in all aspects of life if it was to be effective in any. India could not hope to win her freedom nonviolently if, at the same time, she prepared to defend her freedom with arms.

The Committee disagreed. For the first time in twenty-five years, Nehru, Patel, Azad, and Rajagopalachari – all veterans of the movement – broke with Gandhi's leadership. Nonviolence could bring them freedom, they argued, but it could not protect their freedom from outside aggression. With real grief, the Working Committee resolved that they were "unable to go the full length with Gandhiji."

Gandhi asked to work along his own lines, separate from the Congress. He would support them wherever they adhered strictly to nonviolence. It was a gentlemen's agreement to disagree. Khan, however, stiffened. He did not want any part of the Congress if it moved away from nonviolence and Gandhi, even in principle. He knew too that if he gave even an inch on the matter, the combustible Frontier – with Hindu-Muslim tensions simmering – might well go up in flames.

"It is difficult for me to continue in the Committee," he announced,

> and I am resigning from it. I should like to make it clear that the nonviolence I have believed in and preached to my

> brethren of the Khudai Khidmatgars . . . affects all our life, and only that has permanent value.
>
> The Khudai Khidmatgars must, therefore, be what our name implies – servants of God and humanity – by laying down their own lives and never taking any life.

In July 1940, the Congress repeated its offer to London. It was ready to throw its full weight behind the British war effort, enlist Indians in the army, and fight as one of the Allies, if the British granted self-government.

Churchill said no. He was prime minister now, as imperial and eloquent as ever. He had "not become the King's First Minister in order to preside at the liquidation of the Empire." But he was looking backward. The days of imperial glory would never return. The Battle of Britain had begun on August 8, and Great Britain was fighting for its life.

Churchill's dogged defense of imperialism drove an embittered – and chastened – Congress back to Gandhi. Both he and Khan rejoined the Working Committee, which now asked Gandhi to lead the country in another satyagraha. He replied that he would have to think about it. He did not know if Indians were ready.

*

Khan, for his part, continued to stay out of politics, devoting his energies to the arduous daily challenge of lifting his people out of poverty and apathy.

From his stay at Wardha and his long conversations with Gandhi, Khan now understood how the Constructive Program, aimed at building a self-sustaining village economy, could eliminate the exploitation and greed responsible for poverty, violence, and war. He opened his center for village service near Utmanzai and built himself a small thatched hut which became his headquarters. There he could work quietly, out of the public eye. He continued to press for rights and involvement of women. "When freedom has been won," he told a group of women near Kohat,

> you will have an equal share and place with your brothers in this country. We are like the two wheels of a big chariot, and

unless our movements have been mutually adjusted, our carriage will never move.

Khan also started holding weeklong camps – his own innovation – to train Khudai Khidmatgar volunteers in the Constructive Program. Mary Barr, an English missionary teacher who came under Gandhi's influence, attended a camp in the early forties and has left a very personal description:

> After a hot drink – very welcome in the frosty early morning – there was village cleaning for two hours, Bapu's [Gandhi's] teaching about sweeping having at last borne fruit. One Pathan told me with glee that the batch he had been with had even cleaned up the police station in the village he went to. The rest of the day went in spinning, drills, flag ceremonies, meetings, and two hefty meals of large flat *rotis* [flatbread] and *dal,* with no trimmings.
>
> In addition to the four hundred "Red Shirts" there were about a hundred visitors, mostly from Baluchistan, Kashmir and the Punjab. Then Khan came into the big tent where we were all gathered. He stood for what *seemed* a long time, looking round solemnly, even sternly, on the assembled campers. There was a pin-drop silence from the moment of his entry, and when he began to speak in a quiet voice, all listened earnestly, but now and then responded by a unanimous shout to something he had said.

But a Pathan training camp had its own style, in contrast to the more sober atmosphere of Gandhi's ashram:

> More dancing this evening – great fun! The band seemed to enter into the dance as much as the others, swaying about in time with the music. One drummer in his excitement threw his drum six feet up into the air, caught it again and went on with his rhythm.

After visiting the camp, Mary Barr went on to one of the schools Khan had established in Utmanzai – a girls' school, "a rare thing in the Muslim North." Then Khan invited her to spend a few days with his family at their home in Utmanzai. She stayed in the large farmhouse, walking the fields and hillsides, and talked with Khan's son, Wali. "I asked him whether he remembered the early days," she writes.

> He said that he had been too young to know anything about the terrorizing in the early twenties, but it was bad enough in 1931–32. . . . He remembered the way they had been besieged in Utmanzai, when if even a cow wandered out it was shot or bayoneted. No one could go out into the fields, with consequent harm to the crops and cattle, while dirt piled up in the village. He told of beatings – one of which he experienced himself until he became unconscious. . . .

The next morning, Mary Barr says, Khan was up and busy before the rest of the household,

> working with the servants sweeping and clearing up, both outside and inside the house. . . .
>
> Then Khan spent an hour spinning before going to work in the garden. He confessed to me that he disliked doing nothing. All day local men kept coming to hear about the camp, and while chatting helped in whatever work was in progress out of doors.
>
> In the evening the sons took me for a walk, and I asked them whether their father had always been as peaceful as now. Ghani said, "No, he used to beat me terribly when I was young, and thrash and jump on anyone he thought was a *badmash*. . . ."

The words throw suggestive light on the kind of transformation that must have taken place in Khan's early years. He was twenty-three when Ghani was born. We have similar glimpses into Mahatma Gandhi's life in his twenties and thirties – heated quarrels with his wife, instances of an imperious temper; nothing more, but enough to hint at a human side of the man which we can recognize. "As a young boy," Khan openly admitted, "I had had violent tendencies – the hot blood of the Pathans was in my veins." Gandhi's ideas and influence had made all the difference: "They changed my life forever." Like Gandhi, Khan was not born nonviolent: he was a Pathan. He had had to remake himself.

Lesser transformations must have taken place a thousand times over during the years of Khan's work among the Pathans. Even Murtaza Khan, the outlaw of Utmanzai that Ghani Khan wrote of, actually became a commander in the Khudai Khidmatgars after serving his prison sentence for killing Atta Khan. His transformation was not permanent like Badshah Khan's – he "found it hard to be a saint and a khan at the same time." Nonetheless, this violent Pathan whose life had known mostly robbing, killing, and the inside of a Frontier jail underwent a change of heart and action that lasted for four years and left a permanent impression on his life.

Ghani asked Murtaza how nonviolence could have become the creed of a former outlaw. The plainspoken reply offers an insight into the dynamics of satyagraha, soul force, which taps the hidden potential of the human spirit. "I was a little saint for those four years," he told Ghani. "I tried to live up to my dreams instead of my desires. It was great, it was a miracle. I refused fortunes for a hope and spared lovely girls because they trusted me and looked up to me." In his unintended way, Murtaza reveals the infectious power of nonviolence – love in action. "You cannot help loving those that love you," he told Ghani, "and you cannot hurt those that trust you. I tried to live up to what the people thought I was." Thus the grizzled outlaw went to prison again – but this time as a "servant of God" in the cause of his people's freedom.

*

Khan's period of peaceful work did not last long. In December 1941 the Japanese attacked Pearl Harbor and began a swift advance across Southeast Asia. Malaya fell, then Singapore; then, in March 1942, Rangoon. The Japanese were within reach of India's border.

The British government tried again to enlist Congress support for the war, but no agreement could be reached. Congress, mindful of India's treatment after the last world war, insisted on certain rights immediately; and Churchill was not about to give India away. Pressure built for renewed struggle. In July 1942, Gandhi proposed an all-out campaign to rid India of British rule. Previous civil disobedience movements had been aimed at a particular law or issue. This one, Gandhi decided, would make just one sweeping demand of the British: "Quit India." Nothing could be clearer.

The British got the message. On August 9, 1942, Gandhi and the rest of the Congress Working Committee were arrested, along with hundreds of Congress leaders across the country.

On the Frontier, Khudai Khidmatgar volunteers entered government offices and courts carrying the Congress flag and chanting anti-British slogans – criminal acts under the Frontier Crimes Regulations. The government cordoned the buildings and beat volunteers who tried to enter. Dr. Khan Saheb, who had relinquished his premiership in 1939 to protest British policies, now put on his red shirt and walked into the headquarters of the Indian Civil Service – under his command only three years before – to deliver a speech denouncing the war effort.

Ghaffar Khan too courted arrest, but each time he went out to a village the government simply picked him up in a patrol car and returned him to Peshawar. Frustrated, Khan led a group of fifty volunteers from Charsadda to "raid" the court at Mardan. When they saw a phalanx of uniformed police in front of them, they locked arms and kept walking. The police beat them to the ground with lathis, four-foot staffs with steel tips, breaking two of Khan's ribs in the process. He was arrested and sent to the Haripur jail, usually reserved for hardened criminals.

By the end of the year, sixty thousand Indians were in jail. The government, already panicky due to wartime conditions and threatened now by the Japanese in Burma, used tear gas, lathi charges, and bullets to break up Indian demonstrations. With Gandhi and the entire Congress leadership in jail, violence erupted all over India. Police stations, post offices, railway stations – symbols of British authority – were bombed and telegraph and telephone wires cut.

The British responded with massive force. "The number of white troops in that country," Churchill admitted, "is now larger than at any time in the British connection."

Miraculously, however, the Frontier remained nonviolent. The picketing and "raids" continued, but there was no sabotage. When some volunteers asked Khan if they could cut a few communications lines – it wouldn't harm anyone – he told them to go ahead, so long as they turned themselves in to the police afterwards. "This would add to the moral courage of the worker," he added drily. They shook their heads at the unrelenting nonviolence of their badshah.

*

For the rest of the war all of India's political figures were kept in jail, while intense repression kept the freedom movement at bay. As the war neared its conclusion, however, Britain's attitude towards India began to soften. Public sentiment turned in favor of Indian independence, and by the summer of 1945, all political prisoners had been released. A Labour government which promised to grant India its freedom was elected in the autumn, and Churchill was retired as prime minister. In March 1945, Dr. Khan Saheb again came into power as chief minister of the Frontier Province when the Muslim League ministry suffered a vote of no confidence.

Immediately after the surrender of Japan, the new government in London announced its intention of "an early realization of self-government in India." Freedom had effectively been won. The question that remained was, to whom should power be transferred? The question was scarcely academic, since Congress and the Muslim League had been unable to form a coalition government. The Muslim League demanded that it be designated the sole representative of Indian Muslims. But Congress, whose membership was only three percent Muslim, refused; it stood for a united India of Hindus and Muslims together. The League wanted a wholly Muslim state and would have no part of a coalition in which British rule, as they argued, would be replaced by Hindu rule.

When an interim government was finally formed without the Muslim League, the League called for a boycott. It declared August 16, 1946, Direct Action Day, on which Muslims were to express their dissatisfaction.

That day northern India exploded. In Calcutta riots broke out between Hindus and Muslims. Hoodlums from both communities took over the city, burning shops and killing thousands. The police were helpless. After four days the city was calmed, but only after deeply felt emotions had been stirred. Once released, they proved impossible to contain.

In Noakhali, in East Bengal, the Muslims took revenge. Hindus were beaten and killed or forced to convert to Islam. Gandhi watched the violence build. He was seventy-six years old and his health was not good, but he could not stand by passively. He announced he was going to Noakhali. "All I know," he told Congress leaders who feared for his life, "is that I won't be at peace with myself unless I go there."

Gandhi had no plan. He entered the ravaged areas of Noakhali with no protection except the love in his heart. "I am not going to leave Bengal until the last embers of the trouble are stamped out," he told a prayer meeting. "If necessary, I will die there."

In the next flare-up it was the Hindus' turn to take revenge. In Bihar they descended upon the minority Muslims with a fury that almost destroyed them. Gandhi, "burning the candle at both ends" in Noakhali, asked Khan to go to Bihar in his stead. Armed with the same weapons, love and nonviolence, the gentle Pathan entered the firestorm. "You are right," he wrote Gandhi. "Our nonviolence is on test."

Where thousands of police and soldiers had been unable to check the violence, the love of the two Gandhis began to work its magic. Gandhi, staff in hand, walked through some fifty villages in Noakhali. At each village he stayed in the home of a Muslim family, ate their food, and joined them in prayer. In the evenings, the villagers gathered at his prayer meetings – at first only a few Hindus, but gradually Muslims too. He spoke constantly of the unity underlying all religions. God was the same, he reiterated, whether He was called Rama or Rahim. By March, Noakhali was calm. Hindus who had fled felt safe enough to return to their villages.

In Bihar, Khan poured out his heart. "India seems an inferno," he told the villagers. "My heart weeps to see our homes set on fire by ourselves." The terrorized Muslims had fled in such panic that many had left their family savings buried underneath their homes. They were too frightened to return, and not even Muslim government officials were willing to risk entering the areas to help. "I'll go with you," Khan promised, and he led them to their ravaged villages.

With Noakhali quiet, Khan asked Gandhi to join him in Bihar. They stayed in Patna, driving out into the villages every day in an old car. Between stops the aging Mahatma often napped, his head in the lap of his niece, Manu, and his feet on Khan's lap. While Gandhi slept, Khan massaged his feet. In each village Gandhi gathered the shamed Hindus and told them to give him their weapons and pledge never to raise hands against their Muslim brothers and sisters again. Often he told them how the silent Muslim giant next to him had transformed the dreaded Pathans of the Frontier with nonviolence – the nonviolence of the fearless and strong that he wanted Hindus to emulate.

And he would pray. When a Hindu extremist objected to the Koran being recited at the prayer meeting, Gandhi retorted: "You are doing no good to Hinduism by your unreasoning fanaticism. Here is Badshah Khan, a Muslim and a man of God, every inch of him – if you want to see one in the flesh. Have you no respect even for him?"

But the two Gandhis could not be everywhere. In the Punjab, aroused and alarmed by extremists of both religions, Hindus and Muslims began to terrorize each other. The violence infected the Frontier. When Hindus in Peshawar were threatened, Dr. Khan called in ten thousand Khudai Khidmatgars. Muslims every one, armed with nothing but their courage and faith, these red-shirted Pathans protected the Hindu and Sikh minorities and helped restore peace to the city.

But communal violence continued to spread. As independence approached, India was drifting toward civil war. Under great pressure, fearful of seeing all they had worked for destroyed, Congress leaders finally decided to acquiesce to the demands of the Muslim League for a separate Muslim state.

*

On March 22 Lord Mountbatten arrived in Delhi, the twentieth and last viceroy of the Indian Empire. His task was a swift and orderly transfer of power. The year before, after extensive investigation, a British cabinet mission had recommended against a divided India. But the violence was spreading swiftly, and no one knew how to stop it. After long meetings with leaders of both Congress and the Muslim League, Mountbatten concluded that the only way to complete his mission successfully was to partition India into separate Hindu and Muslim states. He drafted a plan which worked out the details of the idea proposed by the Muslim League: in principle, those states with a Muslim majority would become part of Pakistan; those where Hindus were numerically superior would remain part of India.

For Gandhi the partition of India seemed a grave error, worse even than civil war. The violence of tearing India apart, he felt, would be as fearful as war and leave much deeper wounds. He drafted an alternative plan which invited the Muslim League to protect Muslim interests to the extent of naming an all-Muslim cabinet. But the plan got virtually no support, not even from the League. On March 31, 1947, the Congress leadership accepted Mountbatten's plan in principle. India would be divided.

Only Khan and Gandhi objected. Gandhi argued that Hindus and Muslims could work out their differences in a united India once the British had left. Partition, he argued, would not resolve communal violence. It would only worsen the problem, as it would leave millions of Hindus in Pakistan and millions of Muslims in India.

He proved to be right. When partition took place in August 1947, Hindus remaining in Pakistan and Muslims in northern India fled their communities in the largest migration of peoples in the world's history. Fifteen million people left their homes and in the chaos that followed, over five hundred thousand lives were lost. In Bengal and the Punjab, torn down the middle, partition left a legacy of violence and fear that continues to this day.

For Khan, partition would mean abandonment. It would place the Frontier Province under the governance of the Muslim League, which had battled Khan and the Khudai Khidmatgars for a decade. Khan and his compatriots had cast their lot with Gandhi and the Congress, often in opposition to the League. Now partition would leave them in the hands of Muslim League ministers, many of whom resented Khan's influence and opposition.

Gandhi assured him that he and India would not abandon them. "It is my intention to go to the Frontier as soon as circumstances permit," he told Khan. "I shall not take out a passport because I do not believe in division. And if as a result somebody kills me, I shall be glad to be so killed. If Pakistan comes into being, my place will be in Pakistan."

Gandhi confessed later that he could not bear to see Khan's grief. "His inner agony wrings my heart. But, if I gave way to tears, it would be cowardly, and stalwart Pathan as he is, he would break down. So I go about my business unmoved. That is no small thing."

"We shall be outcastes in the eyes of both," Khan told friends in Delhi. But he did not fear the future; Gandhi had promised to protect them. "I do not worry," he told his colleagues, "so long as Mahatmaji is here."

*

May 1947 in Delhi was hot. It would be another month before the summer monsoons began to cool the air. Khan and Gandhi had come to the capital to meet with the Congress Working Committee about partition. Gandhi had talked several times with the viceroy, trying to persuade him to leave India undivided. Mountbatten replied that he too preferred a united India, but he was helpless under the circumstances. Mohammed Ali Jinnah and the Muslim League would accept nothing less than partition.

On May 7, to the displeasure of extremist Hindus, Gandhi went to Jinnah's home. The two leaders talked in a friendly way, but there was no giving in on the idea of Pakistan. The two of them would never agree on India's future. Personally, Gandhi said in a sad, firm voice, he could not bear the thought of partition. It was wrong for both Muslims and Hindus. And as long as he was convinced that it was wrong, he could not possibly give his assent.

At his evening prayer meeting, Gandhi pleaded with those who complained of his going to Jinnah's. What was the harm? They were fellow Indians. They had to live in the same land. He refuted the argument that the Koran was bad because some Muslim fanatics had done evil deeds in Bengal and the Punjab. The Hindus had gone mad in Bihar, but that did not diminish the greatness of the Gita. Not to read from a scripture because hatred for its adherents filled your heart was the negation of true religion. Far from protecting Hinduism, he stated flatly, it was the fastest way to destroy it.

Gandhi looked grave. The day had been a long one and his talk with Jinnah, though cordial, had been a disappointment. He closed his eyes. Then his lips began to move. "O God," he prayed in a strong voice, "I begin every task with the remembrance of Thy name." It was the first line of a prayer that he used every day in his meditation – and it was from the Koran:

> Thou art the Compassionate and the Merciful.
> Thou art the Creator of the universe.
> Thou art Lord and master.
> I praise Thee alone and desire only Thy help.
> Show me the right path,
> The path which Thy saints have taken....

Khan was staying with Gandhi and was sick with a fever. But he did not want to take any medicine, and he could be as obstinate as Gandhi. When his Hindu friends told him not to overstrain himself he turned his bearded face towards them. "Before long we Pathans shall become aliens in India," he said, "away from Bapu, away from India, away from all of you. Twenty-five years – and the end of our long fight shall be to pass under the domination of Pakistan. Who knows what the future holds for us?"

The next day Gandhi was leaving for Calcutta. There was no way to know when – or if – Khan would see him again. Every evening during his stay, Khan had massaged Gandhi's legs. This time, however, seeing Khan's pale, feverish face, Gandhi tried to persuade him to rest instead. Khan looked into the face of his teacher and kindred spirit, whose word was law to him. "Let me do it," the soft voice pleaded. "It is your last night." He added gently, "It will make me well."

Gandhi told his niece, "He is a true fakir. Independence will come, but the brave Pathan will lose his. It is a grim prospect," he added, "but Badshah is a man of God."

The next day Gandhi left for Calcutta on the train. Khan accompanied him to the station. "Mahatmaji," he told him as they parted, "I have full faith in you. I look for no other support."

The two aging warriors stood for a long time on the platform and looked at each other: the Hindu mahatma and the Muslim fakir, joined in a union of sacrifice and service.

What needed to be said? Their understanding had long ago passed beyond words. Their spirits met far above language. They did not know when they would meet again – they did not need to know. They were Khudai Khidmatgars, servants of God. They would serve – and God would decide where and how.

Khan watched the express pull out of the station in a burst of steam and clatter. Hundreds of robed and saried figures swirled around and past him toward the door of the big terminal – and toward freedom. And his Pathans? They would prevail. If they could find out their true strength, it would not matter whether they were part of India or Pakistan. As for himself, Khan was at peace. His surrender long ago to the will of God shielded him like armor from these setbacks. He had not looked for rest in this life, and he would not start looking now. There was work to do.

Khan glanced up at the large board near the top of the terminal: the day's arrivals and departures. He smiled. An express left for the Frontier in two hours. It was time he got back to his people.

He stepped through the rush of travelers toward the ticket window. The plum orchard behind the farmhouse would have exploded in pink by now, he thought. Its splendor would not last much longer. It was time to go home.

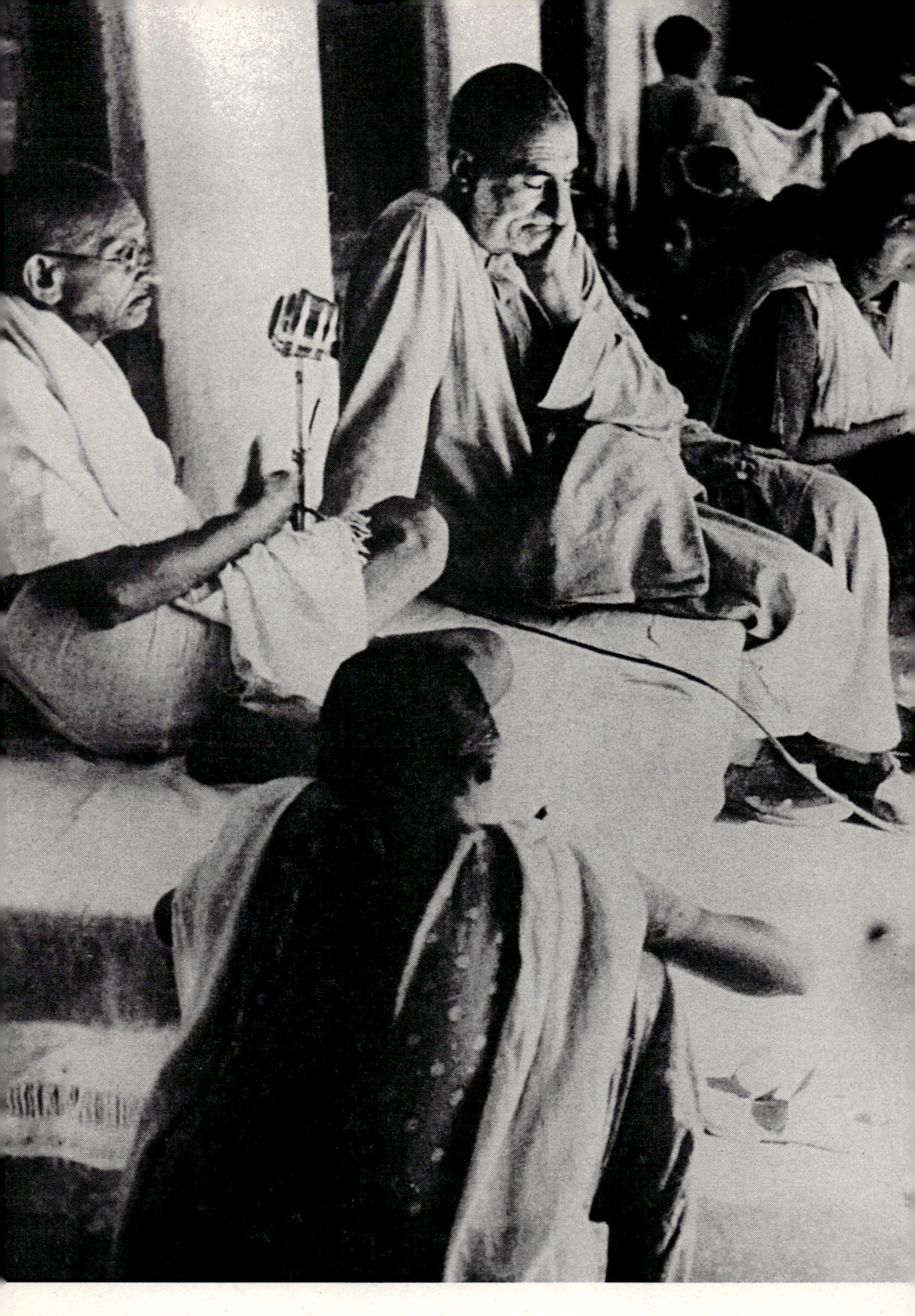

With Gandhi at a prayer meeting (National Gandhi Museum)

AUGUST 15TH, 1947

Epilogue

I consider it a crime to be a slave. Therefore, until we establish in this country a true people's government under which every community secures equal opportunities for expansion, you will Wnd me struggling for freedom, no matter who dominates the scene.

AS MIDNIGHT PASSED, the earl Mountbatten of Burma spent the first hour of India's freedom clearing away the vestiges of the British Raj from his office in the viceregal palace in New Delhi. He wanted the new leaders to begin with a clean slate, and all articles that bore the symbol of British rule were being carried unceremoniously away. "There was an air about him of serenity, almost detachment," his aide, Alan Campbell-Johnson, recalled. "The scale of his personal achievement was too great for elation ... at this historic moment, when the old and the new order were reconciled in himself...."

As servants shuttled silently in and out, Rajendra Prasad, president of the newly created Constituent Assembly, and Jawaharlal Nehru, India's prime minister, entered Mountbatten's office. They had come to convey the first resolution of India's new government: a formal invitation for Mountbatten to continue to serve the republic as its first governor-general.

"In the little scene that ensued," Campbell-Johnson recalled, "friendship completely burst the bounds of formality." Mountbatten, of course, had already been approached privately on the question and had given willing consent, but still he was freshly touched by the magnanimity of the gesture. He accepted gladly, adding that he would serve India "as if he were himself an Indian." Then the new earl – he had just learned that he had been elevated a rank in the peerage by

George VI for his conduct in India – poured out port for his guests and raised his glass in a toast. "To India," he offered, turning toward Nehru, whom he had come to admire deeply. Nehru returned the gesture, raising his own glass in a spontaneous gesture of friendship. "To King George VI!"

Later that day, in the opulent Durbar Hall where twenty British viceroys had held audience, Lord Mountbatten, the great-grandson of Queen Victoria, took a solemn oath "to become the humble and faithful first servant of an independent India." Then he swore in the ministers of the new government – Nehru, Patel, Azad, men who, Mountbatten observed, had all served time in British prisons.

As a twenty-one-gun salute boomed in the background, Lord and Lady Mountbatten stepped into a state carriage and proceeded out into the streets of Delhi toward the palace. The carriage passed through a sea of cheering, waving Indians, former subjects and long-time opponents of the British, who were now reaching with affection and gratitude to grasp the outstretched hand of their new governor-general. All the way back to the palace, the last representative of the Raj which had ruled Indians for three centuries – not without harshness – heard with pleasure the cries that burst from the huge crowd: "*Mountbatten ki jai!* Long live the Mountbattens!"

It was a remarkable, even unprecedented scene, yet it marked the general tenor of the day throughout India as power finally passed from British to Indian hands. No one could have expected the outburst of mutual good will that was expressed in countless ways between former rulers and subjects; it was unique in colonial history. "No power in history but Great Britain," K. M. Munshi wrote that day, "would have conceded independence with such grace, and no power but India would have so gracefully acknowledged the debt."

The Mountbattens deserve great credit for the courage, warmth, and style with which they carried out their mission, effecting the transfer with uniform dignity and respect for the citizens of their former colony. To this day they are remembered in India with deep affection. But the overwhelming sense of amity that enveloped British and Indians alike at the moment of independence came as a direct and logical consequence of the unique revolution Indians had waged against their former masters. They had chosen to resist nonviolently, to defy the will of the Empire and accept, without retaliation, the consequent suffering. The good will of that decision continues to the present time.

For this, of course, the credit is Gandhi's. Never hating his enemies, seeking compromise at every turn, insisting that Indians respect and even love their rulers even while they defied their rule, Gandhi set the stage for a remarkable triumph. Indians had fought against the greatest empire in world history, without weapons, and they had won their freedom. At the same time, they had won Great Britain's admiration and affection. Of all the transitions from colony to nation that would take place over the following decades, none would approach the tenor of fellowship that accompanied the British as they left India.

For the Indians, the changes were sweeping and abrupt. Indian officers found themselves suddenly in charge of an army they had never before been allowed to command. The few Indian members of the Indian Civil Service found themselves overnight in control of the heartbeat of a large, teeming nation. And for those who had led the freedom movement, independence brought sudden power and responsibility. Nehru became prime minister; Sardar Patel, deputy minister. Change – sweeping, abrupt, and unpredictable – would characterize the country for some time to come.

For the two Gandhis, however, independence only brought more of the same opportunities to serve and to suffer in the cause of truth. These two servants of God were called upon to bear witness to enormous suffering and to stand, in the darkness that engulfed the country, as lamps of light and truth. For when independence came to India and Pakistan, it did not bring peace. Hundreds of thousands died in the conflagration of communal violence that followed partition. Unable to reach his people in any other way, Gandhi finally undertook a "fast unto death" in January 1948, to be broken only if he could be assured that the slaughter had stopped – and that it would never be provoked again. In the anguishing days that followed, all eyes in India turned toward this frail, beloved old man. Fear of losing him finally brought an end to a seizure of communal madness that no amount of police action had been able to touch.

Following his fast, Gandhi wanted to go to Pakistan. Jinnah, now governor-general, agreed to his coming. Still masterful in riveting the attention of his countrymen on a particular problem, Gandhi decided he would walk – directly through the Punjab, which had experienced the worst of the communal violence. His mere presence would do much to salve the deep wounds left by the riots.

Gandhi was almost eighty and still suffering the effects of his last fast, but he was feeling buoyant. Indians and Pakistanis alike had responded to his fast with an immense outpouring of sincerity and affection, and he felt the promise of greater things to come. Also, of course, Badshah Khan was in Pakistan now. Gandhi still had much to say to the Khudai Khidmatgars – and he had made them a promise which he wanted to fulfill, although he did not yet know how.

But he never got his chance. Mahatma Gandhi died shortly after five o'clock on the afternoon of January 30, 1948, blessing with the name of God the man who had just fired three shots into his frail body. The assassin, a fanatical Hindu, was angered because Gandhi kept giving away too much to the Muslims – among other things, he had just pressured the Indian government to make good its debt of 550 million rupees to Pakistan as part of the partition settlement. He believed the Mahatma was pro-Muslim.

With Gandhi's death, his promise of protection for the Khudai Khidmatgars evaporated amidst the animosity that broke out between India and Pakistan over the disputed territory of Kashmir. But it is doubtful what even Gandhi could have done. Badshah Khan's sacrifice had already been made. He had accepted Pakistan.

By the logic of the Mountbatten plan, the Frontier would have remained with India. Though almost entirely Muslim, it had chosen Khudai Khidmatgar representatives over the Muslim League. But the League would not have Pakistan without the Frontier. Finally Mountbatten had insisted on another election – a referendum to choose between Pakistan and India. It is difficult to exaggerate the horror of the communal violence that surrounded those times. Badshah Khan, like Gandhi, felt he was watching the cause he had given his life for go up in flames. If he pressed his case, the Frontier would explode in violence like the rest of northern India – but among Pathans, that violence would tear villages and families apart for generations. Everything he had helped his people gain in unity and self-respect would be undone. In an agonizing act of renunciation, Badshah Khan finally urged the Khudai Khidmatgars to abstain from voting in the referendum. The rest of the Frontier, in that climate of communal hatred, voted for Pakistan.

The consequences followed swiftly. One week after independence, Dr. Khan Saheb's government in the Frontier was disbanded and replaced by a Muslim League ministry.

Shortly thereafter, a large gathering of Khudai Khidmatgars met at Sardaryab and resolved that "the Khudai Khidmatgars regard Pakistan as their own country," pledging to "do their utmost to strengthen and safeguard its interest and make every sacrifice for the cause." At the same time, Khan asked for a united Pathan province within Pakistan, in which all Pathans would be reunited under "rule of the Pathans, by the Pathans, and for the Pathans." In this scheme, all five major peoples of Pakistan would have their own semiautonomous provinces. Like Bengalis in East Bengal, Sindis in Sind, Punjabis in the Punjab, and Baluchis in Baluchistan, Khan argued, Pathans deserved Pushtunistan, the "land of the Pathans."

The rest of his life would be devoted to realizing this dream.

Khan toured the Frontier and spoke out boldly for his plan and the democratic rights of his people. The government, at war with India over Kashmir, claimed he was disloyal and in league with India. On June 15, 1948, he was arrested for "fomenting open sedition" and sentenced to three years' rigorous imprisonment. The Khudai Khidmatgars were banned and their headquarters razed. More than a thousand of them went to jail. The *Pushtun*, Badshah Khan's journal, was silenced forever.

Thus, within less than a year of the night that Mountbatten handed over the reins of power to India and Pakistan, Mahatma Gandhi had been assassinated by a Hindu who feared he was pro-Muslim and Badshah Khan had been jailed by an Islamic government that claimed he was pro-Hindu. The irony could not have been more complete. Two of India's foremost men of God had been sacrificed in the name of religion.

So began Khan's second long ordeal in the cause of freedom. His sentence was extended twice, so that he actually served seven years before being released – only to be imprisoned again the following year. During the first three decades of Pakistan's existence, he would spend fifteen years in prison and seven years in exile, while Pakistan itself labored much of the same time under military dictatorships and martial law.

Whenever he was out of prison, Khan continued to plead for a united Pathan province and the rudiments of democracy for his people. In 1956, he and three other leaders founded the National Awami (People's) Party, the first social-democratic party in Pakistan, which functioned as the major opposition party through the sixties and seventies with Khan's son Wali as its Frontier leader. Badshah Khan was jailed several more times "for antistate activities." Since he refused to be silenced, his life since partition was a history of prison terms broken occasionally by interludes of freedom.

Counting from 1910, with the opening of his first school in Utmanzai, Badshah Khan went on serving, reforming, and resisting tyranny for almost eighty years. I cannot imagine finding anywhere in the world's history a life of more unbroken service in the cause of freedom.

Despite his thirty years in jail – the equivalent of every third day of his life –Badshah Khan never ceased to stand by the principles of love and service with which he began his mission. As one biographer wrote, "He will not bend." Through all the suffering and setbacks, he remained a dedicated servant of God, compassionate, forgiving, and resilient– and as dogged as ever.

*

Pyarelal, Gandhi's last personal secretary, visited Badshah Khan in Kabul in 1965, when Khan was a state guest of the Afghanistan government while in exile. He left us a vivid personal description of Khan's character that still stands today.

Pyarelal found his friend seated in front of his residence, "a lovely villa, roomy and well furnished, with every modern convenience," surrounded by a score of visitors. He looked much the same as when Pyarelal had seen him last, before independence: "Bare-headed, with graying hair, and in sandals, he was wearing his flowing blue-dyed shirt and pyjamas as of yore." The two veteran soldiers of nonviolence listened to the news on the radio and then ate a simple dinner: Khan had declined the sumptuous meals the government wanted to provide for him. After dinner the two went for a walk. "For all his seventy-five years," Pyarelal wrote,

> he seemed, indeed, extraordinarily fit. He walked with a firm, steady step.... The countenance bore marks of intense suffering but the eyes beamed deep compassion and an air of kindliness surrounded him. Even more striking was the complete absence of rancor or bitterness on his part after all that he and his people had suffered as a result of India's partition and as a result of their subsequent neglect. It speaks volumes for his large-heartedness that he retains his regard and affection for his friends, Congress colleagues and the people of India, unaffected by all that he has been through....
>
> As I took leave of Badshah Khan, the feeling uppermost in my mind was one of wonder and amazement at the unconquerable spirit of this man of God, who, having watched from behind the prison bars [as] the things he had given his life to [were] broken, had now, in the evening of his life, set about undeterred by the overwhelming odds arrayed against him, to build them up....

Badshah Khan said many times that he would not seek rest in this life. Certainly he found little. Yet his long years of suffering seem only to have enlarged his sweeping spirit and magnified his strength and capacity to love. "One learns a good deal in the school of suffering," he once said with more than a touch of Gandhi. "I wonder what would have happened to me if I had had an easy life and had not had the privilege of tasting the joys of jail and all it means."

*

Judged by the normal standards of human affairs, the lives of men and women of God may look overburdened with suffering, and even inconclusive. This would have seemed true of St. Francis of Assisi, with whom I have compared Badshah Khan's beginnings. In his latter years, Francis watched helplessly while the institutions he had built faltered and languished. But the profound currents he released into the stream of history were already stirring the Western world at the time of his death, and they continue, a thousand years later, to be felt today.

It was the same with Gandhi. Today, fifty years after his death and the partition of his country that he so strongly opposed, the impact of his ideas is being felt more, by a larger part of the world, than at any time during his life. His influence grows year by year, informing the visions of seekers in many parts of the world. As the political and intellectual leaders of the world fail to grapple with the monstrous problem of violence, more and more people in both East and West will be examining his nonviolent alternative.

And so with Badshah Khan. It is only a matter of time before his special light will begin to shine in many corners of the earth. For his contribution to the legacy of nonviolence has special significance today, when so many countries of the Islamic world are torn by violence. Just as Gandhi reminded Indians of their long-forgotten legacy of truth and nonviolence, it has been given to Badshah Khan to perform the same great service for Islam. His life is a perfect mirror of the profound values of love, faith, and selfless service embedded in Islam since its inception. His nonviolent "army of God" stands as a beacon to all Muslims who seek an alternative to the self-destructive violence of our times.

Like Gandhi in Hinduism and Martin Luther King Jr. in Christianity, Badshah Khan demonstrated conclusively that nonviolence – love in action – is in perfect harmony with a vigorous, resurgent Islam. Khan's simplicity, deep faith, and selfless service represent the Islamic tradition at its purest and most enduring.

But Khan's message is scarcely limited to Islam. It can help the non-Muslim world to understand the true greatness of Islam, but more than that, it should help all nations to understand their own potential for love in action. If Badshah Khan could raise a nonviolent army out of a people so steeped in violence as the Pathans, there is no country on earth where it cannot be done. The message he sent for this book is simple and urgent: "The present-day world can only survive the mass production of nuclear weapons through nonviolence. The world needs Gandhi's message of love and peace more today than it ever did before, if it does not want to wipe out civilization and humanity itself from the earth's surface."

The world may yet come to know of this simple, courageous, nonviolent freedom fighter and his eloquent message of love in action.

Part Four

The "Muslim Fakir" (Tendulkar)
Previous pages: In Bihar, 1947 (J.V. Mehta)

AFTERWORD

The Good Fight

BY TIMOTHY FLINDERS

NONVIOLENT MUSLIMS. Nonviolent Muslim *Pathans* in an "army of God" sworn to lay down their lives in the cause of freedom, without fighting back.

One could be forgiven a stir of doubt, some puzzlement.

Yet when Mahatma Gandhi first heard of the nonviolent resistance of Badshah Khan's Pathan tribesmen during the Salt Satyagraha of 1930, though he may well have been surprised, even awed, he would not have been puzzled. No doubt Pathans seemed to the rest of India like a kind of eastern Mafiosi – ruthless, clannish, vengeful, without scruple. But to Gandhi, who understood better than anyone else the inner dynamics of satyagraha, Khan's "miracle" was entirely consonant with his idea of nonviolence. In fact, Gandhi had been looking for a decade for the Pathans – or someone like them – in order to make a point.

Gandhi's search went back to the Kaira struggle of 1918, during which he had led Indian peasants in a nonviolent revolt against unfair taxes. The Kaira peasants won the struggle, but in the process they unmasked a truth about their nonviolence which Gandhi found disturbing. They had taken to nonviolence, they admitted, only because they lacked the courage to fight with

Tim Flinders is a longtime student of Eknath Easwaran. An educator and writer, he has taught gifted children for many years and is the co-author of The Making of a Teacher.

violence. "With me alone and a few other co-workers," Gandhi reported, "[nonviolence] came out of our strength and was described as Satyagraha, but with the majority [of resisters] it was purely and simply passive resistance, which they resorted to because they were too weak to undertake the methods of violence."

This was not Gandhi's idea of nonviolence. True nonviolence did not issue from weakness but from strength. It was a matter of the powerful voluntarily withholding their power in a conflict, choosing to suffer for the sake of a principle rather than inflict suffering – even though they could. Gandhi called this the "nonviolence of the strong," as opposed to the "nonviolence of the weak" that he had found in his Kaira peasants. "My creed of nonviolence is an extremely active force," he insisted. "It has no room for cowardice or even weakness."

After much thought about the implications of the peasants' admission, Gandhi stunned his colleagues by starting a recruiting campaign in Kaira to raise an army of Indians to fight for the Empire in the First World War. If Indians were afraid of violence, he argued, then they should first learn to fight *so that they could renounce fighting.* "I do not infer from this that India must fight," he explained. "But I do say that India must know how to fight." To perplexed colleagues who thought he had lost his way, Gandhi gave a simple explanation: "A nation that is unfit to fight cannot from experience prove the virtue of not fighting." True satyagraha required fighters, fearless, impassioned, and dogged. If he could not find natural fighters, he decided, he would create them, even if it meant sending them to war.

Gandhi's recruitment campaign of 1918 proved a failure. The majority of Indians were not prepared to take up arms. "But do you know that not one man has yet objected [to recruitment] because he would not kill?" Gandhi wrote a colleague. "They object because they fear to die. The unnatural fear of death is ruining the nation."

When the war ended, so did his recruiting campaign. But Gandhi never stopped looking for those born fighters who would prove to the world that nonviolence was especially meant for the strong. "There is hope for a violent man to be some day nonviolent," he insisted, "but there is none for a coward."

In 1930 Gandhi heard about the heroics of Badshah Khan's Khudai Khidmatgars, and he must have known that he had found what he was looking for. Pathans *knew how to fight.* They were an unlikely lot, to be sure. But the Hindus' image of the menacing Pathans was incomplete: they were vengeful and they could be ruthless, but they were not without scruple. Honor was everything. They were capable of self-discipline and temperate in their habits. Raised with a Spartan abandon for comfort, they lived with a deep-running faith in God and legendary contempt for fear and cowardice: "The coward dies," we read, "but his shrieks live on. So [the Pathan boy] learns not to shriek." Gandhi could not have invented a people better fitted to his radical notion.

But he did not have to invent them. More than that, he did not even need to transform them: Badshah Khan had done it for him. Khan's genius, as Easwaran has pointed out, was to sense the underlying nobility of the Pathan temperament – with its profound and compelling passion – and to tap it for a high purpose. "Being fighters," Khan explains, "they had learnt discipline. All that he had to do was to give it a nonviolent turn." And to everyone's amazement – except Gandhi's – it worked: Khan's Pathans became, we read, "the bravest and most enduring of India's [nonviolent] soldiers."

Even Khan was baffled at the extent of his success. "I started teaching the Pathans nonviolence only a short time ago," he told Gandhi once. "Yet in comparison, the Pathans seem to have learned this lesson and grasped the idea of nonviolence much quicker and much better than the Indians. . . . How do you explain that?"

Gandhi, almost laconic in his self-assurance, told the Pathan leader: "Nonviolence is not for cowards. It is for the brave, the courageous. And the Pathans are more brave and courageous than the Hindus. That is the reason why the Pathans were able to remain nonviolent."

Thus the unique place of Khan's Khudai Khidmatgars in the history of nonviolence. They proved Gandhi's claim that nonviolence is meant for the strong – no insignificant matter in today's world, where violence is seen almost as a natural response to conflict and nonviolence is dismissed as a refuge of those who are too weak or too fearful to fight with guns.

But Gandhian nonviolence has another side to it: a side more personal than political, which aims at transformation. We can call this "transformative" nonviolence, to distinguish it from the more overt political forms. Here nonviolence is used as a tool to reform and regenerate human personality. The story of Khan's movement among the Pathans demonstrates the power of nonviolence to harness the negative forces in personality and use those same forces to transform an individual, a community, or even a society. Transformative nonviolence could find a special place in the regeneration of our own postindustrial democracies, wherever political tyranny has been replaced by subtler forms of oppression – meaninglessness, alienation, pervasive dissatisfaction, ennui.

Like Gandhi, Khan was essentially a reformer. He first seized upon nonviolence not as a political weapon – he was forced into politics by British suppression, he claimed – but as an antidote to the violence which had long paralyzed his vigorous but indiscriminate people. His first concern was not British repression, but the Pathan cult of violence and revenge. Khan found that Gandhi's nonviolence had the power to recast the Pathan temperament into a potent, positive force without diminishing its vigor.

"To me nonviolence has come to represent a panacea for all the evils that surround my people," Khan said. "Therefore I am devoting all my energies toward the establishment of a society that would be based on its principles of truth and peace." In his "Servants of God" Khan released a powerful, socially benign force equal but opposite to the destructive forces embedded in the Pathan temperament and culture. In doing so, he was following almost to the letter the powerful dynamics of transformative nonviolence that Gandhi had discovered twenty-five years earlier in South Africa.

Dissatisfied with the hopeless inadequacy of the phrase "passive resistance" to describe the innate *power* of nonviolence, Gandhi coined his own term in 1906: *satyagraha. Satya* means truth in Sanskrit, and *agraha* comes from a Sanskrit root meaning "to hold on to," which Gandhi used as a synonym for "force." Thus *satyagraha* carries a double meaning: it signifies a determined holding on to, a *grappling* with truth; while at the same time it implies the force that arises from that grappling, what Gandhi called "soul-force." *Satyagraha* stands for both the means and the ends, the struggle and the force that is generated in that struggle.

As heat is generated by friction, Gandhi contended, power is released from within the depths of the human spirit in its struggle toward truth. The raw material for this power is passion. "I have learned through bitter experience," Gandhi explained, "the one supreme lesson to conserve my anger, and as heat conserved is transmuted into energy, even so our anger controlled can be transmuted into a power which can move the world." In this "truth-struggling" nothing is lost or repressed; energy is conserved and transmuted. Thus in its transformative aspect nonviolence is not nonviolence at all, but violence transmuted, harnessed, *used.* We could more properly call it *trans*violence, where the power of passions like anger, hatred, and fear is reshaped into a potent fighting force.

With his truculent, explosive Pathans, Khan had an abundance of raw material to work with. Because of their powerful tendencies toward violence, they had great potential for nonviolence. Their grappling toward nonviolent truths sometimes provoked excruciating suffering, and required a demanding psychical and emotional about-face. A Khudai Khidmatgar who took Khan's oath renounced not just violence but the code of revenge itself, badal, the cornerstone of his value system and the cult of the heroic Pathan. "To bear this *zulum* [tyranny] without retaliation is hard indeed," we read one villager telling Verrier Elwin at the height of the British repression in 1932.

"But do you still believe in nonviolence?"

"With all our hearts."

Because of their demanding inner struggle, Pathans under Khan's leadership were able to invoke resources of courage and will that far exceeded their known limits, and came into possession of that inner strength – "soul-force" – which Gandhi claimed we all possess but do not know about. It is a power released from within the depths of the human spirit. Gandhi called it the strength of God.

When he visited the Frontier in 1938, Gandhi made clear the profoundly spiritual nature of transformative nonviolence. "To realize nonviolence means to feel within you its strength – soul-force – to know God." At Utmanzai he told Khan's red-shirted officers, "If the Khudai Khidmatgars really felt within themselves an upsurge of soul-force as a sequel to their renouncing arms, they would have the strength of God behind them." Call it what you will, there is no denying the display of this power in the lives of both Gandhi and Badshah Khan, or in the collective force of Khan's Khudai Khidmatgars.

It is a tribute to the Pathans' capacity for faith, as much as to their bravery, that they could so genuinely accept such a foreign code of conduct and use it to work the reversals of thinking and action we read of here. Their transformations were not always complete or permanent, as in the case of the outlaw Murtaza Khan, but they were often profound, and even in Murtaza Khan's example they left permanent marks.

The full effect of Khan's movement on the progress of his people can never be measured. What remains unmistakable in the story of the Khudai Khidmatgars is that nonviolence, properly undertaken, recasts and empowers the human personality. Very little is known about this kind of transformation. While some attention has been given by scholars to nonviolence as a political weapon, virtually nothing exists in the literature regarding the effects of nonviolence upon those who practice it. Since we are dealing with such intangibles as "soul-force," faith, and "conscious suffering" – difficult qualities to quantify and observe – these dimensions of nonviolence may well lie outside the scope of traditional scholarship.

And perhaps this is as it should be. For in the last analysis, such nonviolence – this "truth-grappling" – is a private affair carried out mostly within the human mind and heart. To move it into a wider sphere of acceptance, what is needed is not study so much as committed individuals ready to undertake its disciplines.

The lack of work on this subject does not mean that we must proceed alone or unguided. There was Gandhi, after all, and now there is Badshah Khan to throw some light across the path. It is especially fitting in this regard that Khan's story is being presented to western audiences by Eknath Easwaran, for his primary interest in both Khan and Gandhi has been their personal transformations from flawed human personalities to permanent forces for good. This is not the place to enter into detail about the exact nature of the disciplines that nonviolence requires; Easwaran has done this exhaustively in other books. But to those who would follow in Khan's footsteps, the extraordinary story of his courage and doggedness in his fight against tyranny leaves no illusions about what is required. Nonviolence, whether political, social, or personal, is a battle, an unflagging engagement of the will against tyranny using the weapons of fearlessness, love, and faith. As Khan told his Khudai Khidmatgars, "You have to be against all tyrants, whoever they may be; whether individuals or nations ... you will oppose them" – even, we can assume, if the tyranny is found to be those turbulent forces of the soul which tyrannize from within the recesses of one's own heart.

Those who would take up this call step into the stream of an ancient tradition of fighters that includes the Buddha and Jesus, continues through St. Francis, and is passed on today, among others, by Gandhi, Martin Luther King Jr., Mother Teresa, and Badshah Khan. The fight, as Khan says, "is always noble," and those who make the attempt to enter its "holy edifice" will find their powers on the rise. The world needs such men and women. May they flourish – or as Badshah Khan himself might say to them, *Stre mashe:* may they never grow tired.

PHOTO RETROSPECTIVE

Seeds of the Future

KHAN ABDUL GHAFFAR KHAN, 1890–1988

No true effort is in vain. Look at the fields over there. The grain sown therein has to remain in the earth for a certain time, then it sprouts, and in due time yields hundreds of its kind. The same is the case with every effort in a good cause.

BADSHAH KHAN (OPPOSITE)
(Photo: Vithalbhai Collection / Peter Rühe Archive)

THE KHUDAI KHIDMATGARS (NEXT PAGE)
History's First Nonviolent Army (Photo: Nehru Memorial Library)

MAULANA ABUL KALAM AZAD AND KHAN ABDUL GHAFFAR KHAN
Maulana Azad was the first leader of Muslim politics to ally himself with India's freedom movement against the British Crown. His newspaper, Al-Hilal, *inspired Khan in 1928 to start his own journal,* Pushtun, *to encourage the development of Pathan culture.* *(See pages 67, 105.* *Photo: DAWAT Afghan News)*

WANDERING FROM VILLAGE TO VILLAGE
Khan's love and service of his people made him the ruler in "the undisputed kingdom of their hearts," according to Mahatma Gandhi. "There is no humbug about him. He is an utter stranger to affectation." (Photo: Vithalbhai Collection / Peter Rühe Archive)

VILLAGE ROOTS OF FRONTIER NONVIOLENCE

With a genius for organization, Khan set up a network of committees called jirgahs modeled after the traditional tribal councils that have maintained Pathan law for centuries. *(See page 112.* *Photo: Vithalbhai Collection / Peter Rühe Archive)*

WITH LEADERS OF THE FREEDOM MOVEMENT

Khan was banned from the North-West Frontier Province in 1934, allowing him to spend time with Gandhi at his community in Central India. Here he met many key figures of the freedom movement, such as Jawaharlal Nehru (speaking, left) and Jamnalal Bajaj, pictured with him above. (See pages 142–145. Photo: Vithalbhai Collection / Peter Rühe Archive)

CHARGED WITH SEDITION
Sardar Vallabhbhai Patel (second from left) and Bhulabhai J. Desai (middle) confer with Khan over his courtroom defense on charges of sedition against the Crown in 1934. (See pages 147, 151–152. Photo: Vithalbhai Collection / Peter Rühe Archive)

A GIFT FROM GANDHI
Awaiting a visit from Mahatma Gandhi, Khan accepts a gift from him – a goat – sent ahead by his secretary, Mahadev Desai (in vest at right). (Photo: Vithalbhai Collection / Peter Rühe Archive)

MAHATMA GANDHI AND BADSHAH KHAN

The "two Gandhis" talk during Gandhi's tour of the North-West Frontier Province in 1938, when Khan invited him to to study and guide the Khudai Khidmatgar movement. (See pages 154–162. Photo: Kanu Gandhi Foto World / Peter Rühe Archive)

AT EDWARD'S COLLEGE

Gandhi bristled early in his Frontier tour in a speech at Edward's College, when his nonviolence was described as "passive resistance" as he was being introduced. "Passive resistance is a negative thing and has nothing of the active principle of love," Gandhi said. "Satyagraha proceeds on the active principle of love which says, 'Love those that despitefully use you.' . . . I find it difficult in spite of my conscious practice of it for the last fifty years." (Photo: Kanu Gandhi Foto World / Peter Rühe Archive)

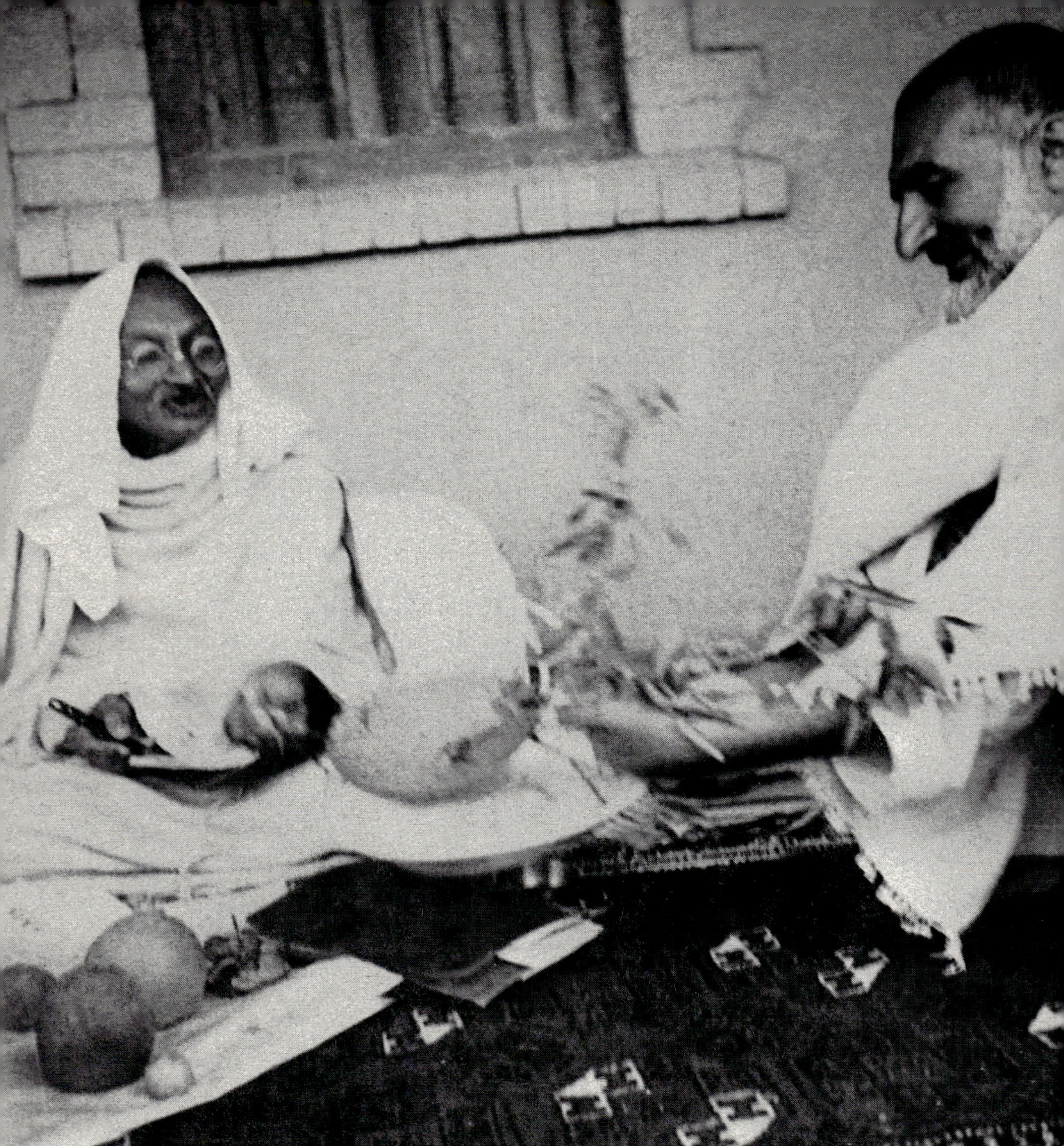

KHAN SHARES A HONEYCOMB WITH GANDHI

Mahatma Gandhi and Khan Abdul Ghaffar Khan held almost identical views on many problems of the day; they reacted in the same way to similar situations, and they enjoyed each other immensely. The ideal of nonviolence was a great bond between them, but they also shared a love of nature, a child-like laugh, and an affinity with the poor. Both craved periods of silence and possessed a deep sense of spirituality. (Photo: Kanu Gandhi Foto World / Peter Rühe Archive)

MEETING THE KHUDAI KHIDMATGARS

Gandhi stopped at dozens of villages in the month he toured the Frontier. "As Badshah Khan believes in my nonviolence, he wanted me to be as long as I could among the Khudai Khidmatgars," said Gandhi in meeting the "Servants of God." "For me, I needed no temptation to go to them. I was myself anxious to make their acquaintance. I wanted to reach their hearts." (Photo: Vithalbhai Collection / Peter Rühe Archive)

KHAN AND GANDHI IN THE LAND OF THE WARRIOR TRIBES

"People laugh at me for believing the Khudai Khidmatgars could become full-fledged nonviolent soldiers," said Gandhi, "but their mockery does not affect me. Nonviolence is a quality not of the body, but of the soul. Human nature in the Khudai Khidmatgars is not different from mine." (Photo: Vithalbhai Collection / Peter Rühe Archive)

VISITING AN ANCIENT BUDDHIST MONASTERY

The ruins of Taxila were the last stop on Gandhi's Frontier tour. "Our land has been witness to various cultures," Khan told Gandhi. "At one time this land was the cradle of Aryan civilization. Later it saw the flowering of Buddhism under which we made rapid progress." Long-forgotten ancestors of the Khudai Khidmatgars had meditated on the Buddha's injunction, "Hatred does not cease by hatred; hatred ceases by love. This is an unalterable law." Antagonisms of the day were an aberration of the Frontier's history, Khan said. (Photo: Kanu Gandhi Foto World / Peter Rühe Archive)

LESSONS IN SPINNING (ABOVE)
Badshah Khan hosts Jawaharlal Nehru.
(Photo: Kanu Gandhi Foto World / Peter Rühe Archive)

GANDHI AND KHAN RELAX BETWEEN ACTIVITIES (UPPER RIGHT)
(Photo: Kanu Gandhi Foto World / Peter Rühe Archive)

KHAN SUPPORTS GANDHI WHEN CONGRESS BREAKS WITH HIS LEADERSHIP (RIGHT)
In a sign of greater separations to come, the Indian National Congress stated in 1940 it was "unable to go the full length with Gandhiji." The Working Committee voted to defend India with weapons rather than with nonviolence should aggression reach its borders during World War II. Front row, from left to right: Mahatma Gandhi, Maulana Azad. Second row, behind Gandhi: Khan Abdul Ghaffar Khan next to Sarojini Naidu. (See page 167. Photo: Vithalbhai Collection / Peter Rühe Archive)

BIHAR RIOTS, 1947 (ABOVE AND RIGHT)
Comforting victims; bringing people together. *(See pages 174, 177.* *Photo: Vithalbhai Collection / Peter Rühe Archive)*

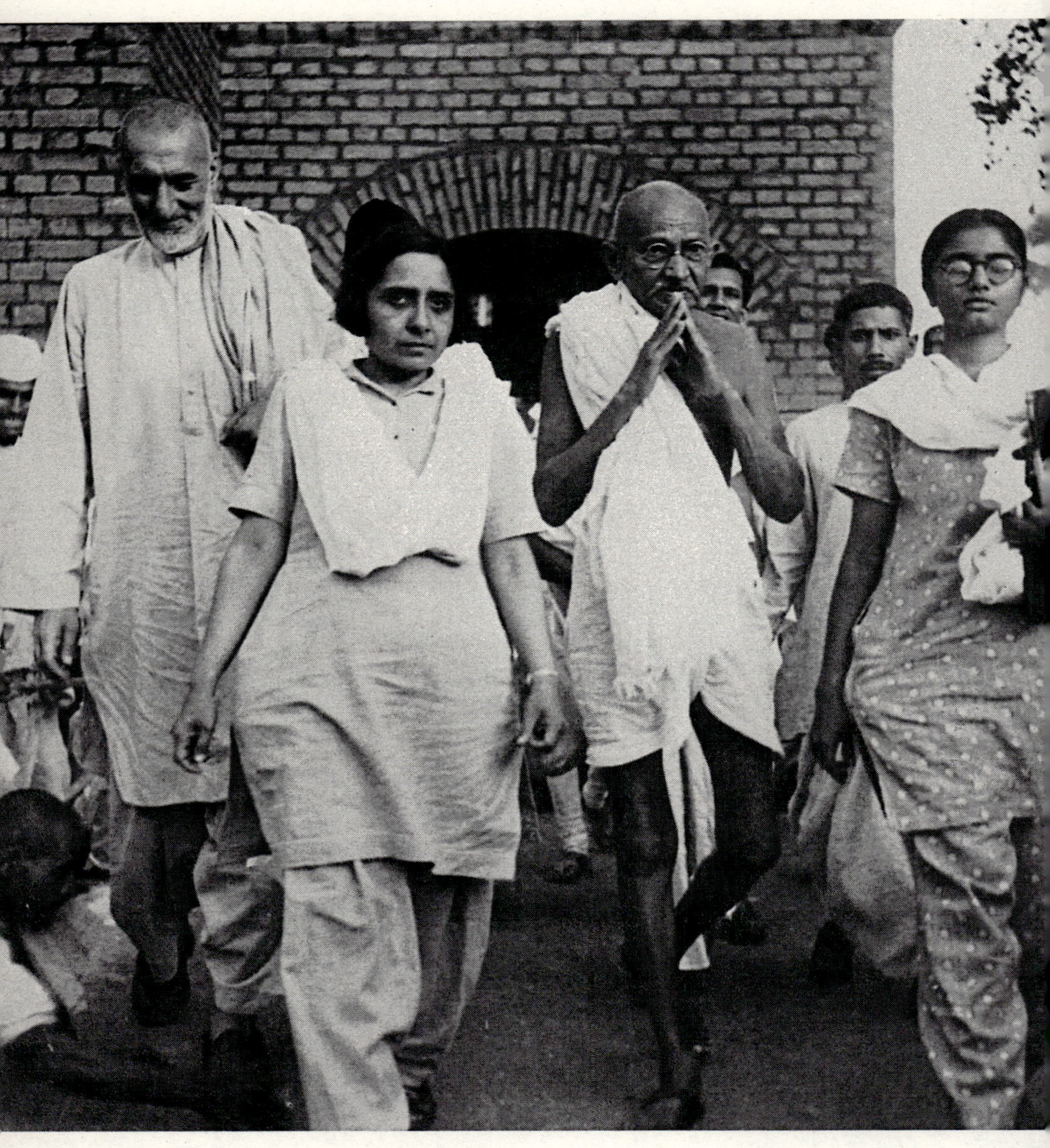

BIHAR RIOTS, 1947

Congress worker Mridulabehn Sarabai, followed by Khan, Gandhi, and Gandhi's niece Manu. (Photo: Vithalbhai Collection / Peter Rühe Archive)

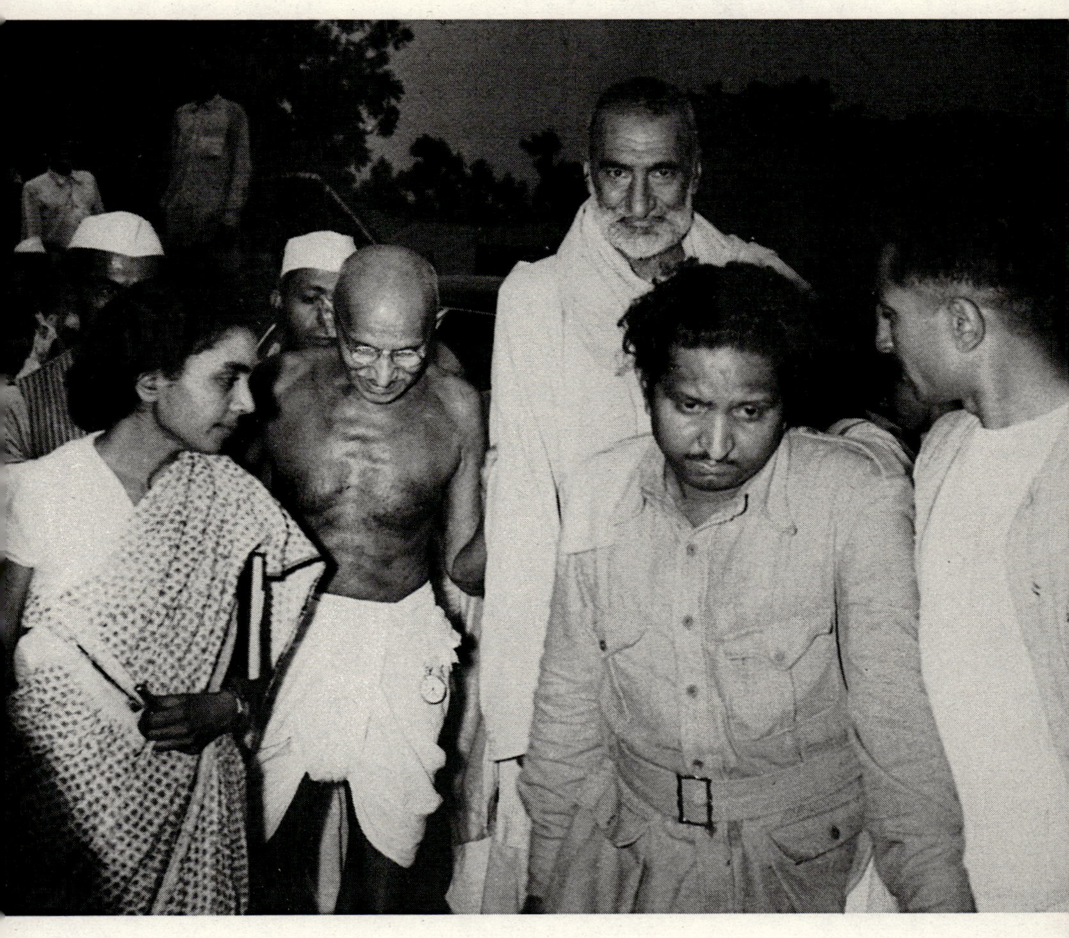

RETURN TO DELHI: FINAL ENCOUNTERS

*One of the last photographs of Khan Abdul Ghaffar Khan with Mahatma Gandhi as they arrive in New Delhi in June 1947, just as Congress takes a formal vote to partition the country. (**See pages 175–179.** Photo: Vithalbhai Collection / Peter Rühe Archive)*

AMONG HIS FAMILY (ABOVE)

Khan was having a meal with his son in a nearby village when he heard of Mahatma Gandhi's assassination. They could not finish eating. They held a condolence meeting of the Khudai Khidmatgars. "He was the only ray of light to help us through these darkest days," said a grieved Badshah Khan. (See page 184. Photo: Kanu Gandhi Foto World / Peter Rühe Archive)

DURING THE FRONTIER REFERENDUM (LEFT)

Badshah Khan reads of Sir Olaf Caroe's decision to resign as governor of the Frontier during the referendum on Partition. (See pages 184–185, 249–250. Photo: Vithalbhai Collection / Peter Rühe Archive)

WORKING WITH THE TRIBAL COUNCILS

Though his mentor was gone, Khan continued his campaign for nonviolence. He told his people the Frontier province could demonstrate to the world the constructive power that is released in returning love for hatred. Perhaps, he said, one day the Frontier could serve as a "golden bridge" to bring India and Pakistan together. (See page 185. Photo: AP/Wide World Photos))

PAKISTAN CONSTITUENT ASSEMBLY

In February 1948, Khan took the oath of allegiance to the new nation of Pakistan. Though he had opposed partition, he accepted the division and said all should move forward for the good of the country. He hoped ultimately to sway Pakistani opinion in support of the Khudai Khidmatgars so that they could continue as a service organization. Four months later, only six months after Mahatma Gandhi's assassination, Khan was sentenced to six years in prison. During his imprisonment many Khudai Khidmatgars were killed, and the organization was banned. (Photo: D.G. Tendulkar)

RELEASED FROM PRISON

Abdul Samad-Khan Atsakzai, the leader of the Pathans in Baluchistan, Badshah Khan, and Khan's brother, Dr. Khan Saheb, were released from prison in January 1954. Pakistan had declared a state of emergency and imposed a government without a vote of the people. Badshah Khan tried to revive the Khudai Khidmatgar movement to fight for representative government. In 1956, he was arrested and imprisoned again and his property was confiscated. In 1957, Amnesty International voted him Prisoner of the Year, saying, "His example symbolizes the suffering of upwards of a million people all over the world who are in prison for their conscience." Khan had been incarcerated for most of the ten years that India and Pakistan had been free. (Photo: Kanu Gandhi Foto World / Peter Rühe Archive)

RENEWED ATTENTION ON BADSHAH KHAN

For years Indian prime minister Jawaharlal Nehru had been trying without success to find some way to support Khan. In the mid-1960s, Nehru encouraged Gandhi's secretary, Pyarelal, to write a book about Khan to draw attention to his plight, and his last assignment to the prominent Indian historian D. G. Tendulkar was to write a detailed biography of Khan along the lines of his epic biography of Mahatma Gandhi. Above is a signed photo that Khan sent Tendulkar. Nehru hoped somehow that renewed attention would help Khan in his human rights struggle. When Nehru died in 1964, Badshah Khan lost his foremost champion in India. A few months later, Khan left Pakistan for about six years of self-imposed exile in Afghanistan. (Photo: D.G. Tendulkar)

INDIA'S VICE PRESIDENT PAYS A VISIT TO KHAN (ABOVE)
Dr. Zakir Husain and Badshah Khan had shared time in prison before freedom. Above is their reunion after nineteen years during Khan's exile in 1966. "Now that the door has opened, we will not let you alone for long."

KHAN ARRIVES IN INDIA FOR GANDHI CENTENNIAL (RIGHT)
In 1969, only weeks away from his eightieth birthday, Badshah Khan was a special guest of India for the centennial of Mahatma Gandhi's birth. Hearing that India was again torn by communal riots, Khan appealed for an end to the violence. Newspapers described Khan as "pulling no punches and speaking with touching sincerity reminiscent of his mentor." The riots had been cloaked as Hindu-Muslim differences, but Khan said the violence had little to do with religion. The truth of the matter, he said, was that selfish people exploited communal differences for economic and political gain. (Both photos: Corbis/Bettman-UPI Images)

FAST FOR AN END TO VIOLENCE

Just one day after his arrival in India for the centennial, Badshah Khan announced a three-day fast for an end to violence. It was his first fast since the seven-day fast he had observed for the same reason in 1947 in sympathy with Mahatma Gandhi. Khan's action electrified India and the bloodshed stopped. "I have considered myself a part of you and you a part of me," he told his former countrymen. "I have come to see for myself if I can be of some use." (Photo: Archive Photos / London Daily Express Newspapers)

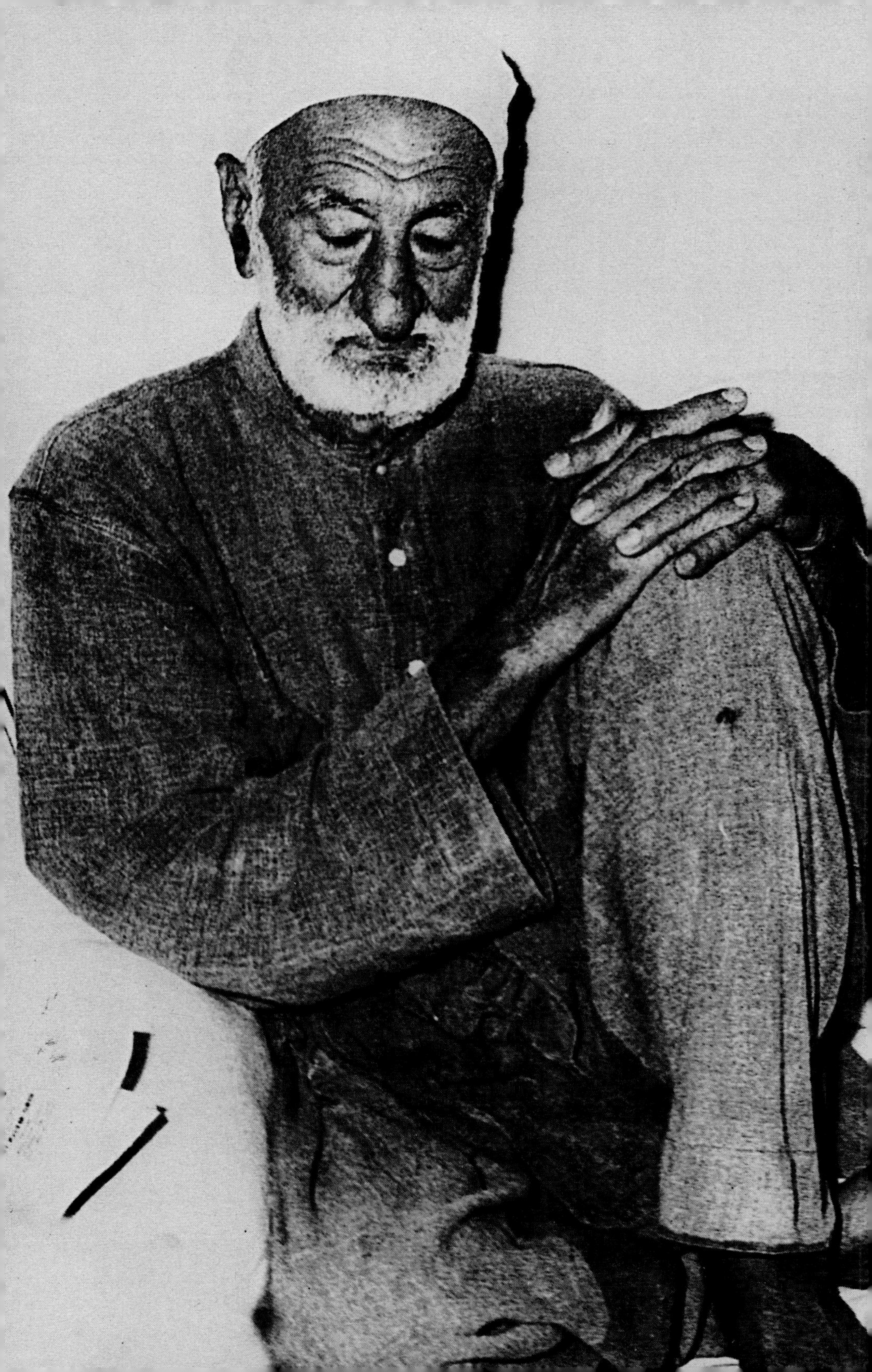

CAMPAIGNING FOR HUMAN RIGHTS AT AGE NINETY-FIVE

Khan Abdul Ghaffar Khan was placed under house arrest at a government "subjail" at age ninety-five after protesting military rule in Pakistan.

Even when Badshah Khan was in Bombay for treatment during his final illness in his late nineties, prime minister Gandhi recalled, "the fight was in him" still. Khan had no concerns for himself, the prime minister said. Instead he worried about building spiritual and moral character for the future, emphasizing that nonviolence was the only effective defense for the world. In his last message to the public from his sickbed, Khan asked reporters, "Why are they producing weapons of mass destruction? Gandhiji worked for nonviolence." (Photo: DAWAT Afghan News)

Khan Abdul Ghaffar Khan, the uncrowned king of the Pathans, died on January 20, 1988, at the age of ninety-eight. Badshah Khan was a tireless advocate of nonviolence to the end of his life. His dream of Pushtunistan, a united province of Pathans with autonomy over internal affairs, was never realized. Nonetheless his deep faith in God and his forgiveness even of those who attacked and imprisoned him touched something deep in millions of hearts.

Badshah Khan's memorial service induced the first visit to Pakistan by India's prime minister in three decades. The estranged governments set aside their differences. The late prime minister Rajiv Gandhi delayed a flight to an international summit in Stockholm, and Pakistan issued without question an emergency visa so that he could visit Peshawar where Khan's body lay in state.

Though Pakistan's prime minister, Zia ul-Haq, had himself imprisoned Khan, he rushed to Khan's memorial service in Peshawar. "History knows very few persons who spent nearly a century in pursuit of a mission they cherished," said Zia in a condolence note to Badshah Khan's son Wali Khan. "May Allah bless his soul and grant fortitude to his bereaved family and followers to bear the loss."

Badshah Khan asked to be buried in Jalalabad, Afghanistan, in the heart of the Pathan homelands. His funeral was in a war zone about one hundred miles from Peshawar, where the Soviet-backed government fought the U.S.-backed mujahedin guerrillas. Tens of thousands of Pakistanis made the historic crossing into Afghanistan for the rites. It was the first time they had stood on Afghan soil in decades.

Though both the government and the rebels called a ceasefire for the funeral, two blasts marred the peace and killed more than a dozen mourners. In death as in life there were great setbacks to Badshah Khan's goal for peace. Yet he never lost faith. "Why do you despair of unity?" he asked a skeptic of nonviolence amid the violence before independence. "No true effort is in vain. Look at the fields over there. The grain sown therein has to remain in the earth for a certain time, then it sprouts, and in due time yields hundreds of its kind. The same is the case with every effort in a good cause."

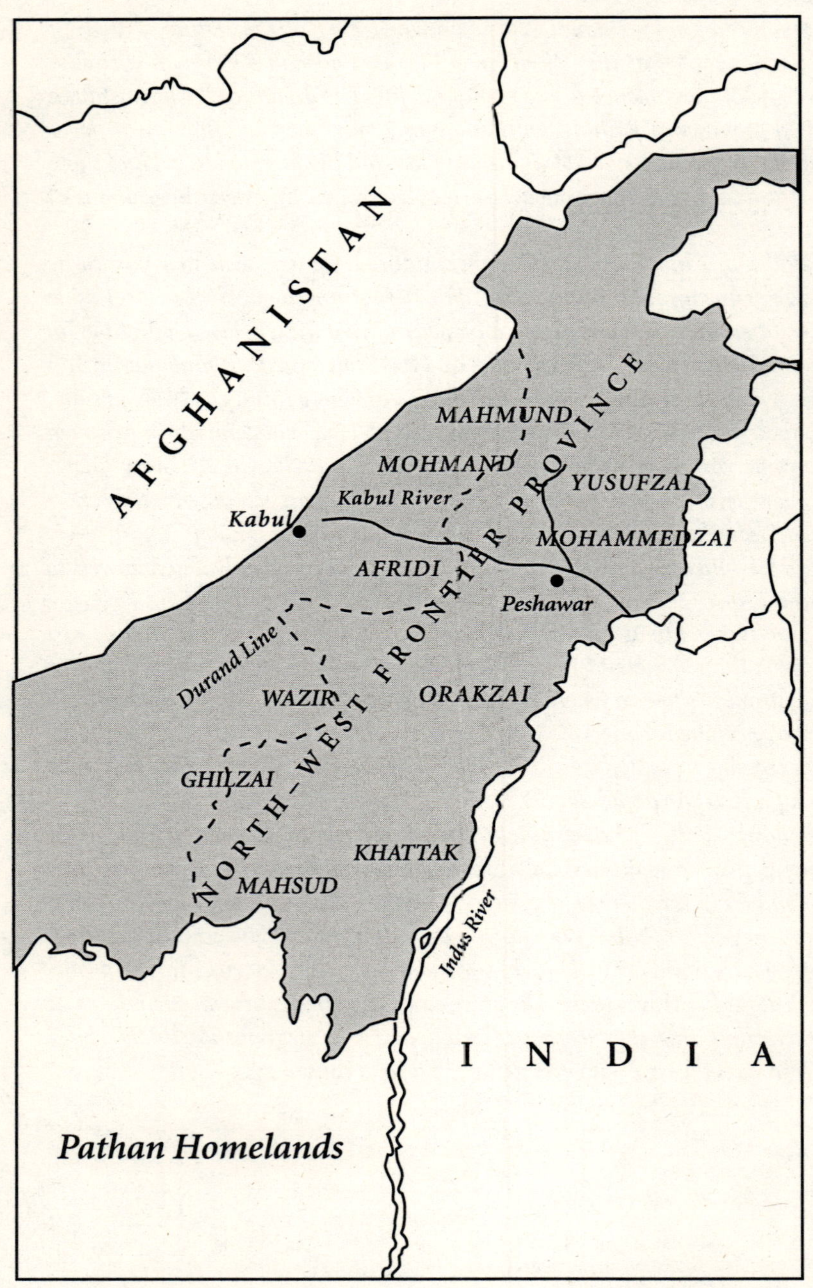

Pathan Homelands

Sources & Historical Notes

BY TIMOTHY FLINDERS

Full citations to references in these notes will be found in the Bibliography which follows. ("Tendulkar" and "Desai" without further title reference always signify these authors' biographies of Abdul Ghaffar Khan; their other works are specified.) The numbers at the left refer to page numbers in the text.

Notes for this edition have been revised and brought up to date by the editorial staff of Nilgiri Press and include corrections suggested by Afghan scholars who knew Badshah Khan intimately. We are deeply grateful for their assistance.

General Notes

THE "PATHANS," OR PUSHTUNS In Pushto, Badshah Khan's native language, the word *Pushtun* or *Pakhtun* (see note on LANGUAGE below) simply means "one who speaks Pushto." In British India, *Pakhtun* became *Pathan,* pronounced to rhyme roughly with *baton,* and this is the name that has come into English usage. Throughout "Gandhi's India," in which most of this story unfolds, Badshah Khan's people were called Pathans whenever English was being used, and this is the word used in this book.

Today, however, the word *Pathan* has decidedly colonial overtones reminiscent of British manipulation. When the British established boundaries around India, they used different words for inhabitants on either side of the line: "Afghan" meant someone in free Afghanistan, "Pathan" meant a resident of British India. Among themselves, Badshah Khan's people continued – and continue – to refer to themselves as one, calling themselves (without distinction) Afghans, Pushtuns, or some dialectical variant. In these historical notes, we chose to follow current usage and keep the word "Pushtun"– as Badshah Khan himself did even in English after the British left, to emphasize the unity of his people.

Afghan, incidentally, was once no more than a synonym – originally Persian – for *Pushtun.* (Dupree, *Muslim Peoples,* 323) To Pushtuns and their neighbors, the name "Afghanistan" still carries connotations of its literal meaning, "land of the Afghans," and in fact the original kingdom of Afghanistan took shape as an attempt to establish not so much a territorial entity as a union of all the Pushtun tribes (Fletcher, 245). Pushtuns are and have always been the dominant ethnic group in Afghanistan. Yet by one of the perversities of political boundaries, the "Durand Line," drawn by the British in 1893 and still preserved (though disputed) as the boundary between Afghanistan and Pakistan, arbitrarily divides Pushtun tribes and even villages. The result is that today roughly half of the Pushtuns (some six million) live in Afghanistan and the other half (perhaps five million) in the North-West Frontier Province of Pakistan. Remembering how arbitrary this division is in Pushtun eyes will help a Western reader to understand the importance of Afghanistan at certain junctures in Khan's story.

Pushtun origins are lost in antiquity. Their lands were the home of the prophet Zoroaster, the Vedic hymns of the Hindus, and a flourishing Buddhist culture long before Islam came.

LANGUAGE The language spoken by Pushtuns is called Pushto – or, depending on the dialect, Pukhtu, Pushtu, Pashto, or a number of other variants. The main division in dialects is between "hard" and "soft": roughly, a Pushtun from north of the Kabul River would speak of "Pakhtu" and "Pekhawar" when someone from the south might say "Pushto" and "Peshawar." This leads to all kinds of confusing variations which we have tried to avoid, though keeping spellings established in English (such as *Pathan, Khyber,* and *Peshawar*).

ABDUL GHAFFAR KHAN: NAME AND VARIANTS *Abdul* is included in the names of most aristocratic Pushtun boys, but is not generally what we in the West call the given name. Abdul Ghaffar Khan was called Ghaffar as a boy, and that is the name we use throughout the chapters on his youth. As a man he became known formally as Khan Abdul Ghaffar Khan (the first *Khan* being a title) or as Badshah Khan (*badshah* meaning "king"). To add to the confusion for Westerners, Indians and Pushtuns would often speak or write of him as "Khan Saheb," the word *saheb* being customarily added to a man's name as a matter of respect, while his elder brother, Abdul Jabar Khan (1883–1956), was known in India consistently as "Dr. Khan Saheb." We have reserved "Khan Saheb" for Ghaffar Khan's brother, who is generally known by no other name.

Specific Notes and Sources

3 "I have one great desire": Ghaffar Khan, 124-125.

12 Death and funeral: Associated Press wires, Jan. 20, 21, & 22, 1988; obituaries and tributes in the *New York Times* (Jan. 21), the *Times of India* (Jan. 20), and the *Hindustan Times* (Jan. 21).

15 THE BRITISH RAJ The British reign in India began to be called the "British Raj" (from the Hindi word for "reign" or "rule") after 1858, when Queen Victoria took over the holdings of the East India Trading Company and began to govern India through a viceroy responsible to

Parliament in London. In a looser sense, however, the Raj may be said to date from 1757, when Colonel Robert Clive established military control of the state of Bengal by defeating its nawab on the battlefield of Plassey. The implication of the term was that the British were successors to the mighty Mogul Empire.

15–16 The transfer of power in Karachi and Delhi is drawn from Collins and Lapierre and from Campbell-Johnson.

17 "To have to carry destruction": quoted in Yunus, 75–76.

18 Guernica stands out in the minds of most Westerners, but it was the colonies of Western powers – Great Britain, France, Italy – that first experienced the aerial bombing of civilians for no military purpose but terrorism. Kabul and Jalalabad were bombed by the Royal Air Force in the Third Afghan War, 1919 (Dupree, 442); villages in the Frontier were bombed thereafter to destroy the homes of Pushtuns who participated in anti-British raids (Caroe, 408).

At the Air Disarmament Conference in Geneva in 1933, it was not Germany but Great Britain that objected to a proposed ban on aerial bombing of civilians. Sir Anthony Eden asked that an exception be made in the case of "certain . . . inaccessible mountain districts, sparsely inhabited, where wild and armed hill tribes had sometimes passionate appetite for disturbing the tranquility of their neighbors. Unless order was maintained in those districts by this method [i.e., bombing], the only alternative was to use land troops, involving in normal times a large number of troops [and] casualties perhaps of a heavy nature. . . . That was bluntly the problem," he concluded – "the policing of these areas." (Quoted in Tendulkar, 154)

19 "The brutes": Tendulkar, 73. Wolpert (324) verifies that "the Frontier had suffered the harshest British repression during the second satyagraha campaign . . . as a result of Lord Willingdon's no-nonsense policy."

20 "The man who loved his gun": Yunus, x.

"That such men": Tendulkar, dust jacket.

25 "O Pathans": Ghaffar Khan, 226.

25–27 The Jubilee is drawn from Morris and Tuchman.

26 Newspaper quotes : Morris, 31.

27 "The largest military force" : Morris, 31
"No one ever": quoted in Tuchman, 55.
"A cherished conviction": quoted in Collins and Lapierre, 17.

29 The estimated population of the Frontier is from figures for 1901 given in the 1911 edition of the *Encyclopaedia Britannica.*

29–32 Information on Khan's childhood and his parents is taken from Ghaffar Khan, Desai, and Tendulkar. The descriptions of Pushtun life draw on Spain, Tendulkar, Dupree, Pennell, and the author's acquaintance with Indian Muslim village life.

31 KHUSHAL KHAN "The idealized Pushtun male," writes Louis Dupree (in *Muslim Peoples,* 327), "is the warrior-poet, brave in battle and eloquent in *jirgah* [council]. Few men fulfill both requirements, but those who do become the heroes of their age, as did a special hero, Khushal Khan Khattak. . . ." The poetry of Khushal Khan is still recited with relish in the derahs of the Pushtuns and quoted with respect by outsiders who write about his people. Warrior, poet, philosopher, and historian, he sings of the Pushtun spirit, its love of honor and passion for freedom, its longing for the hills and rivers of home, and its acceptance of the transiency of worldly fame and fortune. (See Caroe, 221–246; Spain, 107–116)

32 Mullah Mastun's story is from Miller, 265–266.

35 "The history of my people": Yunus, 115.

35–38 The history of the East India Trading Company is drawn from Miller and from Collins and Lapierre.

37 "First an English Resident": Annie Besant, in Yunus, 79–80.

"To pick a quarrel": Miller, 90.

"To interfere decidedly": Miller, 30.

"Avowed schemes": Miller, 32.

38 Strictly speaking, the North-West Frontier was not so named as a province until 1901. At the time of the Jubilee, the area was simply a backward (and largely ignored) part of the Punjab, which had been annexed by the East India Company just fifty years earlier.

38 "Thus is verified": quoted in Miller, 79. "Mahommed Akbar" was the son of Dost Mohammed, first amir of Afghanistan – and, incidentally, a Pushtun. The East India Company designed to depose the amir and put on the throne one Shah Shuja, who, though despised by his people, was favored by the British because he promised to resist any Russian advance through his country.

38 "As swiftly as permitted" and "Would leave it": Miller, 85.

38–39 THE "GREAT MUTINY" Though triggered by a revolt of Indian troops, the "Mutiny" was actually a popular rebellion. But it was not truly a nationalist one, and it was finally suppressed because the British were still able to secure the help of some Indian regiments (notably the Gurkhas and Sikhs) against others. Pushtuns are not proud to recall that at this time in their history, when ties with the rest of India were slight, many of their men helped to put down what is now known in India as the First War of Independence.

It is difficult to exaggerate the shadow this uprising cast over the remaining years of British rule. There is no doubt that every subsequent act of Indian resistance, even those in which nonviolence was strictly pledged and preserved, evoked the terror of those days in 1857 when a comparative handful of British soldiers and civilians faced an angry population out of their control.

The British, understandably, remembered cruelties they suffered at the hands of the Indians in the course of the uprising. "But there is another side to the picture also," Nehru writes, "that impressed itself on the mind of India, and in my own province especially the memory of it persists in town and village. One would like to forget this, for it is a ghastly and horrible picture showing man at his worst, even according to the new standards of barbarity set up by nazism and modern war. . . ." (Nehru, 238–239) The rebellion was followed by a full month of indiscriminate reprisal which even the official report to Parliament admits was directed simply against Indians in general, women and children included. These reprisals left a scar in Indians' minds at least as deep as that left on the English by the revolt itself.

One lesson the British learned from these cataclysmic events dominated policy thereafter: that they had won only because of India's lack of unity. Any attempt at organization or unification – of Hindus and Muslims, or caste Hindus and "untouchables," or the Frontier and the rest of India – was seen as a potential threat to British control.

41 "Revenge is a word": Pennell, 71–72.

45 "Our fault": Tendulkar, 186–189.

"In the small hours": Churchill, 88.

"Like most young fools": quoted in Miller, 269. Churchill had pulled strings to get a leave from his own regiment, stationed in India, to cover the Frontier uprising as a war correspondent.

45-46 "The tale I have to tell": Churchill, 82-83.

47 The description of Forward School policies follows Miller. More information is in Caroe and James.

"'The Great Game,' of which Kipling writes so stirringly," writes Spain (34), "became a frantic scurry for advantage between two expanding empires. Peace and progress on the Frontier was of little concern to the men who ruled India. Security was the all-important objective. To this end, Afghanistan was looked upon as a buffer state. The settled Pathan districts along the Indus were made an integral part of India. Tribal territory in the hills [in between] was a marshland which must be dominated." The degree to which the Pushtun homeland was carved up by Great Game geopolitics can be seen from the map on page 234.

48 "If you should cut": quoted in Yunus, 77–78.

49–52 The Frontier War is from Churchill, Miller, and James.

50 "It is no exaggeration": Churchill, 94–95.

"Sir Bindon Blood": Churchill, 90.

51 "The autumn tints": James, 147.

52–53 "We loudly proclaimed": quoted in Yunus, 80.

55 "The Holy Prophet Mohammed": Ghaffar Khan, 231.

56 "Those who learn in schools": Ghaffar Khan, 12.

The reference to standard examination questions on the benefits of the Raj is from Tandon, 13.

59 The dialogue between Khan's friend and the English officer is from Ghaffar Khan, 20.

60 The conversation between Khan and his mother is from Ghaffar Khan, 22–23, and Mehta, 241.

64 "I know these men": quoted in Miller, 284.

64–65 The Curzon material is from Miller, 283–293.

66 The talk with the mullah is from Ghaffar Khan, 27.

67 *Al-Hilal* was founded by Maulana Abul Kalam Azad, a brilliant Muslim scholar and staunch nationalist who was one of Gandhi's earliest and most loyal co-workers. Azad and Gandhi came together in 1920, when they were co-workers in the three-man committee that launched the first noncooperation movement as a united Hindu-Muslim front.

68 Ghaffar Khan (29) describes the Haji Saheb as essentially a social reformer whose struggle was to found Islamic schools where "outdated and useless traditions" could be replaced with newer ideas still consonant with Islam. This was scarcely the contemporary British view; to them he was simply an outlaw. He unified the Mamunds and roused them against the British on several occasions, prompting the British to complain that letting him escape was the first big mistake they made on the Frontier. In British military accounts of the time, the Haji of Turangzai figures only as a regrettably long-lived enemy.

68–69 "Had to bow low": Tendulkar, 25. Caroe, the last in the line of British commissioners and governors-general of the Frontier, comments that justice in the Frontier agencies was mostly a matter of the agents' character.

70 The accounts of Khan's *chilla* are all sketchy. This version follows Yunus (105), who knew Khan intimately.

77 "Like flowers in the desert": Ghaffar Khan, 122–124.

78 Ghani's illness and the death of his mother are drawn from Ghaffar Khan, 39–40. Ghani Khan wrote later (51): "She did not live long to see [her husband's] long silences and dark moods turn into strength and action. She died before she was twenty-five. They covered her with flowers and took her to the burial ground in her wedding robe. She left behind two baby boys with a bewildered, terrified look in their eyes. . . . He [Ghaffar Khan] left his children in the tender care of his old mother and drowned his sorrow in work and service."

80 "Nonviolence in its dynamic condition": *Young India,* August 8, 1920, p. 3. Quoted in Gandhi, *Mind of Mahatma Gandhi,* 121.

"Truth implies love": Gandhi, *Satyagraha,* 102.

"Satyagraha is soul force": Gandhi, *Satyagraha,* 105.

"There is no time limit": Gandhi, *Young India,* February 19, 1925, p. 61. Quoted in Gandhi, *Mind of Mahatma Gandhi,* 173.

81 Ironically, the same year as the Rowlatt Acts – 1919 – King George V announced the so-called Montagu-Chelmsford reforms, which aimed at placating Indian sentiment with a system of "dyarchy" or parallel government. Provinces were to elect Indian ministers to govern provincial affairs (agriculture, health, education, etc.), while the central Government of India would remain wholly British. This scarcely satisfied the Indian demand for home rule, but it was a significant concession.

Montagu-Chelmsford went into effect in 1920 in every Indian province except the North-West Frontier, which was deemed "unfit" for democratic reforms – despite the fact that the Pathan jirgah is one of the most ancient and egalitarian forms of indigenous democracy in the world. "No franchise for Pathans, no elections, no legislature, no ministry – not even elections for local bodies." (Caroe, 425)

The events surrounding Montagu-Chelmsford help to explain why it seemed so hollow. The Rowlatt Acts became law on March 18, 1919; in most Indian cities, the hartal (day of prayer and fasting) to protest the act was observed on April 6. One week later Brigadier-General Reginald Dyer, who had been in charge of the volatile province of Punjab for all of four days, blocked with troops the sole viable exit available to a peaceful meeting of unarmed men, women, and children in Amritsar, the sacred city of the Sikhs, and ordered his men to fire on the crowd until ammunition was exhausted – producing, according to the official British inquiry, 1516 casualties with 1650 bullets.

The Amritsar massacre, together with the public floggings and humiliations of martial law which followed, offended many British (though far from all) at home and in India; but it aroused Indians universally, and was never forgotten. The Montagu-Chelmsford system was announced less than eight months later. Since it left veto, police, and military control in the British hands, and since the Rowlatt Acts – martial law – were not withdrawn, it seemed clear that British rule could never be separated from "Dyerism," the mentality of the British military in India.

82 Dialogue with the commissioner is taken from Ghaffar Khan, 48.

83 The mass pilgrimage of Pushtuns to Afghanistan, an Islamic kingdom, protested another grievance of Indian Muslims. In World War I, the British had sent Muslim soldiers in India against Turkey. Since the sultan of Turkey was not only the temporal ruler of the Turkish Empire but the caliph or spiritual leader of all Islam, Muslims in India mounted a strong caliphate or *khilafat* movement after the war was over, fueled by anger at British rule. Gandhi, by urging a united protest against the Rowlatt Acts and British treatment of the caliph, brought Hindus and Muslims together for the first (and only) time in a joint nonviolent noncooperation campaign.

85 The incident of Khan bending the bars was reported to the author by Sri Gurudayal Mallick.

87 "One learns a good deal": Desai, 23.

87–90 Khan's prison experiences are from Ghaffar Khan, 58–81.

90 "She had been most keen": Tendulkar, 45.

91 "It is better": quoted in Fischer, 203.

92 "O people": Ghaffar Khan, 78.

"One day a lioness": Ghaffar Khan, 83–84.

95 "Is not the Pathan": Desai, 68.

95–101 Material in this chapter is all from Ghani Khan.

103 "There is nothing surprising": Ghaffar Khan, 195.

106 "A deplorable lack of tact": Alan Campbell-Johnson is quoted in Fischer, 256.

108 "The world, once weak": Khushal Khan is quoted in Spain, 110.
"There are two ways": Ghaffar Khan, 93–94.

110 The scene describing the founding of the Khudai Khidmatgars is a dramatization of the account Khan gives in his autobiography. "We did not want this movement to have anything to do with politics," Khan adds (Ghaffar Khan, 95–96), "but later on the cruel oppression the British subjected us to made it impossible for the movement to keep away from politics." Caroe (432) acknowledges that "the impetus [of Khan's movement] came originally from the British failure to grant to the Pathans the system of representative institutions set up elsewhere in the subcontinent in 1920 [the Montagu-Chelmsford reforms]."

Khan's notion of a professionally trained nonviolent army based upon military models stands as one of the pivotal moments in the history of nonviolence, much like Gandhi's spontaneous decision on September 11, 1906, to fight discriminatory legislation in South Africa through "passive resistance." (See Gandhi, *Satyagraha*, 95.)

111–112 The Khudai Khidmatgar oath is from Ghaffar Khan, 97.

113 "We are the army of God": Yunus, 114.

117 "I am going to give you": Tendulkar, 129.

"We believe": Tendulkar, 64.

NONVIOLENCE IN ISLAM Since Islam is so poorly understood in the West, it may be helpful to give some explanation of how Khan can speak of nonviolence as the "weapon of the Prophet." *Sabr,* often inadequately translated as "patience" or "endurance," is counselled repeatedly in the Meccan suras of the Koran, but the context makes it clear that if a one-word translation were possible, "satyagraha" comes closest to what is meant. The reference is to the early years of the Prophet's teaching in Mecca, when he and his few followers had to endure torment ranging from ridicule to the harshest persecution. Their stance was consistently to "hold on to truth," the literal meaning of *satyagraha,* without either retaliating or retreating, in perfect submission (*islam*) to God's truth and the consequences of their faith.

Sabr is all this and more: it means tenacity in a righteous cause, cheerful resignation in misfortune, forgiveness, self-control, renunciation, refraining from revenge, "bowing before the blow without a sound or complaint." One saying is reminiscent of Gandhi: "*Sabr* is revealed at the first blow." An epigram attributed to Umar suggests the high value ascribed to this virtue in some circles in medieval Islam: "We have found the best of our life in *sabr.*" In the mystics, particularly al-Ghazzali, *sabr* becomes a cardinal virtue in the "holy war" (*jihad*) between good and evil that every human being is called upon to wage in his or her own heart. (*Shorter Encyclopedia of Islam,* s.v. "Sabr")

Sabr is not Khan's nonviolent resistance, of course. It was his genius to extend its meaning to the renunciation of all retaliation by the strong.

119 "The strangest communication": Fischer, 269–271.

121 The British had much more on their hands than the Khudai Khidmatgars at this time. While Badshah Khan and his followers were courting arrest with nonviolent activities, some of the Pushtun hill tribes took advantage of the confusion to stage some raids, including two major assaults on Peshawar. (Caroe, 272) British writers like Caroe and Barton (and Miller, an American, following them) associate these violent uprisings with the Khudai Khidmatgars, and thus impugn the nonviolence of Khan's movement. Barton, a British administrator on the Frontier for twenty years, writes in 1939 that Khan, "a fanatical, bitterly anti-British Pathan . . . preached sedition along the Frontier. . . . Red Shirt agents preached war against the British in Dir, Bajaur and in the protected areas of the Malakand." (Barton, 164) The British, of course, had never allowed Khan to work with the "free" tribes of the hills, and in any case these uprisings occurred while he was in jail.

Of particular importance are the raids on Peshawar, which immediately followed Khan's arrest. When Afridis, the tribe around the Khyber Pass, heard about the treatment of the Khudai Khidmatgars, they marched on Peshawar and delivered an ultimatum: "Release Badshah Khan and Malang Baba [the "naked holy man," i.e., Gandhi], release the Khudai Khidmatgars, and stop the atrocities and repression against the Pathans. If you don't, we shall declare war on you." (Tendulkar, 74) The Afridis were stopped by British cavalry and fighter planes; but in the meantime, in the south, Waziri tribesmen had besieged a British garrison.

It is instructive to note that while the tribal violence was quickly repulsed by overwhelming British military power, Khan's nonviolent movement flourished in spite of repression, so that by 1932 it had gained the Pushtuns significant political concessions. (See p. 129.)

Interestingly, the British Government of India report comments that during these raids "the tribesmen altogether abstained from looting in their customary manner the villages they had passed through." (Tendulkar, 74) If Khan had been able to work among these hill tribes during his two decades of reform prior to 1930, he might have been able to inspire them with nonviolent ideals.

122–124 The Congress report is quoted in Tendulkar, 67–70.

122–123 When Western writers mention the Khudai Khidmatgars, the one event most likely to be included is the Peshawar "disturbances" of 1930. Since Khan's nonviolence is often judged on this event, some remarks about sources are warranted. Writers like Miller and Barton rely solely on British military accounts, ignoring the other eyewitness testimony collected in the Congress Inquiry Committee report on Peshawar.

Miller's story, like the rest of his book, makes colorful reading. By his account, the "disturbances" amounted to a "full-scale insurrection" in which "regular infantry and cavalry regiments sometimes came close to being scattered and routed in volleys of bricks that were supported by charges of Red Shirts carrying clubs and knives. . . ." (Miller, 349)

Neither Barton nor Miller asks why Pushtuns, who would ordinarily not consider themselves dressed without at least a rifle and a knife or two each, would throw their armories away and choose to fight off cavalry, armored cars, and machine guns with bricks and stones.

123 "When those in front": Sharp, 110.

Sentences of the Garhwal Rifles are from Tendulkar, 70.

124–125 Dr. Khan Saheb's report is in Tendulkar, 66.

125 In addition to the Pushtuns' nonviolence, another very disturbing factor for the British was the fact that Khan had aligned the Khudai Khidmatgars with the Congress party instead of the Muslim League, which had cooperated with the British since the twenties. The leaders of the Muslim League "were not prepared to help us," Khan writes (110–111), "because we were opposing the British." When the Khudai Khidmatgars then joined hands with the Congress, the government "sent me a message . . . 'The Frontier Province,' the message said, 'will immediately enjoy all the reforms that have been brought about in India, and in future we will do even more for you than we are doing for India. But on the condition that you resign from the Congress.'" True to form, Khan refused the offer.

126 The story of the Khudai Khidmatgar captain is from Tendulkar, 70–71, and Ghaffar Khan.

126–127 Wali Khan's rescue is from Tendulkar, 71.

127 The incident with Abbas Khan is from Tendulkar, 71.

128 "You must prevent": Desai, 51.

"The two years": Yunus, 118.

129 "Thanks largely to": Miller, 350.

"The nauseating . . . spectacle": Fischer, 281.

131 "I have but one": Desai, 92.

"Do not add": Tendulkar, 179.

132 The description of Khan's touring is from Yunus, 133.

132–133 Pyarelal (in Tendulkar, 525–526) gives insight into the importance of Khan's village work. When asked how he had had "such spectacular success in turning the fiercest warriors on earth into matchless soldiers of nonviolence," Khan answered that "it consisted simply of education through direct, personal touch. Most of the time he lived in the villages like and with the people in their homes. 'We taught them elementary things of daily life: how to keep clean and healthy and at peace with one another. . . .' Being fighters, [he said,] they had learned discipline already. All that he had to do was to give it a nonviolent turn."

133 "My sisters": Tendulkar, 101–102.

133–134 Devadas Gandhi is quoted in Tendulkar, 107, 109.

134 The newspaper quotes are from Tendulkar, 130-131.

"Do not fear death": Tendulkar, 126.

It is uncertain to what extent the British in India believed that Khan was a communist; in our own times, lack of evidence has scarcely prevented similar allegations from being made and believed. But in any case the fear of Russian expansion was powerful and genuine, both on the Frontier and at home in England. Much of the British activity and policy regarding the Pushtuns can only be understood if it is remembered that British foreign policy has been dogged by fear of the "Russian menace" for well over a century. "The Tsar Nicholas II," comments Morris (491), "once observed that all he had to do to paralyse British policy was to send a telegram mobilizing his forces in Russian Turkestan." (See note for p. 47 above.)

134-135 The conversation with Sir Ralph Griffith is from Tendulkar, 132–133, and Ghaffar Khan, 141.

136–138 Verrier Elwin is quoted in Tendulkar, 144–150.

138 "To gain independence": Tendullkar, 161.

141 "As a young boy": Mehta, 241.

"The political atmosphere": Tendulkar, 160.

Gandhi's Constructive Program, in contrast with the noncooperation movement, anticipated independence and attempted to rebuild India's ravaged village economy while forming a just social order. The spinning wheel stood at the center of the program because it offered work and an inexpensive source of income for the millions of villagers who were normally idle during six months of the year. Other aspects of the program were sanitation, the boycotting of foreign cloth, Hindu-Muslim unity, the emancipation of women, and the removal of untouchability.

143 "The more I knew": Desai, i–ii.

"The greatest thing": Desai, 90.

"You will have": Tendulkar, 176.

"The brothers' friendship": Tendulkar, 171.

143–144 "To be with them": Tendulkar, 193.

144 "It is these brothers": Desai, 86–87.

145 "You will be surprised": Desai, 34, and Tendulkar, 172–173.

Ahle Kitab is the Prophet's term, used frequently in the Koran, for Jews and Christians: those who share with Muslims the earlier books of revelation (the Torah, the Psalms, and the Gospels) which Islam regards as completed and perfected by the Koran. The *Shorter Encyclopedia of Islam* (s.v. "Ahl al-Kitab") states that in the interests of mutual religious tolerance, "Islam extended very early the circle of the Ahl al-Kitab beyond its original limits," even in India.

146 "I appreciate": Tendulkar, 171.

"I would like to": Tendulkar, 177.

"I have never found": Desai, 91–92.

147 "What is our fault": Tendulkar, 186–189.

148 The description of Khan's arrest is from Desai, 104–106.

151 "Whenever Gandhiji takes": Desai, 91.

"And indeed, it amazed": Tendulkar, 205.

"I am a loyal": Tendulkar, 199.

153 "The province has": Tendulkar, 207.

The Government of India Act of 1935 made the chief minister of each province an elected official for the first time (previously the position had been filled by British appointment). In 1937 the first elections were held; Dr. Khan Saheb was chosen chief minister as the Khudai Khidmatgars won a strong majority in the Frontier legislature.

153–154 "At long last": Yunus, 126.

155 "I noticed wherever": Tendulkar, 238.

"We can never forget": Tendulkar, 238.

"I congratulate you": Tendulkar, 239.

155–162 Gandhi's conversations with Khan and the Khudai Khidmatgars are taken from verbatim reports recorded by Pyarelal (*Pilgrimage*, 57–76), Gandhi's personal secretary, who accompanied him on his Frontier tour.

158 "We want you to": Tendulkar, 249.

159 "Even as the rose": Pyarelal, 87.

"If I had my way": Pyarelal, 95.

160 "My impression": The conversation between Gandhi and Khan is from Pyarelal, 71–76.

162–163 "Whatever the Khudai Khidmatgars": Tendulkar, 284–288.

165 "The Prophet faced": Yunus, 132.

"A free democratic India": Fischer, 354.

166 "*Divide et Impera*": quoted in Yunus, 85.

Jinnah is quoted in Tendulkar, 306.

167 "Unable to go": Fischer, 356.

"It is difficult": Tendulkar, 327.

168 Churchill ("I have not become the King's First Minister") is quoted in Fischer, 357.

168–170 The descriptions of the camp and Khan's home are from Barr, 228–234.

171 "As a young boy": Mehta, 241. Transforming and harnessing anger did not come easy to Khan and seems to have been a long-fought struggle. He gave some indication of the nature of this struggle when he told some of his workers in 1938, "I know it is difficult to curb one's anger altogether. But you have pledged yourselves to it before God. Man is by nature weak but God is all-powerful. By yourselves you may fail in your efforts to be completely nonviolent but God helping, you will succeed. It may not be all at once. The progress will be slow and there will be setbacks. But each effort will take you a step higher on your path. Do not lose heart." (Pyarelal, *Pilgrimage*, 69)

Murtaza Khan's story is from Ghani Khan, 16–21.

173 "The number of white troops": quoted in Tendulkar, 359.

174 "All I know": Fischer, 444.

"I am not going": Fischer, 444–445.

"Burning the candle": the expression is Dr. Sushila Nayyar's, who was with Gandhi at this time. Quoted in Fischer, 468.

174 "You are right": Tendulkar, 403.

175 "India seems an inferno": Tendulkar, 403.

177 "It is my intention" and "His inner agony": Tendulkar, 422.

177 "We shall be outcastes": Tendulkar, 416.

177–178 Gandhi's talk at the May 7 prayer meeting is from Tendulkar, *Mahatma*, 391.

178 "Before long": Tendulkar, 416

179 "He is a true fakir": Tendulkar, 416–417.

"I have full faith": Tendulkar, 417.

181 "I consider it a crime": quoted in Yunus, 132.

"There was an air": Campbell-Johnson, 156–157.

"In the little scene": Campbell-Johnson, 157.

181–182 Mountbatten's transition from viceroy to governor-general is from Campbell-Johnson, 156–157, and Collins and Lapierre, 266–267, 275–277.

182 "No power in history": quoted in Campbell-Johnson, 162.

"As if he were": Collins and Lapierre, 266.

185 "Rule of the Pathans": Tendulkar, 465.

"The Khudai Khidmatgars": Tendulkar, 450–451.

THE REFERENDUM The Mountbatten plan divided India not where Muslims were predominant, but where the elected representatives belonged to the Muslim League. By this criterion, the Frontier would have remained part of India, on the same basis as any of the other Indian provinces. Less than a year earlier, in a clear majority, it had voted in Dr. Khan Saheb and other Congress and Nationalist candidates over the Muslim league.

Yet Jinnah would not accept a "moth-eaten Pakistan" that did not include the Frontier. Further, the League could not "claim to be the unqualified representative of Muslim India" with a ninety-five percent Muslim province voting against it. (Gopal, 333) Many British officials – including Sir Olaf Caroe, governor-general of the Frontier since 1946 – personally supported the Muslim League. The League had cooperated with them loyally since the twenties; the Khudai Khidmatgars and the Congress had been thorns in their sides. To such men, a Congress-governed Muslim province was an aberration to be cleared up. Caroe "acted openly on the premiss that 'the Congress is not natural here,'" and a letter from him to Mountbatten indicates that he "repeatedly urged [Dr. Khan Saheb] to oust the Hindus in his ministry and sever his connection with the Congress – advice which was hardly in keeping with the governor's constitutional position." (Gopal, 348)

Caroe argued to Mountbatten that another election was needed to allow the Frontier to ally itself with its Muslim neighbors. It was, he felt, the only way to make Pakistan a reality. Mountbatten adopted Caroe's plan into his own and pressed the whole package on the Congress, whose leaders finally acquiesced as the violence around them went from horrible to worse. Northern India was being torn to pieces by Hindu-Muslim riots and a kind of panic had set in; self-government was wholly blocked until the issue of partition could be resolved.

186 "He will not bend": Tendulkar, 1.

186–187 Pyarelal's account of his visit with Khan is quoted in Tendulkar, 523–528.

189 "The present-day world": From a letter to the author sent by Abdul Wali Khan, February 2, 1984.

193–194 "With me alone": Desai, *Day-to-Day*, 174.

194 "My creed": Gandhi, in *Mind of Mahatma Gandhi*, 143.

"I do not infer," "A nation," and "But do you know": Desai, *Day-to-Day*, 166.

195 "There is hope": Gandhi, in *Mind of Mahatma Gandhi*, 143.

"The coward dies": Ghani Khan, 30.

"Being fighters": Tendulkar, 526.

"The bravest": Nehru is quoted in Yunus, x.

"I started" and "Nonviolence is not": Ghaffar Khan, 193–194.

196 "To me": Yunus, xlii.

197 "I have learned": Gandhi, in *Mind of Mahatma Gandhi*, 16.

"To bear this": Tendulkar, 148.

198 "To realize nonviolence" and "If the Khudai Khidmatgars": Pyarelal, *Pilgrimage*, 59.

199 "You have to be against": Tendulkar, 187.

"Is always noble": Yunus, 132.

201 "No true effort": Pyarelal, *Pilgrimage*, 166.

Glossary

In an English context, all these words may be pronounced approximately as in Spanish or Italian.

ahle kitab "People of the Book": see note for p. 145
amal Selfless service
amir An Afghan ruler
ashram A community based on spiritual disciplines
badal Revenge, vendetta, blood feud
badmash Scoundrel
badshah King
chilla A period of meditation and fasting
chillum Small, bowl-shaped clay pipe used for smoking
derah Guest house for travelers and communal gatherings
fakir A renunciate, holy man
haj Pilgrimage
haji Title taken by one who has gone on *haj* to Mecca
jirgah Council of elders, tribal leaders, or heads of families
khan A village or tribal chief; generally, an honorific title
maktab A school run by a mosque
melmastia The Pathan code of hospitality
muezzin Crier who calls the faithful to prayer
muhabat Love; compassion
mullah Muslim religious leader
namaz The daily prayers prescribed in Islam

nanawati The Pathan code of giving sanctuary to fugitives

pyjama (Hindi) The baggy trousers and long shirts worn in some regions in north India and beyond

Pushtun Pathan; see note, p. 235

Pushtunwali The "way of the Pathan": the social codes of *badal, melmastia,* and *nanawali* by which Pathans rule themselves

Pushto or *Pakhtu* The language of the Pathans; see note, p. 256

pir A Muslim saint

purdah Veil; the custom of keeping women in seclusion

qahwa Green tea, salted or sugared; the "Pathan national drink"

raj (Hindi, "reign") An empire, esp. Mogul or British India

satyagraha "Soul-force," Gandhi's nonviolent campaigns

satyagrahi One engaged in or training for satyagraha

sepoy A native Indian soldier, generally from one of the so-called martial tribes: Sikhs, Gurkhas, and Pathans

sitar A stringed instrument of northern India

surnai A reed instrument of the Pathans

tulwar A curved sword

yakeen Faith

zulum Tyranny, oppression, injustice

Chronology

Events in Badshah Khan's life are chronicled in the left column, general events in the right. Before 1947, the right-hand column generally follows developments in British India; after 1947, in Pakistan.

Born (Utmanzai)	1890	
	1894	Lord Elgin, viceroy
	1895	Chitral punitive expedition
	1897	Queen Victoria's Diamond Jubilee "Great Frontier War"
Enters Municipal Board School, Peshawar	1898	
	1899	Lord Curzon, viceroy
To Edwardes mission school, Peshawar	1901	North-West Frontier Province created
	1903	Frontier Crimes Regulation Act
	1905	Lord Minto, viceroy
Refuses Guides commission	1906	Muslim League formed
Enters Islamic school at Aligarh	1908	
Decides against college in England	1909	

Opens first school in Utmanzai	1910	Lord Hardinge, viceroy
Marries; given leadership of the reform movement of Haji of Turangzai	1912	
Attends Muslim League conference in Agra First son, Ghani, born	1913	
To Bajaur; long fast (*chilla*); returns to work with settled tribes	1914	World War I begins (Aug.)
Second son, Wali, born Wife dies	1915	Gandhi returns to India from S. Africa
Exposure to Muslim renaissance in *Al-Hilal* etc.	1916	Lord Chelmsford, viceroy
	1918	World War I ends
	1919	Rowlatt Act passed (Mar); Gandhi calls nationwide strike to protest (Apr. 6) Amritsar massacre (Apr. 13); martial law in India
Arrested & sentenced to 6 months in prison		Khilafat movement begins Gandhi publishes *Young India* (Oct.) Montagu-Chelmsford reforms (Dec.)
Released; remarries To Khilafat conference in Delhi; sees Gandhi, Azad, et al. Joins mass pilgrimage to Afghanistan as part of Khilafat protest	1920	
Attends Nagpur session of Indian National Congress (Dec.)		Nagpur Congress, at Gandhi's urging, declares policy of self-rule & nonviolence for the first time (Dec.)

Founds high school in Utmanzai Established Anjuman-e Islah ul-Afaghena (Reform Assoc. of the Afghans) Arrested & sentenced to 3 years' imprisonment (Dec.)	1921	Lord Reading, viceroy
	1922	Gandhi announces satyagraha, calls it off (Feb.); arrested (Mar. 18) & sentenced to 6 years' imprisonment
Mother dies	1923	
Released from prison; given title of Fakr-e Afghan, "Pride of the Afghans" Pilgrimage to Mecca & tour of Muslim countries; wife dies in Jerusalem	1924	Gandhi released from prison
Father dies	1926	Lord Irwin, viceroy
Anjuman-e Zamindaran (Peasant Association) established under Khan's direction; "cooperative enlightenment centers" improve local agriculture Pushtun Jirgah (Pushtun Youth League) founded under his direction	1927	Simon Commission boycotted Punjab unrest: Lajput Rai killed by police; police chief assassinated (Dec.)
Attends Khilafat conference & Congress session in Calcutta (Dec.)	1928	
Forms Khudai Khidmatgars; starts journal, *Pushtun* Attends Lahore session of Congress (Dec.) & meets Gandhi & Nehru	1929	Congress declares independence (Dec. 31)

Arrest Apr. 23 triggers mass demonstrations and shootings in Peshawar Repression in Utmanzai (May 13)	1930	Gandhi's Salt March begins (Mar.) Salt Satyagraha launched at Dandi (Apr. 5): many thousands attacked and jailed in nonviolent activities throughout India; worst repression on Frontier in history of British Raj Gandhi arrested (May 4)
Released (Mar.); starts village tours Attends Karachi session of Congress (Mar.);member of Working Committee with Gandhi	1931	Gandhi released (Jan.); Gandhi-Irwin Pact; civil resistance suspended (Mar.) Lord Willingdon, viceroy Gandhi to London for Round Table Conference on Indian independence (Sept.–Dec.)
Imprisoned in arrest of all Congress leaders		Gandhi-Irwin "truce" breaks down under new viceroy; Congress leaders arrested; repression & martial law in Frontier & elsewhere (Dec.)
	1932	Gandhi imprisoned without trial (Jan.) Civil resistance resumed; Elwin report on Frontier repression
	1933	Gandhi released at start of fast (May) Gandhi arrested; released; rearrested; released(Aug.)

Released; banned from Frontier (Aug.), joins Gandhi at Wardha Visits Muslims in Bengal	1934	Gandhi retires from politics to concentrate on Constructive Program of village uplift (Sept.)
Declines presidency of Congress Gives speeches in Bombay; arrested (Dec.)		Bombay session of Congress (Oct.); Gandhi resigns, pledging support
Released from prison (July); banned fromFrontier	1935	Govt. of India Act provides for election of provincial officials (including the Frontier)
	1936	Lord Linlithgow, viceroy
Banishment lifted by new Frontier government; returns home (Aug.)	1937	Congress wins majority of provincial elections; Dr. Khan Saheb chief minister of Frontier
Begins Constructive Program in Frontier	1938	Gandhi visits Frontier (May & Oct.)
	1939	World War II starts; Congress ministries resign
Opens center for Constructive Program at Sardaryab (near Peshawar) Resigns from Congress (June) out of commitment to nonviolence	1940	Muslim League passes resolution for separate Muslim state (Mar.) Congress offers war support to UK if independence promised (June); refuses support when promise refused (Aug.)
	1941	Gandhi gives up leadership of Congress; starts individual civil resistance movement Pearl Harbor attacked (Dec.)

	1942	Singapore falls to Japan; Rangoon follows
Pledges support of “Quit India (Aug.); Frontier begins civil resistance		Gandhi launches “Quit India” campaign (Aug.); Gandhi & Congress Working Committee arrested
	1943	Lord Wavell, viceroy
Imprisoned (Oct.)	1944	Gandhi released (May)
Released (Mar.)	1945	World War II ends; general release of all political prisoners; Dr. Khan Saheb reinstated as chief minister of Frontier
		New Labour government in London prepares for Indian independence
	1946	Simla conference on transfer of power fails on issue of Pakistan
		Muslim League “Direct Action Day”; riots in Calcutta (Aug. 16)
		Interim govt. formed in India (Sept.)
		Noakhali massacre (Oct. 10)
Tours riot-torn Bihar		Gandhi to Noakhali (Oct. 28); riots in Bihar
	1947	Gandhi joins Khan in Bihar (Jan.)
		Riots in Punjab & Frontier
		Lord Mountbatten, viceroy, arrives in Delhi (Mar. 22)
		Congress accepts partition in principle (May 1)
Asks Khudai Khidmatgars to boycott referendum		Referendum (July 6–18); Frontier votes to join Pakistan
Pushtun suspended by Pakistan govt. (Aug.)		Independence granted India & Pakistan (Aug. 15)

Calls meeting of Khudai Khidmatgars to accept Pakistan (Sept.)	1947	Khan Saheb's Frontier ministry dissolved by Pakistan Fighting begins in Kashmir, disputed by Pakistan & India (Sept. 24)
Takes oath of allegiance to Pakistan (Feb. 23) Elected head of Pakistan Peoples Party (Mar. 13) Imprisoned (with Dr. Khan Saheb); Khudai Khidmatgars suppressed (June)	1948	Gandhi undertakes "fast unto death" (Jan.); assassinated (Jan. 30) Jinnah dies (Sept.11); Khwaja Nazimuddin govenor-general of Pakistan
	1951	Ghulat Mohammad governor-general of Pakistan
Released from jail under house arrest	1954	Dr. Khan Sabeb released from prison; joins central cabinet of Pakistan
Returns to Frontier after 7 years' detention	1955	Gen. Iskander Mizra assumes presidency of Pakistan "One Unit" plan incorporates Frontier & other provinces of W. Pakistan under central govt.; Dr. Khan Saheb chief minister of W. Pakistan
Arrested; property confiscated in lieu of fines (June)	1956	Pakistan proclaimed Islamic republic; constitution adopted (Mar. 23)
Forms National Awami Party (July)	1957	Dr. Khan Saheb assassinated (May 9)
Arrested & jailed (Oct. 11)	1958	Pres. Mizra declares martial law; abolishes constitution; dismisses central & provincial govts. & dissolves all political parties (Oct. 7)

	1958	Mizra exiled; Gen. Ayub Khan takes power in coup (Oct.28)
Released "on consideration of age & health" (Apr.); disqualified from holding any public office	1959	
Arrested & jailed with hundreds of co-workers for "spreading disaffection" (Apr. 12)	1961	
Named Prisoner of the Year by Amnesty International	1962	Ayub Khan proclaims new constitution (Mar. 1)
Released ("poor health") to house arrest (Jan.); allowed to go to England for medical treatment (Sept.) Exile in Afghanistan (Dec.)	1964	Jawaharlal Nehru, Khan's foremost champion in India, dies (May 27)
	1965	Fighting between India & Pakistan over Kashmir
	1968	Thousands of Khudai Khidmatgars demonstrate for end of One Unit Rule & restoration of Frontier province (Apr.); student & opposition leaders arrested
Visits India to speak at Gandhi's birth centenary; fasts for Hindu-Muslim unity in India	1969	Student & labor unrest throughout Pakistan; Ayub Khan resigns to General Yahya Khan, who proclaims martial law (Mar. 25)
	1970	New Pakistan constitution Martial law continues; tensions between E. & W. Pakistan break into

Returns from exile (Dec.) with end of 12 years' military rule in Pakistan	1971	Civil war (Mar.), ends (Dec.); E. Pakistan secedes as independent state of Bangladesh Yahya Khan resigns (Dec.20); Ali Bhutto president; Frontier, Baluchistan, etc. again declared separate provinces
	1972	Pakistan withdraws from British commonwealth (Jan. 30)
	1973	New Pakistan constitution (Aug.); Bhutto chief executive Civil war begins as Baluchistan attempts to secede (war continues until 1977)
Jailed; National Awami Party outlawed Released "in consideration of old age"	1975	
	1977	Ceasefire in Baluchistan; Gen. Zia proclaims martial law & postpones elections; army assumes control (July)
	1979	Bhutto hanged USSR invades Afghanistan (Dec.)
	1980	UN calls for immediate withdrawal of foreign troops from Afghanistan (Jan.); mass emigration of Afghans to Pakistan, India, etc.

Arrested with son Wali & all opposition leaders; kept under house arrest in govt.-designated "sub-jail" Released (Dec.); to hospital for medical treatment	1983	Movement for Return to Democracy (coalition of all opposition parties) attempts nationwide non-violent resistance against military rule
To hospital in Kabul	1984	
Visits India with son Wali for centenary celebration of Indian National Congress party	1985	Mohammed Khan Junejo prime minister of Pakistan
To India for medical treatment as guest of government; receives Bharat Ratna ("Jewel of India") award, the first non-Indian recipient Hospitalized (summer) for stroke in Peshawar	1987	
Dies 6:35 a.m. Jan. 20 in Peshawar at Lady Reading Hospital after a series of strokes and a lung infection. Buried at his request in the garden of his home in Jalalabad, Afghanistan Factions in Afghanistan observe ceasefire in honor of his funeral in Jalalabad as 20,000 mourners cross border through Khyber Pass accompanying his coffin	1988	UN-initiated Geneva peace talks agree on withdrawal of Soviet troops from Afghanistan by Feb. 15, 1999 (Apr.) Gen. Zia killed in plane crash (Aug.); Benazir Bhutto elected prime minister of Pakistan

Bibliography

ABDUL GHAFFAR KHAN

The primary sources of biographical information for Khan's life are both based on oral interview: Desai (1935) and the autobiography as narrated to K. B. Narang (1969). Other biographies rely heavily on these two sources. The definitive history of Khan's life and movement remains to be written.

Barr, Mary. "A Tribute to the Frontier Gandhi." In *Bapu: Conversations and Correspondence with Mahatma Gandhi.* 2nd ed. Bombay: International Book House, 1956. The most intimate glimpse of Badshah Khan yet produced by a westerner. Mary Barr lived in Gandhi's ashram and draws on personal experience of Khan during the Bombay Congress session of 1934 and a visit to the Frontier in 1941, when she was a guest at Khan's house.

Desai, Mahadev. *Two Servants of God.* Delhi: Hindustan Times Press, 1935. The first biography of Badshah Khan, commissioned by Gandhi during Khan's stay with him at Wardha. Desai bases it upon extensive conversations with the two Khan brothers at the time.

Khan, Abdul Ghaffar. *My Life and Struggle.* Delhi: Hind Pocket Books, [1969]. Khan's autobiography as told to K. B. Narang.

Kumar, Ravinder. *Khan Abdul Ghaffar Khan: A Centennial Tribute.* Har-Anand Publications [1995]. Papers presented at a centennial seminar, published "under the auspices of Nehru Memorial Museum and Library."

Pyarelal. *A Pilgrimage for Peace: Gandhi and Frontier Gandhi Among the N.W.F.P. Pathans.* Ahmedabad: Navajivan Publishing House, 1950. Describes Gandhi's two tours of the Frontier in 1938. Pyarelal, Gandhi's personal secretary, accompanied him on these tours and kept detailed stenographic records of Gandhi's words and actions.

———. *Thrown to the Wolves: Abdul Ghaffar.* Calcutta: Eastlight Book House, 1966. Based on the Desai biography and Pyarelal's personal experience.

Tendulkar, D. G. *Abdul Ghaffar Khan: Faith Is a Battle.* Bombay: Gandhi Peace Foundation (Popular Prakashan), 1967. The most comprehensive biography to date, commissioned by Nehru after the model of Tendulkar's eight-volume biography of Gandhi, *Mahatma.* Tendulkar had access to the unpublished autobiography and draws on it heavily for Khan's story, along with the Desai biography. He quotes extensively from such primary sources as British government files and official reports, the records of the Indian National Congress and its Working Committee, handwritten transcriptions of Khan's and Gandhi's speeches, issues of the *Pushtun* (Khan's journal), and other periodicals.

Yunus, Mohammad. *Frontier Speaks.* Bombay: Hind Kitabs, 1947. Primarily a social and political history of the Pathans, with a section on Khan's life and movement. Yunus was a Pathan colleague of Khan's.

Zutshi, G. L. *Frontier Gandhi: The Fighter, the Politician, the Saint.* Delhi: National Publishing House, 1970. A condensation of material from the above biographies with the author's commentary.

THE PATHANS AND THE NORTH-WEST FRONTIER

Barton, Sir William. *India's North-West Frontier.* London: John Murray, 1939. Barton was a British official on the Frontier for twenty years. Writing during the height of the independence movement, he reflects the attitudes of those officials who saw the Indian nationalist movement as "insurrection" and its leaders (Khan, Gandhi, Nehru, et al.) as disloyal opportunists.

Caroe, Olaf. *The Pathans: 550 B.C.–A.D. 1957.* New York: St. Martin's Press, 1958. The most complete scholarly work on the Pathans. Caroe, the last governor of the North-West Frontier Province before independence (1946–1947), writes of the Pathans with understanding, respect, and affection. His treatment of Khan's movement, however, and the Indian independence movement in general, is understandably characterized by a staunch pro-British attitude.

Dupree, Louis. *Afghanistan.* Princeton: Princeton University Press, 1980. An authoritative discussion of the history and cultures of Afghanistan by the area's foremost anthropologist. Includes a good deal about the Pathans.

———. "Pushtun." In *Muslim Peoples,* ed. by Richard V. Weekes. Westport, Conn.: Greenwood Press, 1978.

Khan, Ghani. *The Pathans: A Sketch.* Bombay: National Information and Publications, 1947. A small but sensitive and often moving description of Pathan life and temperament by Badshah Khan's eldest son, a respected poet. Unfortunately the book is still difficult to obtain.

Mayne, Peter. *The Narrow Smile.* London: John Murray, 1955. An engaging account of a return to the Frontier by an Englishman who lived with Pathans in the last years of British India.

Miller, Charles. *Khyber: British India's NorthWest Frontier; The Story of an Imperial Migraine.* New York: Macmillan Co., 1977. A lively but often sensationalized history of the Frontier, which relies heavily on British military sources.

Pennell, T. L. *Among the Wild Tribes of the Afghan Frontier.* London: Seeley & Co., 1909. Pathan life at the turn of the century, described by a missionary doctor who lived on the Frontier for many years.

Said Khan, Mohammed. *The Voice of the Pukhtoons.* [Lahore: 1972]. "The story of the Pukhtoons of the twentieth century living in Pakistan today." Mostly articles written for the *Khyber Mail*, the *Pakistan Times*, and the *Peshawar Times* (now suppressed).

Singer, André. *Guardians of the North-West Frontier: The Pathans.* Peoples of the Wild series. Amsterdam: Time-Life Books, 1982. A sensitive, readable record of an anthropologist's stay among the Mohmands, including a rare firsthand description of life behind *purdah* from one of the photographers, Toby Molenaar. Lavish color photographs in the Time-Life Books tradition.

Spain, James W. *People of the Khyber: The Pathans of Pakistan.* New York: Frederick A. Praeger, 1962. A balanced and most readable account of Pathan history, written by a sympathetic American scholar. Includes a brief account of an interview with Khan in the early sixties.

OTHER WORKS CITED

Campbell-Johnson, Alan. *Mission with Mountbatten.* London: Robert Hale, 1951.

Churchill, Winston S. *Great Destiny.* Edited by F. W. Heath. New York: G. P. Putnam's Sons, 1965.

Collins, Larry, and Dominique Lapierre. *Freedom at Midnight.* New York: Simon and Schuster, 1975.

Desai, Mahadev. *Day-To-Day with Gandhi.* Benares: Sarva Seva Sangh Prakashan, 1968. Cited: vol. 1, *From Nov. 1917 to March 1919.*

Fischer, Louis. *The Life of Mahatma Gandhi.* New York: Harper & Brothers, 1950; Collier Books, 1962.

Fletcher, Arnold. *Afghanistan: Highway of Conquest.* Ithaca, N.Y.: Cornell University Press, 1965.

Gandhi, M. K. *All Men Are Brothers.* Ed. by Krishna Kripalani. Ahmedabad: Navajivan Publishing House, 1960.

———. *The Mind of Mahatma Gandhi.* Ed. by R. K. Prabhu and U. R. Rao. Ahmedabad: Navajivan Publishing House, 1967.

———. *Satyagraha in South Africa.* Ahmedabad: Navajivan Publishing House, 1950.

Gopal, Sarvepalli. *Jawaharlal Nehru: A Biography.* Cambridge: Harvard University Press, 1976. Cited: vol. 1, 1889–1947.

James, Lionel. *The Indian Frontier War: Being an Account of the Mohmund and Tirah Expeditions, 1897.* London: William Heinemann, 1898.

Mehta, Ved. *Mahatma Gandhi and His Apostles.* New York: Penguin Books, 1976.

Morris, James. *Pax Britannica: The Climax of an Empire.* London: Faber and Faber, 1968.

Nehru, Jawaharlal. *The Discovery of India.* Ed. by Robert I. Crane. Garden City, New York: Doubleday & Co., Anchor Books, 1960. (Original ed.: The John Day Co., 1946.)

Sharp, Gene. *Gandhi Wields the Weapon of Moral Power: Three Case Histories.* Ahmedabad: Navajivan Publishing House, 1960.

Tandon, Prakash. *Punjabi Century: 1857–1947.* Berkeley: University of California Press, 1968.

Tendulkar, D. G. *Mahatma: Life of Mohandas Karamchand Gandhi.* 2nd ed. 8 vols. Delhi: Publications Division, Ministry of Information and Broadcasting, 1962. Cited: vol. 7, 1945–47.

Tuchman, Barbara W. *The Proud Tower: A Portrait of the World Before the War, 1890–1914.* New York: Macmillan Co., 1966.

Wolpert, Stanley. *A New History of India.* 2nd ed. Oxford: Oxford University Press, 1982.

Index

Eknath Easwaran grew up in Mahatma Gandhi's India when Badshah Khan's influence was at its zenith. Meetings with both men, together with a close observation of their lives, convinced him that Khan perfectly embodies the transformation behind what Gandhi called the nonviolence of the brave.

Eknath Easwaran was a Professor of English Literature at the University of Nagpur, India, as well as an established writer and speaker when he came to the United States on the Fulbright exchange program in 1959 and taught at the University of California at Berkeley. He founded the Blue Mountain Center of Meditation in 1961 to move, as he puts it, from education for degrees to education for living. He has written more than 25 books on spirituality and finding peace of mind.